Modernity as exile

The Stranger in John Berger's writing

«*Για τους γονείς μου*»

Modernity as exile

The Stranger in John Berger's writing

Nikos Papastergiadis

Manchester University Press
Manchester and New York
Distributed exclusively in the USA and Canada by St. Martin's Press

Copyright © Nikos Papastergiadis 1993

Published by Manchester University Press
Oxford Road, Manchester M13 9PL, UK
and Room 400, 175 Fifth Avenue, New York, NY 10010, USA
Distributed exclusively in the USA and Canada
by St. Martin's Press, Inc., 175 Fifth Avenue, New York,
NY 10010, USA

British Library Cataloguing-in-Publication Data
A catalogue record for this book is available from the British Library

Library of Congress Cataloguing-in-Publication Data
Papastergiadis, Nikos, 1992-
  Modernity as exile: the stranger in John Berger's writing/Nikos Papastergiadis.
    p. cm.
  Includes bibliographical references.
  ISBN 0-7190-3876-6 (hardback)
  1. Berger, John--Characters--Outsiders. 2. Outsiders in literature. 3. Modernism (Literature) 4. Exiles in literature.
  I. Title.
  PR6052,E564Z83   1993
  823',914--dc20   92-2492

ISBN 0 7190 3876 6 *hardback*

Typeset in Great Britain
by Megaron, Cardiff, Wales

Printed in Great Britain
by Biddles Ltd, Guildford and King's Lynn

Contents

	Acknowledgements	*page* vi
Introduction	This exilic shuttle	1
1	The method of metaphor	8
2	A romantic Marxist	35
3	Death of a stranger	90
4	Under the silken sky	143
Postscript	Faith without certitudes	191
	Select bibliography	196
	Index	210

Acknowledgements

This book began as a doctoral dissertation at the University of Cambridge. My studies were made possible by the Cambridge–Australia Scholarship and the Le Bas Research Scholarship. To my supervisor Anthony Giddens I owe a deep thanks for his rigorous attention. The energy for working was regularly boosted by the companionship and example of my friends Musa Ahmed, Teresa Brennan, Shaun Gorvy, Gary Kelly, Deborah Levy, Peter Ravenscroft, Ingrid Schiebler and Jo Stockham. With Pavel and Alexandra I found understanding *in* the compulsion to narrate journeys and dreams. Had it not been for Rasheed Araeen and Jean Fisher, and all the team that passed through *Third Text* the context and the urgency of my project may have been lost to me. *Third Text* allowed me to see the question of migration and estrangement from a truly global perspective. And in this light I am in debt to Homi Bhabha, John Forester, Stuart Hall and Gayatri Chakravorty Spivak for their incisive commentaries.

This book is also deeply rooted in the diasporic condition of Australia. It was with Don Miller, Michael Healy, John Hutnyk, Kike Martinez and Scott McQuire that I first began to think through the problematics of the subject, and it was with Antigone Kefala, Peter Lyssiotis and George Michelakakis I was able to find examples of how this re-thinking can be staged. Sneja Gunew and Fiona Mackie showed me the intersections between the passions of theory and experience.

I also owe profound thanks to Teodor Shanin for arranging my first meeting with John Berger. To Teodor, my relatives and the Tan family I feel the humblest gratitude for their boundless generosity and open-ended hospitality, their enduring kindness was a pillar of support and a spur for inspiration.

My deepest thanks must be extended to Scott, Vassili and Erika for they lived with all the emotions of production.

Introduction

This exilic shuttle

Migrants have made modernity what it is, and modernity has changed the parameters of global migration. From this perspective we can ask who is the native and where is the home in modern times? Can there be levels of displacement in the culture of modernity? This book concerns itself with the radical instability of contemporary experience. It attempts to trace this theme by focusing on the representation of exile in John Berger's writing. Exile is taken to signify not just the consequence of political banishment but also to refer to the dislocations of peoples by economic pressures and the redefinition of values and norms through cultural transformation. In this sense exile embraces the totality of ruptures that pervade the mechanisms and constitute the dynamism for social change. I argue that exile is not just the consequence *of* modernity, but also a metaphor for the processes *within* modernity. Exile will also be used as a component in the methodology for a critical representation of modernity. To raise exile as the dominant force in contemporary culture and as a trope for criticism is not without its problems. However, one of the advantages of this strategy is that it releases the migrant from carrying the burdened privilege of victimage as it obliges the reader to examine the multiple levels of displacement and rootedness in modernity.[1] Migration is not a problem that is confined to the traumas of departure, the imbalances in social injustice, the mistakes between languages, the dreams of release, and the nostalgia for return, rather migration with all its asymmetrical contours and uneven times is a metaphor for the modern condition. Modernity is a sensibility which is obsessed with journeys. It is articulated by a particular type of consciousness and in so far as my aim is to characterise these amorphous discursive practices I have followed the writings of an author who has managed to speak with the voices that have emerged from its hardest roads. Berger's writing is an ongoing portrait of the strangers in our midst, and he articulates a consciousness which the social sciences have either passed over in silence or invoked with clumsy abstractions.

The stranger is the person who has entered 'our' space but without an *a priori* claim for staying. Strangers arrive from the beyond but what is it that they have entered? Would we ask ourselves the question of what makes us what we are, would we define our space if it wasn't for the presence of strangers? To know oneself is to confront the stranger within and beside you. But where does this confrontation occur, on the street, in the heart or in language? We have many names for strangers. But what names does this self-constituted 'we' give to its own identity? Take away the geographic and political affiliations in which you are inserted and then try to give yourself a name. The local, the citizen, the native? Is that enough? Does it even sound real? This is the contradiction that the stranger must wear. He or she can no longer say, 'I am what I am and you know what I mean.' They must find other terms. Yet by some curious transposition of value in the opposition between foreigner/local, migrant/native, exile/citizen it seems that it is the former term which is recognisable instantaneously. It is the negative term of the stranger with its heavier sense of gravity that is capable of setting loose the myriad flock of images, clichés and stereotypes, whereas the positive term of belonging is blockfilled like an invisible hypothesis. What this suggests is that the problem of the stranger is not that he or she lacks a name, but that it precedes his/her arrival, action and voice. The identity of the stranger begins in dreams of hope and fear, and the dream of exile begets modernity. From here we must examine how this process of naming and the phenomenon of estrangement are integral to the cultural dynamics of modernity. The stranger is always located within society and we must ask what are the available categories for defining these levels of interaction. The etymology of words or the existence of synonyms at times reflects the scope for differentiating and understanding the complex patterns of social interaction.[2]

John Berger's diverse writings which range from art criticism to literature, from sociology to philosophy offer us the unique opportunity not only to reflect on the utility of each genre but also to engage with the specificity of particular forms of exile. At first this diversity can appear as a problem for a study which seeks to use it as the object of investigation. The difficulty of locating Berger's writing in the context of British culture or the empirical procedure of a psychobiography which tracks the genesis of a system through the parallel development of character has been bypassed because no clear-cut relationship exists between the space of writing, the culture of a nation state and the life of the author. The boundaries between writing, culture and author do not present themselves in analogical terms, rather the borderline between these 'bodies' is constantly traversed.[3] However, this difficulty of defining the context within the conventional categories does not lead to a cul-de-sac but opens up as a chronicle for the decentring of sexual and cultural identities in modernity. For while a reading of say Berger's art criticism in the 1950s may be very revealing of the particular cultural and political barriers in the London art world, what is also necessary is to consider the heterogenous sources of the questions that Berger put to these debates, and from this angle, the portrayal of the minor blockages and conflicts within this milieu can serve as a metaphor for our modernity. Today, with all the upheavals of decolonisation and the intensive trafficking of signs through telecommunications, the relationship between individuals and their culture cannot be represented in discrete terms which presuppose that cultures are hermetically sealed. Culture is the name for the dynamism which regulates social exchange, it does not refer to a closed container. Hence the terms culture and exile must be linked to unfold the productive as well as the disruptive processes of transgression.

The three chapters in this book are concerned with tracing parallel co-ordinates and processes: in the first chapter I have attempted to relate Berger's commentary on the artist's position in society to the question of attachment and detachment; in the second chapter I have brought Berger's discussion on migration into play with the Simmelian co-ordinates of near and far; and in the third chapter I have examined Berger's fictional representation of the ruptures in sexual identity through the psychoanalytic concepts of self and other.

In an illuminating essay on the migrant perspective, Paul Carter takes Artistotle's opposition between history as 'the telling of that which had happened' and poetry as 'the narrative of that which *could* happen' and *joins* them to illustrate both Husserl's notion of 'concomitant modes of production' and his own evocation of the migrational predisposition.[4] With the combinatory genius of the bricoleur Berger also integrates the poetic trope of exile with the historical theme of displacement.

This book does not offer a history of modernity by establishing a causal relationship between Berger's texts and the shifting trajectory of this epoch. Rather it is an exploration which utilises literary, sociological and psychoanalytic concepts to reveal the multiple connections and fascinations that are brought to bear on the theme of exile and how the trope of exile can summon up a further exploration of the potentialities of his writing. This method seems justified in the absence of an established discipline that can examine the dynamics of displacement in modernity. For while Edward Said has asked the urgent question of why various theories are travelling across the borders of disciplines,[1] it is also necessary to pose the need for an interdisciplinary approach into the interjacency between the structures of modernity and the dynamics of exile.

The fundamental achievement that I have attempted to draw out is the dialogical relationship between author and subject. The vitality of this dialogue is secured by the methodological axioms of empathy, exile and metaphor. Thus while this book is concerned with expanding upon the theme of exile, it also includes empathy as a necessary correlative. If exile was merely an 'objective' subject, and if empathy was simply a 'subjective' form of understanding, then the exhaustability of the former and the one sidedness of the latter would defeat both the author's compulsion to repeat an approach, and mere persistence would hollow out the resonance of a theme. I argue that exile and empathy are both continuous forms of departure/arrival and projection/introjection. Empathy extends the identity of the self as it approaches the other not as an object for investigation, but as a subject with consciousness. This process of apprehension involves a sense of journeying: a departure from the preconceived certitudes rather than the mere accumulation of already known facts. In this sense empathy with the other approximates a sort of exile from the self, and the term which describes this process of approaching and retreating, putting together and pulling apart, superimposing known with unknown is metaphor. The cycle of this critical perspective reverberates within these three methodological co-ordinates. Thus in Berger's writing the critical pulse of metaphor oscillates within the ceaseless rhythm of exile and empathy.

This procedure must necessarily be distinguished from the 'outsider' principle of discovery. I would suggest that this dialogical mode of writing avoids the pitfalls of critical distance, appropriation and displacement which tend to dominate so much of the contemporary writing on the other. We need a form of recognition that is neither sentimental nor abstract, a code of interaction between the self and the other that admits the reflexivity of both positions, and a mode of criticism which opens that potential space within society for responding to alternatives.

The strategy that I have attempted to follow is to crossweave Berger's texts with and against the more enduring threads of cultural and critical theory. My concern is not to develop a system of interpretation which uses fiction to inform theory or vice versa, but rather to relate both to the discourse on agency in modernity. The resulting pattern infuses all the constitutive components with a new destiny. No overriding theory has guided my overall sojourn. It is an exercise based on the assumption that juxtaposition and comparison furnish productive insights and new formations. But juxtaposition always presupposes a framework. My manoeuvres are bounded on one side by the twin sentinels of critical theory – early German sociology and postwar French philosophy – and on the other side the current debates in cultural studies that Stuart Hall has aptly described as revolving around the 'politics of representation'. This trajectory raised old and unresolved questions, for instance the sociological status of literature. There are certain hesitancies, gaps and flaws which any alert reader will spot. But it is important to note that I am not alone in pondering or stumbling over these aporias. They are certainly not all of my making. For if we are to acknowledge that the humanities are in a crisis, then we cannot separate the epistemological shortfalls of the orthodox sociological explanations of change from the radical transitions that society is undergoing.

The emergence of cultural studies as a discipline is both a symptom and a response to this crisis. It is a symptom in that it has yet to lay down the principles for a new evaluation of the relationship between art and society. It is a response in so far as it has recognised new forms of cultural expression which have not only challenged the aesthetic distinctions between high and low art, canonical and non-canonical literature, but have also questioned the putative neutrality and detachment of the investigator of society. For cultural critics to face the question of modernity they must perform what Giddens calls the 'double hermeneutic', or what Spivak calls 'critical intimacy': that is, to acknowledge that they are engaged in a form of social interaction in which agents transform their actions as they reflect on their performance. It is at this juncture, when the politics of pragmatism and the ethics of commitment seem so irreconcilably distanced, that I take Berger's example as a guide. To look at the 'body' of his writing and to read a particular text with scrutiny is to witness the seeding of freedom and responsibility in every decision and to imagine the potential compatibility of uncertain dualisms and contradictions.

The task of this book is not prescriptive. It is reflective and at best suggestive of a possible reconfiguration which may guide our understanding of the relationship between home and exile; self and other; modern and non-modern. It is not my aim to represent the claims and aspirations of a particular group who lack the institutional power to define their own place in the world. However, I hope to offer a contribution towards the rising challenge against the categories which legitimise domination and exclusion.

John Berger has characterised this epoch as the century of departures; one could qualify this by saying that in fact this is the century of multiple departures and arrivals, and the real difference between the uncertitude of this epoch as compared with others is that the foreignness and uncanniness of a journey is measured not by the distance travelled, but in the unlocatability of the moment of departure and arrival. When did one truly leave? Was it in a dream, with a rumour, on a wish, or in the ship? As for the arrival, is it the place of destination or some way between destiny and return?

With all these entries and exits, what is most truly undermined is the stability of place, the coherence of a space that one can occupy, work on, represent, construct. How can one speak of rootedness or organic attachments or find other metaphors that will evoke some genuine or a serious and rigorous involvement with place? Who can hold on to this claim, who can even enjoy the privilege of earning these rights? These metaphors may seem redundant, but such projects are not. While the accepted language and forms have been fragmented, this does not imply that they should also be eliminated; on the contrary I will argue that they should be re-invented, and this time I hope the question of ethics and justice will be closer to the centre of the project of innovation and transformation.

Notes

1 See also P. Ilie, *Literature and Inner Exile*, Baltimore, Johns Hopkins University Press, 1980, p. 6 where he argues that it is necessary to extend 'the generic experience of exile whose central structure can enfold all forms of migration; physical and psychological, spatial and emotional, external and internal'.

2 John Torrance begins his seminal analysis of alienation and estrangement with a note of discontent against the conflation of these two terms and the blurring of their multiple implications. In the English-speaking world, the singular term alienation is often used to cover a concept that for Marx contained various subject positions, and which he specified through the use of various terms. Furthermore the etymology of such terms not only casts light on the moral and psychological ambit of the German language but is also revealing of the significance of polarities in Marx's dialectic. See *Estrangement, Alienation and Exploitation*, London, Macmillan, 1977.

3 Compare with J. Derrida, *The Ear of the Other*, New York, Schocken, 1985, p. 44.

4 P. Carter, 'Living in a New Country', *Meanjin*, vol. 49, no. 3, spring 1990, p. 435.

5 E. W. Said, *The World, the Text and the Critic*, Cambridge, Mass., Harvard University Press, 1983, p. 226.

1

The method of metaphor

Exile in modernity

I think the experience of emigration, of displacement could be found in almost everything I've written, and that corresponds with something deep in myself that I don't fully understand. But it is also one of the typical experiences, if not *the* typical experience of our century.

John Berger

Banishment or prolonged separation from one's native land is how the *Oxford English Dictionary* defines exile. This definition is illustrated by quotations which suggest that exile can be either a rewarding adventure into the unknown, or the melancholy trauma of moral and spiritual abandonment. This ambivalent trajectory of transcendence or negation is also etymologically presaged by the Latin word *salire* (to leap), which is the root that produces both *exile* and *exult*. There is a further ironic semantic intersection; exilience is an archaic term for the state of exultation.

Literary scholars have often noted not only that exile is a persistent theme in the history of literature but that the most profound works have been written by authors in exile. Yet what has this observation on the conjunction between the experience of exile and the representation of society led to? Have the critics looked into the nexus between detachment and involvement as a metaphor for critical thinking, or have they turned the other way, abandoned the realm of dialectics and merely conformed to the sentimental rhetoric which implies that the persistence of this archetype is also evidence of a 'perpetual' will to transform the island of suffering into the rock of redemption.[1] The condition of exile, I believe, deserves critical attention, not because of its putative universality but in its 'shocking' particularity.

To put a few brakes on the slide into sentimental generalisations, one need only consider the second definition of exile in the *OED*. Here exile means to reduce and to fragment. Although the ultimate etymology of this word is disputed, again it proves to be very illuminating: 'some regard it as contracted from *ex* - (privative) + *ilia* (entrails), the primary sense being assumed to have been "disembowelled"'. While this notion of exile as an eviscerated existence is archaic, the sense of diminution that it suggests compounds a loss of place with the absence of inner unity.[2] This definition also brings us closer to Franz Neumann's argument that as modern society has tightened the fit between politics and culture, it has proportionately *expanded* the impact of exile.[3] Exile in this sense is not measured by the distance or by the type of location to which one has been expelled, but in the disruption of the mechanisms for cultural and political formation. The etymologies of the archaic and modern definition of exile intersect within the suggestion that displacement occurs within the processes of internalisation. In an age where communication is not necessarily diminished by distance and for exile to remain an alternative to execution and incarceration it must take different forms. On the contemporary scale, as Edward Said argues, exile is comprehensible through the internalisation of rupture. Thus modern exile is not exclusively confined to the massive displacement of peoples from their homelands but can also be located in the specific forms of silencing opposition without expulsion.[4]

These conjunctions and qualifications focus our attention on the condition of exile in two directions; firstly, it is a recognition of the invalidity of the romantic vision of exile; and secondly, Said emphasises that a modern vision must confront a number of global as well as local paradoxes. For instance, while the United Nations defines a person as an exile on the basis of 'well founded fear of persecution, for reason of his race, religion, nationality, or political opinion', there remains an unresolved tension between the subjective perception of fear on the part of the exile and the official interpretation on the part of the states involved.[5] As some legal commentators have observed, the dominant concern in international law reflects the vested interests of multinational corporations, whereby the emphasis is heavily weighted on the prevention of appropriation of foreign assets rather than the promotion of the rights of minorities *within* states.[6] As Giddens rightly observed, with the geo-political demarcation of the globe into interlocking nation-states, borders have replaced frontiers. This absorption of the liminal space between countries has not just tightened the control of geographic margins but also redefined the political constituency of individuals.[7] Allegiance to a nation-state cannot be suspended but only transferred.[8] Thus as the establishing of human rights is made synonymous with, and confined to, *national* rights, the meaning of modern exile must be related to the emergence of the nation-state.

Exile and belonging must not be seen as opposites which are exclusive of each other, for there is not just a physical border which both joins and separates these states but also a dialectical tension that informs and constitutes their meaning. Neither term can be grasped in isolation – the word nationalism for instance, first written by an exiled French priest, was the result of the conflict between the love of the particular and the love of the general.[9] Consequently, to perceive nationalism as the consolidation of identity purely through negative identification, or to reduce the paradoxical ubiquity of this 'inwardly determined social necessity'[10] to an expression of the false consciousness of global political economy, is to belie the fictive[11] processes of self-affirmation and to ignore the agonistic[12] tension between the internal and the external in social formation. The perspective on exile and nationalism[13] that I wish to develop is one that does not repeat the binary opposition of lack and plenitude. I would suggest that the border between the two is both fixed and unstable. If the meaning of exile and emigration was confined to banishment by political decree and geographic displacement, then neither would offer any general purchase on the analysis of estrangement within modernity. However, if we consider exile as a metaphor for the act of interpretation as well as the name for the journey from the familiar to the foreign, and if we include the other meaning of exile which suggests diminution and fragmentation and whose etymology is derived from the act of disembowelment, then we can expand the critical force of these terms. From this 'position' we can suggest a new method for understanding the complex patterns of cultural interjacency and the psychological processes of identification in modernity.

The clearest examination of the theme of exile and possibly the best starting point for a study of John Berger's writing occurs in the middle of his most meditative book, *And our Faces, my Heart, Brief as Photos*. It is here that Berger explores the parallelism between the inner dynamics of the migrant, and the ubiquitous experience of estrangement in modernity, by relating both to a consciousness of the transformations in the meaning of home: 'the displacement, the homelessness, the abandonment lived by a migrant is the extreme form of a more general and widespread experience. The term "alienation" confesses all'.[14] Following on from Mircea Eliade's claim that traditional societies locate 'the heart of the real' in the home, that is, as both the site for the ontological reconciliation of time and space, and the axis-point that secures a unity between the spiritual and terrestrial, Berger relates the modern anxiety over authenticity and the struggle for meaning in modernity to the experience of migration: 'to emigrate is always to dismantle the center of the world, and so to move into a lost, disoriented one of fragments'.[15]

This is not to say that the objective walls and corridors within which we live are now devoid of emotional or figurative qualities. Gaston Bachelard has intricately and sensitively analysed the ways in which the properties of a house are saturated with metaphorical qualities, and how this continuous process of projection and introjection grants meaning to the place of residence.[16] However, the metaphoricity of this process which intensifies identity through the imaginative leaps across animate/inanimate, objective/subjective, internal/external, near/far takes a new twist in modernity. In modernity the frame that gives meaning to action has shifted and the link between the home and the social cannot be configured in a transparent hierarchy. It is as if the modern home is at best a process of bricolage, a juxtaposition of disparate elements, where each fissure testifies to the absence of any unitary sense of wholeness.

In modernity the meaning of home has shifted from being a shelter that unifies the dual consciousness of memory and destiny through tradition, to being a container of incommensurable practices and improvisations. 'Home is no longer a dwelling but the untold story of a life being lived.'[17]. From such aphorisms and ruminations we can reflect back over Berger's writings and witness the centrality of exile in his entire project, but we can also project forward into the debates on modernity and modernism and again note the ubiquity of exile and of the figure of the stranger. As I proceed in these two directions I want to emphasise that the contemporary manifestation of exile cannot be contained by the conventional forms that it is associated with, that is, as an expression of romantic disavowal or as a consequence of political banishment. The relevance of any contemporary examination of exile can only be secured if it is located in the broader cultural dynamics of displacement in modernity.

It is now commonplace in social theory to define modernity as a process of radical upheaval. Most social critics have noted that the modern world is characterised by the increasing fragmentation of traditional structures and the pluralisation of social structures of belief within the private sphere. Coupled with this is the ascendancy of bureaucratic and technological institutions that regulate praxis in the public sphere.[18] Berger consistently confronts the conradiction between the modern rationality that validates progress and achievement in linear metaphors of movement – getting ahead, leaving the past behind – and the multi-dimensional experience of displacement and estrangement inherent in the incessant migrations of modernity. The gap between the given and the desired is present in all social structures; however, what is unique about modernity is that the distance between the two is not explained by the will of God. In the absence of God, the narratives of modernity explain destiny by either the agency of the individual or the structure of society. Modernity begins with the consciousness to confront a double rupture; firstly, the displacement and reinvention of comprehensible norms; and secondly, in the dismantling of structured patterns for conferring identity and value. In both lurks the threat of an unknown anomie and the promise of increased agency.

The dynamism for change in the culture of modernity is thus paradoxical. Paradoxes frame the universe of social relations and personal ethics, even the narrative structures which seek to inscribe the form of modernity are framed by paradox. The myths of modernity are of displacement rather than unity, they promise new levels of choice but do so only at the expense of undermining the universal certitudes which guide decisions. To represent the relationship between structure and action when everyday life is so radically unstable is fraught with difficulties. Few paradigms seem secure in a culture which valorises change and constantly provokes a sense of crisis and transformation. To explain the present disjunctures critics are left with invidious choices: to search for monumental 'new' theories, or to refashion 'old' theories. However, even the attempts which consciously refuse to collude with the hollow paeans to modern progress, or lament the loss of authenticity and seek to strive towards a radical synthesis, often conceal an asymmetrical negation of the constitutive tension, or return to a prior position.[19] The critical way out is found not at either end of these oppositions, but by *working through* the dialectic between the threat of exile and the promise of home in modernity.

This dialectic between exile and home in modernity is often bypassed in favour of a simplistic binarism which relegates the plausibility of home to pre-modernity. In this schema the social cohesion and the identity of the home in pre-modernity stands in stark contrast to the social antagonism of anonymity of the home in modernity. The putative homeliness of pre-modernity 'accuses' modernity all the more for its homelessness.[20] But from where do the demands and the desires that define this 'metaphysical' concept of home emerge if not from modernity? To understand the cultural dynamics of modernity the meaning of 'home' needs to be radicalised.

Rather than seeing 'home' as the essential vestige of the premodern, which is lacking in modernity, it might be more accurate to see the presence or absence of home and homelessness as a dialectic 'peculiar' to modernity. Thus the sense of 'freedom', which also ushers forth the ideology of mobility, individualism and progress, is not an expression of an ahistorical 'man' but is the necessary step that guarantees admission into the 'historical' consciousness of modernity.[21]

Between the submission to modernity as an oppressive unity, and the celebration of modernity as an open arena in which a near infinity of possibilities can be assembled and reassembled, we need to probe the 'parameters of choice' not simply through the binary opposition between the past and present which serves as a moral opposition between lack and plenitude, but rather to open a critical space which highlights the ambivalence of the 'freedom' that is gained, as Arnold Gehlen reminds us, *through* alienation.

Metaphor as method

The theme at the centre of Berger's writing is the dynamic instability between social values and social roles in modernity. I call this theme exile because it involves at least an historical disjuncture, if not a geographical displacement. Perhaps what is unique to modernity is not just the unprecedented scale of migrations, or even the nature of the imposition or the obligation to leave home, but rather the experience of estrangement that *precedes* departure. In modernity foreignness is not commensurate with distance travelled.

The proximity of foreignness, or rather the unique interconnection between the foreign and the familiar in modernity, can be explained partly by the increased traffic of visual symbols and the perpetual 'reinvention' of the object of desire by a media culture which operates simultaneously on a local and a global scale. In the first section of this introduction I attempted to define the modern experience of exile by locating it in the context of global transitions. I have argued that the dynamics of exile are generated by both internal and external forces, and that ultimately the experience of rupture and dislocation does not presuppose movement. Exile also occurs in the heart of the home. It is my contention that there is another face to the concept of modern exile. The fascination with exile is related not only to the experience of physical displacement but also to the semantic ruptures in representation. Thus exile is often a crucial component in the methodology of critical thinking. This form of thinking I will call metaphorical. In the following sections of this introduction I want to argue that if exile is considered as a concept for distanciation, and coupled with the concept of empathy, then it can also be utilised to open up the methodological principles of metaphor. Exile and empathy could be seen as analogues to the dual co-ordinates of near and far, as well as to the twin forces of approaching and retreating that are constitutive of metaphor.

The use of exile as a methodological concept is not linked to the romantic association between exile and the putative clarity that is gained by seeing things from a distance. While attempting to address the interconnection between perspective and position, I proceed from the assumption that there is no neutral or exterior point from which vision can claim absolute objectivity. Exile does not connote the space outside society, but the process of crossing borders. If there is a productive and incisive side to this experience, it emerges from the attention to the consequences of shuttling from one position to another and results in an awareness of the unstable equilibrium that regulates both detachment and attachment.

In an essay on photography Berger describes August Sander's method as 'translucently documentary', and quoting from Walter Benjamin's earlier appraisal he tries to illuminate this paradox: 'It is indeed unprejudiced observation, bold and at the same time delicate, very much in the spirit of Goethe's remark: "There is a delicate form of the empirical which identifies itself so intimately with its object that it thereby becomes theory"'.[22] Before looking at Berger's own method in greater detail I would like to unfold the claims that are embedded in this quotation in order to question the categories which define the suitability of certain methodological components for social criticism. This intimate form of observation that delicately entwines the empirical with the theoretical is, I believe, an example of empathy. Just as I argued that the sentimental lament for an irrevocable loss of place, or the regressive 'nostalgia' which encloses itself within an unattainable moment in the past must not overshadow our understanding of modern exile. Similarly we must distinguish empathy from its egocentric variety, which attempts to blur the boundary between self and other in order to rationalise an unearned or an appropriative claim for similitude.

Empathy is a process of understanding which is undervalued in modernity. It is regarded as intuitive rather than as scientific, speculative rather than accountable, imaginative rather than empirical. In short it is seen as subjective as opposed to the objective, because it is incommensurate with the dispassionate principles of critical distance. The value of empathy is denigrated by the same logic which defines distinction via exclusion and isolation. Knowledge which is gained through empathy is considered at best as impure and equivocal and at worst, as an instance of what in psychoanalytic terms is called 'projection'. Empathy is thus measured on a scale that ranges from the dubious to the pathological. However, if we take the common working principle in poetics which suggests that a form of projection is not only present in the complex patterns through which identity is defined with and against the other, but is also central to all representation, then we can begin to radicalise our understanding of knowledge. For rather than attempting to deny this criss-crossing network of traces, what is needed is a certain degree of permeability between the boundaries and the processes of self-understanding. From this perspective, identity would not be perceived as an impervious and homogenous block. It would also open a space which would facilitate a vigorous negotiation between the limits of the self and the beginnings of the other.[23]

Empathy thus serves as a concept for the approach and the reception of the other in the formation of knowledge. However it also leads to a certain type of predisposition, a way of receiving the other which curiously splices the unknown with prefiguration. The fragility of the object that beckons restoration, or the solidity of the unknown place of arrival is always ambiguous. In Berger's writing, there is the faint awareness that, in a partial sense, such 'objects' were already 'there' in his consciousness even before his conscious realisations. The dual consciousness of arrival and departure throughout the process of journeying, which juxtaposes the impressions formed in one place with the contradictory memories of another, constitutes what is often described as the exile's bifocal vision. Edward Said argues that it is this experience of crossing boundaries – with the concomitant discovery that even when borders are permeable the relationships within different cultures are not wholly correspondent – which produces new narrative forms.[24] In this respect Said claims that Berger's work is exemplary, not because it contains the yearning for an unbounded mutuality with the other, but rather for its rigorous attentiveness to 'other ways of telling'. In the performance of this critical task Said explains that

> there must be interference, crossing of borders and obstacles, a determined attempt to generalize exactly at those points where generalizations seem impossible to make. One of the first interferences to be ventured, then, is a crossing from literature, which is supposed to be subjective and powerless, in those exactly parallel realms, now covered by journalism and the production of information that employ representation but are supposed to be objective and powerful.[25]

Said concludes that Berger's work offers a 'superb guide' in the 'opening of culture to the experience of the Other which have remained "outside" . . . the norms manufactured by "insiders"'.[26] Hence the 'gift' of empathy is not in the disappearance of the subject in the object of contemplation, but in the heightening of new subject positions in the dialogue with the excluded, and as a safeguard against what Ashis Nandy calls the asymmetry of objectification and over-definition in cultural inwardness.[27]

Having argued that the propensity for change is the dynamism of modernity I now wish to use the concepts of exile and empathy to comment on the overriding vision that steers all of Berger's writing. If we use exile and empathy as two modes – one which refers to the repulsion that pushes the subject away, and the other which describes the attraction which pulls the subject in – this will offer a bifocal perspective that is adequate for an understanding of the particular method that guides Berger in all his heterogenous projects.

This fascination with the twin axioms of convergence and dispersal, familiarisation and distanciation, polysemy and silence, approach and withdrawal, is articulated in discursive as well as analytical voices. In Berger's novel *G* the narrator repeatedly interrupts the flow of narration in order to comment on the tension between the fragmentary apprehension of reality and the desire for an *a priori* totalisation schema which can ground the particular in the general.²⁸ In his film scripts with Alain Tanner, Berger spliced Brecht's theory of alienation and Eisenstein's narrative technique of 'a montage of attractions', to form a 'push-pull movement between the attraction of the real and the uncoupling from the real' resulting in a method that Tanner calls the 'realism of desire'.²⁹ Whilst commenting on the narrative potential of photography Berger meditates on the profound oscillation between stillness and movement in order to comment on the principles of translation and interpretation. For Berger meaning comes from the transformation of a single disconnected instant into an observation perceived in the terms of a 'subjective revelation'.³⁰ Finally, after writing his first collection of short stories on the peasantry Berger concluded that stories are not guarantors of the known, they do not confirm occupancy, but are ways of habituating the unknowable.

To approach experience, however, is not like approaching a house. 'Life', as the Russian proverb says, 'is not a walk across an open field'. Experience is indivisible and continuous, at least within a single lifetime and perhaps over many lifetimes. I never have the impression that my experience is entirely my own, and it often seems to me that it preceded me. In any case experience folds upon itself, refers backwards and forwards to itself through the referents of hope and fear; and by the use of metaphor, which is at the origin of language, it is continually comparing like with unlike, what is small with what is large, what is near with what is distant. And so the act of approaching a given moment of experience involves both scrutiny (closeness) and the capacity to connect (distance). The movement of writing resembles that of a shuttle on a loom: repeatedly it approaches and withdraws, closes in and takes its distance. Unlike a shuttle, however, it is not fixed to a static frame. As the movement of writing repeats itself, its intimacy with the experience increases. Finally if one is fortunate meaning is the fruit of intimacy.³¹

Thus the metaphor for Berger's method is metaphor itself. For Berger metaphor is not just a rhetorical flourish, but rather it is the origin and the process of meaning. His continuous project has been to formulate ways of seeing the thisness of thatness.

Metaphor is not just a rhetorical trope for expressing the difference or the similitude of things (in most cases Berger sees the lightness of metaphor as the counter to the burden of dogma), the metaphoric 'moment' in language is not confined to its ability to create a novel perception or reveal a hidden significance through its incongruous perspective, rather metaphor in all its luminous elusiveness is the universal basis of all thought, it is the cognitive and the mythological process which discovers validation through the association of contraries.[32]

The attention to the metaphoricity of all meaning also involves a shuttling movement in relation to place and time. Berger is quick to see that embedded within the etymology of metaphor is the 'theory' which links the process of naming through differentiation and the dynamics of movement in creativity. 'The Greek word for "porter" is *metaphor*. And this is a reminder of how deeply the act of transporting, of dispatch and delivery, is intrinsic to the imagination'.[33] If the etymology of metaphor suggests the act of transporting, then we must also question the assumption in everyday and philosophical discourse that makes the link between metaphor and truth conditional on its transparency. When metaphor serves as the invisible 'porter', that is, when metaphor doubles-up as the messenger and the message, then it is recognised not just as the image which serves as a proxy to reality, but as a linguistic fact that is constitutive of reality. My concern at this stage is not to use Berger's various reflections on the relationship between metaphor and thought, or even to contest whether metaphor is the master trope in language, but rather my aim is to describe the structural dynamics of metaphor in order to illustrate both the fluidity and the fixity in Berger's method. Metaphor is like a structure made *in* motion. Metaphor is not the moment of resolution, it does not declare, define, equate or arrive once and for all, but rather the truth of metaphor is in its alliance with disparates, a sign which confirms a destination by suggesting a further direction. The truth of metaphor is not in what it contains but in the possibilities it suggests. It includes opposites not to rebound perpetually within them, but to scaffold up and beyond them. For Berger, metaphor joins and poetry extends:

> Poetry's impulse to use metaphor, to discover resemblance, is not to make comparisons . . . or to diminish the particularity of any event; it is to discover those correspondences of which the sum total would be proof of the indivisible totality of existence . . . Apart from reassembling by metaphor, poetry reunites by its *reach*.[34]

For Berger, whose relationship to place has always been ambivalent and whose consciousness is drawn to the exclusions and contradictions in the given categories of a culture, it is metaphor which serves as the map for imagination, and it is metaphor which surrounds and plots experience.

The boon of language is that *potentially* it is complete, it has the potentiality of

The method of metaphor 19

holding with words the totality of human experience – everything that has occurred and everything that may occur. It even allows space for the unspeakable. In this sense one can say of language that it is potentially the only human home, the only dwelling place that cannot be hostile to man. For prose this home is a vast territory, a country which it crosses through a network of tracks, paths, highways; for poetry this home is concentrated on a single center, a single voice, and this voice is simultaneously that of an announcement and a response to it.[35]

If exile and empathy are concepts for the act of receiving and displacing and metaphor the overall process of combining in interpretation, then it would be valid to characterise Berger's method as metaphor in motion. In the debates over the function of language as the 'house' that interiorises experience, or the 'permanent exile' between language and its content,[36] Berger's writing can be seen as beginning with an appreciation of the estranging tensions and gaps between representation and experience, but also committed to the belief that, at best, descriptions must alleviate as they integrate disparities. This is not to suggest that language can offer a quick panacea or a respite from the exterior tensions for, in Berger's writing, every resolution presupposes an awareness of its constitutive oppositions. Similarly, the unceasing attempt to accommodate the enduring experience of exile within the fragile walls of language is not just a sacrificial act of redemption but the source and the process of criticism. To avoid the egocentric pitfalls of mannerism and moralism, Berger suggests that an artist's convictions must grow from an imaginative identification with: 'the tragedy or energy of his subject matter, instead of using his subject matter as a justification, a dramatic container of his own emotion.'[37] By focusing on the experience of the other Berger is not attempting to conceal the identity of the self, or to suggest that experience categorically precedes language, yet through this emphasis on 'engagement' it does commit him all the more to the belief that the utility of a representation is secured only through its multiple interrelations. It is in the unravelled textures between experience and language, rather than the sovereignty of the one over the other that we forge a critical understanding of the relationship between the self and the other. This process of imaginative identification is best illustrated by tracing Berger's description of the working method of various artists. Like so many of the recurring themes in Berger's writing this question can be approached only tangentially and vicariously.

Amidst Berger's essays there are a number of portraits of other authors and painters.[38] In all these essays Berger's attention has never been simply focused on achievement, his fascination is not just with what is made, but also in how it is made. These portraits reveal character by reflecting on the making of objects and by casting projections on the aspirations that are contained within labour. In the following analysis of these portraits I will attempt to illustrate not just the link between Berger's criticism and the way in which others have worked, but also to draw attention to the critical process of identification in representation. For instance, in Berger's quotation of Victor Serge's thoughts on the function of writing one can witness the formulation of a task which resembles the roles that Berger attributed to his own writing: 'He saw writing as a means of expressing to men what most of them live inwardly without being able to express, as a means of communion, a testimony to the vast flow of life through us, whose essential aspect we must try to fix for the benefit of those who will come after us.'[39] The value of writing is thus determined not just by the author's ability to demonstrate the possibilities for social change, or in the innovative use of language to heighten this potential,[40] but also in the reciprocity that the author establishes with his or her audience.[41] Freedom lies at both ends of the function of writing: there is no response without freedom, and freedom needs to be re-imagined before the author can write. Berger saw writing as offering three levels of meaning that were absent from habitual consciousness. Firstly, writing is the act that gives *form* to experience. Secondly, writing was the means by which a hidden truth was *revealed*. Thirdly, writing was the record of the silent or the silenced histories whereby writing doubles up as a space for *testifying* to the unrecorded parts of history. In this sense writing becomes the atavistic space, or, paradoxically, the forgotten books of a culture. Through this process of construction, revelation and testimony the performative function of writing projects the author to a position of witness, whereby the author moves against detachment by working through the attachments of the 'people' he or she is trying to represent. It is through this oscillating dynamism that Berger invests writing with the function of recognising both the forces of history that traverse time and the ability to inhabit them. Writing thus serves as the refuge of experience; both the means for redeeming it from the exterior and the space in which it is housed.

For Berger the relationship between writing and truth is forged through the identification of the tension between the inner and outer experiences of a subject. This methodology presupposes both the idealism that there is a protean truth and an adversarial social predicament which represses the realisation of such truth. In Berger's metaphors exile heightens the distance *between* and empathy offers an approach *to* the reconciliation between the given and the desired. Hence the role of writing is not a cynical renegation, or a sentimental foreclosure of the tension between the inner and outer life, but the maintenance of a dialogue that increases an awareness of social justice.[42]

The double-sexed Micheletist hero who deposits and conducts Justice within History described so vividly by Barthes is not quite the heroic model present in Berger's writing, nor would it be accurate to suggest that Berger is heroised by simply transmitting the message of other heroes; however, what Michelet calls Heroisation, 'the power of seeing and resuscitating Justice', is illustrative of both the process of the hero and the function of the writer. For if the purpose of Berger's 'joining' with the heroic subject is neither a form of selfless immersion nor a parasitic attachment, but rather a form of extension which possesses the virtues of disclosing the style of both the self and the other, then the nature of this method can be described as metaphorical, for it is in essence the association of contraries. Thus, to examine Berger's relationship with his subject, one has to consider 'fidelity' not in terms of substantive replication, but as an open-ended process that includes the generative tension of transformation.

This relationship between self and other can be further demonstrated by tracing the emphasis that Berger gives to the active role of interruption and reconstruction in Cézanne's analysis of perception and interpretation:

Cézanne, who consciously strove towards a new synthesis between art and nature, who wanted to renew the European tradition, in fact destroyed for ever the foundation of that tradition by insisting, more and more radically as his work developed, that visibility is as much an extension of ourselves as it is a quality-in-itself of things. Through Cézanne we recognize that a visible world begins and ends with the life of each man, that millions of these visible worlds correspond in so many respects that from the correspondences we can construct *the* visible world, but that this world of appearances is inseparable from each one of us: and each one of us constitutes its centre.[43]

After Cézanne art could no longer function as the 'mere' record of things, and if the artist's task involves a combination of projection and introjection, then the artist must 'place himself in the position of another' as well as being 'permeated by the outrages and sins among which he found himself'.[44] For just as the value of love is heightened by the consistent re-negotiation of the borders between the lover and the loved, Berger also argues that the value of seeing is measured by the reverberating intensity of involvement between the seer and the seen, and he repeatedly affirms that faithfulness to the other can only come from the empathy of love,[45] and that understanding proceeds between the spontaneous construction of an order and a perceptual recognition of things.[46]

For Berger, objectivity demands both intimacy and distance, whereas detachment in isolation can only yield objectification. Schemas which exteriorise the relationship between subject and object are considered flawed because they are seen as defensive strategies that simultaneously justify a judgemental moralism as they pre-empt any identification with the other. In the case of La Tour's early paintings Berger argues that all the figures arrive already transformed into signs and designated to some form of moral injunction. In La Tour's schema every representation of a physical gesture and expression is pre-determined by the ineluctable laws of his own symbolic language. Berger claims that in an age which lacks the total faith of the Middle Ages, and when individualism has been gained at the expense of a God-given iconography, the use of a coda to justify distanciation is not just cynical and dispassionate but also a self-aggrandising manoeuvre, for in La Tour's work the use of abstract formality grants him the space to imitate God.[47] Distance offers La Tour the space both to invent his subjects and to pass judgement.

The credibility of an image is thus generated not by the severity of its judgement but by the construction of a perspective that visually reveals an amalgam of multiple experiences or what Said calls the 'non-sequential energy of subjectivity'.[48] In contradistinction to La Tour's failure, Berger argues that Ralph Fasanella's paintings succeed because what is contained in his images of New York is a result of the identification with the perspective of New Yorkers. There is no singular intention to form judgements *against* others, by painting the condition *of* others. Fasanella's approach is far more consensual. He is not situated ahead of, or above the subject, but *within* it. Fasanella shows *how* the pressure of the city, with its 'impersonal ahistoricity',[49] has sucked out the possibility of inhabiting space and time; *how* the city with its 'eviscerated'[50] exteriority remains as a continuous plane of windows and walls – all surface and no refuge; and *how* the dreams of

The method of metaphor

immigrants have been dashed by the insurmountable stigmas and irredeemable suffering of migration.[51] The city is thus shown not as a static place but as a 'circuit of messages'.[52] Yet despite this representation of hardship and estrangement Berger claims that the tone in Fasanella's paintings is not tragic, for neither are they haunted by despair nor do they seek to offer a respite from the tense rhythm they express. In Fasanella's paintings: 'The island of Manhattan is a gigantic metaphoric model of the compression of an immigrant ship that has moored and never left.'[53] While describing Fasanella's paintings, Berger also produces a metaphor which illuminates a perspectival method. Here the paradoxical resemblance between the migrant's home and the moored vessel suggests both the inability to return to the 'old' country and the static journey within the 'new'. Similarly, Fasanella succeeds as an artist because he adapts his perspective to accommodate the density of the metropolis and the radial memories of its inhabitants:

> Thus each painting offers, not an instant view, a postcard, but an amalgam of visual experience, a sequence of memories. Hence the likeness. Hence the fact that those who have lived in these streets, *recognize* corner after corner although Fasanella has 'invented' them.[54]

Berger gives another example of an artist who by inadvertently joining and bending contradictory languages for spatial perspective revealed a further insight into the enigma of time and vision. Seker Ahmet, while attempting to introduce the European optic into Turkish art, created a painting entitled *Woodcutter in the Forest*. For Berger, the peculiar gravity in the perspective of this painting not only revealed the disjuncture between the ontology of European landscape painting and the Turkish pictorial tradition, but also gave expression to an experience for which neither the language nor the tradition were designed. Berger argues that Ahmet painted the forest in such a way that it appears to be both withdrawing and approaching the woodcutter. This spatial ambiguity is primarily sustained by the representation of the woodcutter's path from above. For rather than showing the path disappearing into the horizon, as is the convention in European landscape painting, Ahmet has offered a view which gives the woodcutter's sensation of being led onwards into the eventual clearing and also of being engulfed by the forest.[55]

In Berger's mind's eye Seker Ahmet:

> faced the forest as a thing taking place in itself, as a presence that was so

pressing that he could not, as he had learnt to do in Paris, maintain his distance from it. This, I think, is what caused the disjuncture to open between the two traditions: the disjuncture in which this forest painting has its being.[56] Berger's appreciation of Ahmet's achievement was, however, prepared by his understanding of the passage in Heidegger's *Discourse on Thinking* which describes the reciprocal relationship between the horizon and vision as 'the coming-into-the-nearness of distance'. Heidegger's verb 'presencing' – which contests the measurement of the present in linear units and attempts to include the dual sense of abiding and extension – also becomes the apposite metaphor not only for the relationship between the woodcutter and the forest, but also for the methodological oscillation between absence and presence, rootedness and migration in Berger's writing.

The subtle interplay between exile as a multivalent theme in modernity and exile as an operative component in a critical methodology for representing modernity is the continuous pulse in Berger's writing. But what does this repetition signify? Is it just a reflection of the historical ubiquity of exile in modernity, or is it expressive of a particular starting or end point toward which other themes are directed?

To assess this interweaving between theme and method according to a sociological method which focuses on context or a psychological method which emphasises the predispositions of an individual would fail to relate what Freud calls the 'drive to repeat' to what Berger calls 'that permanent process by which reality is being produced'.[57] To examine the various conjunctions that are at play in Berger's representation of exile we require a method that can draw from the diverse fields of poetics, philosophy, history and psychoanalysis, and in this way we might also revitalise the parameters of sociology. For ultimately, in Berger's texts the utility of theme and method is measured by the construction of a presence that *intercepts* the production of other presences.[58]

Only a method which includes the properties and dynamics of metaphor would be suitable for an analysis of Berger's texts. For given the diverse range in subject matter and genre and the non-linear process of development, a metaphorical method would enable us to discover continuities in the midst of all these diverse approaches. This method would draw attention to the 'on-going-ness' and elasticity of Berger's project without having to justify it in terms of a scholarly assemblage or celebrate it under the chic banner of postmodern

The method of metaphor

partiality and incompleteness. The continuities do not surface in isomorphic reproductions[19] of content, nor does the 'line' of thought develop along well-marked paths, the 'true' path emerges only, in Zen-like stead, *through* the journey. I am not suggesting that Berger conveniently disguises or unwittingly represses his method, but considering the emphasis that he places on the relationship between the mode and the content of representation, it could be seen that this resistance to articulating a 'precise' methodology is both a reflection of his claim about the 'radial' nature of subjectivity in modernity and an obtuse disavowal of academic and commonsensical literality. For the consequence is not an anti-methodology but a methodology which is formed through metaphor. And Berger can rightly claim that the precedent for this lies in the most profound critic of modernity: Karl Marx; and in the most affirmative aesthetic innovation in modernity: cubism:

> in Marx's mode of thinking the degree to which each superceding phase of thought modifies the orientation of the preceding phase is new, because it plays upon a new notion of discontinuity . . . one proceeds by leaps from point to point.[60]

> The proposition that a work of art is a new object and not simply the expression of its subject, the structuring of a picture to admit the coexistence of different modes of space and time, the inclusion in a work of art of extraneous objects, the dislocation of forms to reveal movement or change, the combining of hitherto separate and distinct media, the diagrammatic use of appearances – these were the revolutionary innovations of Cubism.[61]

Berger's analogy between the chiasmatic method of connection in Marx's writing and the cubists' experimentation with interjacency underlines the methodological utilisation of discontinuity and the interactive process of interpretation.[62]

The incorporation of the extraneous is necessary, not simply in order to enhance the identity of the internal, but rather because the continuity of an identity is only realisable to the extent that it can include a 'discontinuous' relationship with that which is non-identical with itself. The critical difference between language as the means of identification and language as the end of objectification is well illustrated by Ashis Nandy's configuration of the master/servant relationship, in which he claims that there is a moral imperative to admit the superior consciousness of the slave: 'because he represents a higher order cognition which perforce includes the master as a human, whereas the master's cognition has to exclude the slave except as a "thing"'.⁶³ Lyotard also warns that for criticism to avoid the functionalist role of crisis management it must incorporate into its mode of inquiry a dynamic that secures an ongoing alertness to the tensions and displacements within each resolution. To this end Lyotard inserts a distinction between the modern, postmodern and romantic addressee and stages the modern as being 'between' constituencies. 'The modern addressee would be the "people", an idea whose referent oscillates between the romantics' *volk* and the fin-de-siècle bourgeoisie.'⁶⁴

However, the implication of Lyotard's distinctions in his discussion of modernity questions the very foundational presuppositions of sociology. Lyotard argues that the two key representational models – functional and conflict theory – share the idea that society forms an organic whole. Lyotard's analysis of contemporary society rejects both these models with his 'infamous' diagnosis that the postmodern condition marks the end of grand narratives. While claiming that traditional models are invalidated as they are 'haunted by the paradisiac representation of a lost "organic" society', Lyotard does not make the counter-claim that the transformation of social relationships in postmodernity can be conceived as free-floating, or disengaged atoms 'thrown into the absurdity of Brownian motion'.⁶⁵ Such a representation of chaos and disunity would be but the underside of the previous representation of order and totality. In Lyotard's terms postmodernity positions the individual in a system with multiple classifications, whereby connections are made over and across each other. If it appears loose and open-ended, it is not because it is unstructured but because it is structured without a centre.

Clearly, one of the crucial lessons that critical theory offers to us is that the social transformations of modernity cannot be understood without a radicalisation of the language in which transition is articulated. Therefore the relationship between traditional and modern culture, or even between the cultural dynamics of exile and identity, are best understood not with mutually exclusive terms or through self-defeating binarisms, but as a composition of cross-hatched categories. The benefit of locating Berger's discussion on exile with the debates on the constitution of modernity in critical theory is twofold: it alerts us to the transitions and ruptures in modern society and also focuses our attention to the pitfalls of the conventional paradigms for representing identity.

In conclusion one can ask, what is gained by articulating such method? Am I not merely stating the obvious? By outlining the structural principles between critical thinking and metaphor and by suggesting that this method is not only an accurate description of the process at play throughout Berger's texts but also a useful mechanism for the representation of the other in modernity, I hope to have made a few steps in critiquing the principles of critical distance and the dominant categories which distinguish between the subjective and the objective, as well as the rooted and the displaced. If, as Said suggests, culture may be represented as 'zones of control or of abandonment, of recollection and of forgetting, of forces or of dependence, of exclusiveness or of sharing, all taking place in the global history that is our element',[66] then it is *with metaphor* that borders are both made and crossed, that memory becomes history, and that violence is named. Metaphor is the act of transportation that simultaneously defines its zone and its border, that includes itself and its other. Shuttling between absence and presence, metaphor is the means for articulating action. This process however seems most evident in moments of extremity when the incongruity between language and practice is most glaring. At these points the very process of metaphor is akin to prophecy.

Notes

1 In Tabori's encyclopaedic book *The Anatomy of Exile*, which includes a narrative recorded on Egyptian papyrus circa 2000 B.C., the Homeric epic, Judeo-Christian myths of exodus, and the modern myth of the intellectual as 'perennial metic' he describes exile as 'the story of the Good Samaritan, and of homo hominis lupus combined; the story of compassion and charity running parallel with man's inhuman cruelty to man'.

While Tabori's study implies that there is an interesting but unexplored connection between the experience of exile and the making of narratives, I don't think his stated assumption that exile as both a primordial and a universal mechanism for resolving social conflict is an appropriate starting point for further investigation, and neither do I think that this literature suggests that there is a seamless link in the experience of exile across time and cultures. P. Tabori, *The Anatomy of Exile*, London, Harrap, 1972, p. 12.

2 This configuration of exile, in terms of lack and plenitude, is a key conceptual tool for most contemporary critiques of society. Hannah Arendt commences her critique of totalitarianism with the story of the pariah. It is the 'politically anomalous' person who is used to explain the politics of the nation-state. H. A. Arendt, *The Origins of Totalitarianism*, London, André Deutsch, 1986, see pp. 3–88 and 267–304. Conversely, Kedourie notes that the nineteenth century philosophical debates on consciousness and self-realisation (which were premised on the belief that the meaning of the past is

derived from its organisation into the whole) were also related to a need to redefine the civic relationship between the freedom of the individual and the identity of the state. Fichte, for instance, would have seen an exile as an individual deprived of identity. See E. Kedourie, *Nationalism*, London, Hutchinson University Library, 1960, p. 40.

3 Franz Neumann, *The Cultural Migration: The European Scholar in America*, Philadelphia, University of Pennsylvania Press, 1953, p. 12.

4 See also E. W. Said, 'Reflections on Exile', *Granta*, 13, autumn 1984, p. 160.

5 The definition is set out in the Statute of the Office of the United Nations High Commissioner for Refugees (December 1950). See Tabori, p. 25. Peter Nobel has argued that the 1969 O.A.U. Convention which was Africa-centred made important steps to expand 'the refugee definition from the Euro-centric and individual-oriented one of the Geneva Convention into a concept that could correspond to the demands of the massive groups of safety-seekers in the Third World and the causes of their fears'. However, he concludes that these 'humanitarian and realistic' steps have been consistently blocked by the powers that be in the western-dominated councils. See 'Refugees and other Migrants Viewed with the Legal Eye – or How to Fight Confusion', in *Displaced Persons*, ed. K. Holst Peterson and A. Rutherford, Sydney, Dangaroo Press, 1988.

6 I. Brownlie, *Principles of Public International Law*, Oxford, Clarendon Press, 1979, p. 520.

7 A. Giddens, *The Nation-State and Violence*, Cambridge, Polity, 1985, p. 50.

8 I. Brownlie, *op. cit.*, p. 556.

9 E. Kamenka, *Nationalism: The Nature and Evolution of an Idea*, London, Edward Arnold, 1976, p. 8.

10 T. Nairn, *The Break Up of Britain*, London, Verso, 1981, p. 333.

11 B. Anderson, *Imagined Communities*, London, Verso, 1983, p. 40.

12 H. K. Bhabha, 'DissemiNation', in *Nation and Narration*, ed. H. K. Bhabha, London, Routledge, 1990, p. 302.

13 J. Plamenatz, 'Two Types of Nationalism', in E. Kamenka *op. cit.*, p. 34.

14 J. Berger, *And our Faces, my Heart, Brief as Photos*, London, Writers and Readers, 1984, p. 65.

15 *Ibid*, p. 57.

16 G. Bachelard, *The Poetics of Space*, translated by M. Jolas, Boston, Beacon Press, 1969, p. 38.

17 J. Berger, *And our Faces*, p. 64.

18 Fredric Jameson, for instance, highlights the following transformations in social structure as marking the origins of modernity: 'commodity reification; monetary abstraction and its effects on the sign system, the social dialectic of reading publics; the emergence of mass culture; the embodiment of new forms of the psychic subject on the physical sensorium' (F. Jameson, *Modernism and Imperialism*, Derry, Field Day Pamphlets 14, 1988, p. 6).

Raymond Williams characterises modernity as a period of 'endless border-crossing', the confrontation with strangers, and more specifically he emphasises the displacement of the artist from an organic constituency. (See R. Williams, *The Politics of Modernism*, London, Verso, 1989, p. 34).

Max Raphael's characterisation of modernity rejects the conventional narrative of linear progress and explains the patterns of transformation as an ongoing exchange between the old and the new, the material and the symbolic (M. Raphael, *Proudhon, Marx, Picasso*, translated by Inge Marcuse, London, Lawrence & Wishart, 1980, p. 116).

John Berger's perception of the uneven but interlocking hegemony of early modernity is also based on the jostling for position of a number of conflicting ideologies and principles: incommensurable dualities of Cartesian reasoning; the civil contradictions between humanism and imperialism. This oscillation between extreme opposites led him to characterise its 'developments' as a series of contractions and expansions (J. Berger, *The Look of Things*, ed. N. Stangos, Harmondsworth, Penguin, 1972, p. 203). Coeval with these transformations is the individual's heightened awareness of the 'simultaneity and extension of events and possibilities' (p. 40). In short, a new social order has emerged as the relationship between time and space has been redefined. For the western metropolitans, accessibility to space increased as the time necessary for the relay of messages decreased. Technological inventions allowed the building of new urban spaces, electricity domesticated the night, and mass circulation newspapers offered the chance to inform the polity democratically. Following from Marx, Berger argued that in early modernity there was the belief that the ascendancy of mechanisation and rationalisation was not a threat to the historical diversity of modernity, but offered the revolutionary promise of liberation. (For a critique of this blindness in Marx's theory, see J. F. Rundell, *Origins of Modernity*, Cambridge, Polity, 1987).

19 In a spirited attempt to reconcile the differences between two dominant discourses in modernity; Marxism and modernism, Berman lapses into the very sentimentalism which, as he rightly notes, is what distinguishes the modernists and Marxists from the romantics. In Berman's hands the point of departure returns as the place of arrival. See Marshall Berman, *All That is Solid Melts Into Air: The Experience of Modernity*, New York, Simon and Shuster, 1982.

20 In Peter Berger's terms this means that in pre-modern societies, the individual both in conduct and in consciousness shares the same 'life-world' as all other members in her or his society. See P. L. Berger *et al.*, *The Homeless Mind*, Harmondsworth, Penguin, 1973.

21 Peter Berger argues that Marx's concept of 'alienation' and 'false consciousness', Heidegger's 'authenticity' and Sartre's 'bad faith' are all responses to the process which Arnold Gehlen defined as the 'deinstitutionalization' and 'subjectivization' in modernity. *Ibid.*, p. 86. The crisis that emerges from the non-correspondence between social values and private roles is a subject that John Berger has repeatedly investigated. For instance, he argues that the decline in the status of portraiture cannot be explained away by the mechanical multiplication of images through photography nor confined to the diversification of modes in pictorial representation. Rather he relates it to the disjunctures emerging from the pluralisation of the available self-images. Modernity is thus witnessed not only through the eye of the camera but also in the instability between the symbolism of the posture and the social position of the individual. In a world where the ontological and metaphysical certitudes are continuously displaced, portraiture is left without a subject, for the difference between classical and modern portraiture is in the absence or presence of a tension between the personal and the social self (J. Berger, *The Look of Things*, p. 38). The first consequence of secularisation was not the freedom of choice, but the necessity of deciding *how to decide* in the absence of God. The underside of modern innocence was the experience of individuation, or what Berger calls 'inverted suffering' (p. 141).

22   J. Berger, *About Looking*, New York, Pantheon Books, 1980, p. 27.

23   On the question of the author's subject position and the identity formations that are strategically excluded from narratives, a valuable comparison could be made between Spivak and Berger. For Spivak the perception of identity is integral with the realisation of the boundary which marks the 'not-self'. See 'Strategy, Identity Writing', *Melbourne Journal of Politics*, vol. 18, 1986–7, p. 47, reprinted in *The Postcolonial Critic*, ed. S. Harasym, New York, Routledge, 1990.

24   E. W. Said, 'Representing the Colonized: Anthropology's Interlocutor', *Critical Inquiry*, winter 1989, p. 225.

25   E. W. Said, 'Opponents, Audiences, Constituencies and Community', in *Postmodern Culture*, ed. by H. Foster, London, Pluto, 1985, p. 157.

26   Ibid., p. 158.

27   A. Nandy, *Traditions, Tyranny and Utopia: Essays in the Politics of Awareness*, Delhi, Oxford University Press, 1987.

28   J. Berger, *G*, London, Chatto and Windus, 1985, p. 77.

29   *Jonah who will be 25 in the year 2000*, screenplay by Alain Tanner and John Berger, Berkeley, North Atlantic Books, 1983, p. 167.

30   J. Berger, *Another Way of Telling*, London, Writers and Readers, 1982, p. 284.

31   J. Berger, *Pig Earth*, London, Chatto and Windus, 1985, p. 6.

32   For a seminal account of both the ubiquity and the resistance to metaphor in western thinking see D. F. Miller, *The Reason of Metaphor*, New Delhi, Sage, 1992. See also J. Derrida, *Margins of Philosophy*, translated by A. Bass, Brighton, Harvester Press, 1982, pp. 207–272.

While reflecting on the paradoxical journey into the absence and presence of an identity that is framed in the pursuits of cross-cultural traditions, Wilson Harris stated that it is by the metaphorical process of linking, which he calls 'Quantum Immediacy', that both the 'fluidity' in the interrelationship of opposites and the 'embeddedness' of reality are 'animated' into meaning (W. Harris, 'The Fabric of Imagination', lecture delivered to the University of Cambridge, 24 October 1990). To acknowledge the metaphoricity of meaning is at first to question the exclusiveness and purity of cultural or cosmological zones, and then to reject the singular and the linear grip of literal or empirical realism; it is to see the emotional overlap of contrary moral concepts, and it is to negotiate the contingency of social values by anticipating the space *between* the open and the closed. The genesis of metaphor is ceaselessly unfinished, provided, warns Harris, that 'we are

The method of metaphor

not compliant with adversarial schemes that deny the overlapping emotional textures of the modern age' and 'we do not exclude the intuitive potential that allows us to revise our sense of locality and the link between various theatres of activity, (W. Harris, 'The Fabric of Imagination').

33   J. Berger, *And our Faces*, p. 92.

34   *Ibid.*, pp. 96–7. Yet if the promise of poetry is that it approaches language as if it were a place that could envelop time (*ibid.*, p. 21), then this promise of co-existence is not separate from the intended effect of metaphor. For when Berger compares stories to battles and poems to prayers, whereby stories rebound in adversarial contestation while poems find consensual assurance (*ibid*, p. 22), he is saying that poems are like metaphors whose metaphoricity is either no longer visible, or whose transparency is plausible.

35   *Ibid.*, p. 95.

36   In contrast to Berger's view that language eternally re-discovers the categories of justice and hope (*And our Faces* ... pp. 98–9), there is Foucault's view that language has no permanent or sovereign relation to truth. Going against the grain of the tradition in modernity which located the truth of experience in the 'interiority' of language, Foucault puts forward the example of de Sade and Holderlin to question the processes of discovering an inner confirmation between language and experience. See 'Maurice Blanchot: The Thought from Outside', *Foucault/Blanchot*, New York, Zone, 1987, p. 17.

37   J. Berger, *New Statesman*, 1 October 1955.

38   More recently, these portraits are also of people engaged in activity that would not normally be considered as artistic. See J. Berger, *Keeping a Rendezvous*, New York, Pantheon, 1992, and for a discussion of this process see John Berger with Nikos Papastergiadis, 'Approaching Stories, Writing Critically', *Arena*, vol. 97, 1991.

39   J. Berger, *The Look of Things*, p. 75.

40   See W. Benjamin, 'The Author as Producer', in *The Essential Frankfurt School Reader*, ed. A. Arato and E. Gebhardt, Oxford, Basil Blackwell, 1978.

41   J.-P. Sartre, *What is Literature*, London, Methuen, 1976.

42   Similarly, Roland Barthes observed that for Michelet the function of historians is both to administer and to redeem the truth of their subject: to make intelligible the form and meaning of their existence, to receive 'their actions, their sufferings, their sacrifices' (Roland Barthes, *Michelet*, translated by R. Howard, Oxford, Basil Blackwell, 1987, p. 82). The historian is thus both the magistrate and the high priest of the past, giving history both a 'social and a sacred order'. In this ceremonial approach to the past, the historian, in order to represent the dead, must not just excavate but re-stage temporality. While Michelet's methodology and cosmology are both subject to the Christian dialectic of reversal – the first will be last – it involves a serious limitation: representation guarantees neither the resurrection of the dead nor the incorporation of the historian within history. For, despite Michelet's claim that the ideal position for the historian involves total immersion, 'the best historian is the one who has emerged from the people, the one who is closest' (p. 185) whereby writing is not just an individualistic act but also an expression of collective will: 'it is not he who writes

history, it is the People that dictate...' (*ibid.*). Barthes notes that nevertheless it is language that separates Michelet from the people, language has kept him at the 'People's frontier', and ultimately Michelet despairs: 'I have not been able to make the people speak' (p. 186). Barthes concludes that it is this confrontation with the alienating effect of language that makes Michelet an author of modernity.

43 J. Berger, *The Look of Things*, p. 192.
44 J. Berger, *About Looking*, p. 151.
45 *Ibid.*, pp. 129–30.
46 J. Berger, *The Look of Things*, p. 195.
47 See *About Looking*, pp. 107–8.
48 E. W. Said, 'Representing the Colonized', p. 225.
49 J. Berger, *About Looking*, p. 102.
50 *Ibid.*, p. 99.
51 *Ibid.*, p. 101.
52 *Ibid.*, p. 97.
53 *Ibid.*, p. 96.
54 *Ibid.*, p. 97.
55 An interesting counter-example to Ahmet's success is Berger's discussion of Millet's attempt to democratise the language of painting by introducing a subject that was historically excluded from it: the peasant. Berger argues that Millet failed 'because the language of traditional oil painting could not accommodate the subject he brought with him... there was no formula for representing the close, harsh, patient physicality of a peasant's labour *on*, instead of *in front of*, the land. And to invent one would mean destroying the traditional language for depicting scenic landscape' (*About Looking*, pp. 77–8).
56 *Ibid.*, p. 84.
57 J. Berger, *And our Faces*..., p. 75.
58 This attempt to define a 'metaphorical method' is drawn from Barthes's and Foucault's 'infamous' essays on authorship. (See M. Foucault, 'What an Author?', in *Language, Counter-Memory, Practice*, Ithaca, Cornell University Press, 1977; and R. Barthes, 'The Death of the Author', *Image Music Test*, London, Fontana, 1982). I agree with their dissatisfaction over the conventional paradigms in social criticism which privilege either the link between the author's biography and the text, or the embeddedness of the text in social context. Their attempt to go beyond this opposition of individualism versus structure was not inspired by an ulterior motive of displacing the legitimacy of the author's ego, but marks an attempt to open a third space, one which addresses the broader dynamics between individual and society, as well as between language and innovation. The name given to this field is discourse. When Foucault and Barthes proclaim the death of the author, they challenge neither the empirical life nor the civil status of the person but question the authority of the literary discourse which reduces the intentionality within the text to the intentions of the author. Rather than assessing the authenticity of work in terms of how it reflects the socio-economic conditions of a given historical period, or measuring the originality of authors by using their range in language as an index to the depths of their 'self', Foucault urges

us to examine the formation, source and transmission of discourse. By scrutinising the relationships and function that discourse constructs for possible subjects he develops the nexus of power/knowledge. Via the transportation of critical emphasis from author to text, it is discourse which is called forward to explain culture. Thus, it is no longer possible to elevate individuality as evidence to be used for or against cultural value. The subject must be recognised in relation to specific historico-social processes, a heterogeneity of structures, codes, languages and the particular position that a text imposes. (See also S. Heath, 'Comment on "The Idea of Authorship"', *Screen Reader 2*, London, The Society for Education in Film and Television, 1981, p. 184). On Berger's 'recognition' of Barthes as the critic of his time see *New Society*, 26 February 1976, p. 445.

59 For instance, in the afterword to a recent publication of *A Painter of Our Time*, New York, Pantheon, 1989, p. 199, Berger expresses some delight in the realisation that his latest play, *Goya's Last Portrait* written in collaboration with Nella Bielski, is the 'sequel' to his first novel. J. Berger and N. Bielski, *Goya's Last Portrait, The Painter Played Today*, London, Faber and Faber, 1989.

60 J. Berger, *The Look of Things*, p. 85.

61 *Ibid.*, p. 160.

62 J. Berger, *Permanent Red*, London, Writers and Readers, 1981, and *The Success and Failure of Picasso*, London, Writers and Readers, 1980; for another account which explores the parallelism between cubism and dialectical materialism, see M. Raphael, Proudhon, Marx, Picasso. In 'The Moment of Cubism', *The Look of Things*, Berger argued that modern subjectivity was born with the destruction of the Renaissance position and the change in the artist's relationship to nature. The cubist did not imitate, transcend, or experience nature, but 'realized that his awareness of nature was part of nature' (p. 150). Nature could no longer be expected to confirm or enhance the gaze of the artist in the act of investigation. If the relationship was no longer one of reciprocity then the estrangement, which was also the precondition for the romantic sensibility, then it was no longer the experience that was to preoccupy the sense of reality that the cubists were to represent.

The legacy of cubism's formal innovations has often been disputed in antithetical terms of whether it re-opened the question of subjectivity or bypassed such claims of the interiority of experience to discover the 'plenitude' of discourse. Thus the cubists in certain contemporary debates are portrayed as proto-postmodernists.

Two types of argument which invert or differ with Berger's claim that the 'moment of cubism' was the brief possibility for an objective humanist integration, are Fuller's that cubism was the penultimate representation of social disintegration and the dissolution of the human subject (P. Fuller, 'Understanding Picasso', *New Society*, 16 July 1981); and Rosalind Krauss's that cubism was not concerned primarily with experience and subjectivity but with the construction of a 'metalanguage of the visual'. Krauss suggests that the cubists' use of collage did not confirm the modernist's 'search for perceptual plenitude and unimpeachable self-presence', rather it problematised the objectification of an experience by the formal constituents of language. It highlighted the disembarkation into the endless mediation between discourse and the subject (R. Krauss, 'Re-Presenting Picasso', *Art In America*, December 1980, p. 96).

Stammelman offers a more plausible argument, that Cubism asserted that each interpretation is an intervention with the surface which displaces both the consciousness of the seer and the substance of the seen object, hence each representation necessitates a 'sense of perpetual recommencement'. Collage, through what Stammelman called 'the rhetoric of reprise and rectification', created a system which was neither about, nor sustained by, the presence of a general truth; rather its orientation was towards an absent origin which was both decentred and supplemented with every attempt to represent 'it' (R. Stammelman, 'The Object in Poetry and Painting: Ponge and Picasso', *Contemporary Literature*, vol. 19, no. 4, 1978, p. 421).

But Berger argues that against this multiple perception of space, the cubists built a universal form which could be interchangeably transposed to re-establish a relationship with objects. While any view of space is at best partial: 'The totality is the surface of the picture . . . the origin and the sum of all that one sees' (*The Moment of Cubism*, p. 177). Rather than inviting infinite contemplation of the *part* cubism offered a new syntax with which one could make connections and draw conclusions for the *whole*. Cubism 'rejected simple causality and the single permanent all-seeing viewpoint' (p. 180) as it redefined the spectator's position for perceiving totality from outside to inside.

63 A. Nandy, *The Intimate Enemy*, p. xvi.
64 J.-F. Lyotard and J.-L. Thebaud, *Just Gaming*, translated by W. Godzich, Manchester, Manchester University Press, 1985, p. 16.
65 J.-F. Lyotard, *The Postmodern Condition: A Report on Knowledge*, translated by G. Bennington and B. Massumi, Manchester, Manchester University Press, 1979, p. 15.
66 E. W. Said, 'Representing the Colonized', p. 225.

2
A romantic Marxist

Writing critically: the positions within commitment

Whenever I look at a work of art as a critic, I try – Ariadne-like for the path is by no means a straight one – to follow up the threads connecting it to the early Renaissance, Picasso, the Five Year plans of Asia, the man-eating hypocrisy and sentimentality of our establishment, and to an eventual Socialist revolution in this country. And if the aesthetes jump at this confession to say that it proves that I am a political propagandist, I am proud of it. But my heart and eye have remained those of a painter.
  John Berger, 'Exit and Credo', *New Statesman*, 29 September 1956

I would like to emphasize two things that are so deeply inside me that they are hardly even at the level of informed ideas. One is a relation to what I have always felt to be the 'mystery' of art. The other is a gut solidarity with those without power, with the underprivileged. Where perhaps I am a bad Marxist is that I have an aversion to political power whatever its form . . . I am a romantic – without any question. I wouldn't deny that for a moment. I see it as something positive . . . If one denies too much those subjective intuitions which romanticism is about and which are frequently expressed in love then something withers. The consistent, logical political line cannot bring them back. When that withering takes place there is a political danger.
  John Berger, 'Ways of Witnessing', *Marxism Today*, October 1984, pp. 37–8

There persists this illusion that everything can be resolved – and the great tragedies have been a result of this impatience with contradiction. It's interesting: the peasant will live with contradiction, the dualisms of life and death, hope and despair. And fiction is about this dualism. Perhaps this is why some of my readers have such a problem with my stories.
  John Berger, *The New York Times Magazine*, 29 November 1987

Romanticism and Marxism: a suspect paradox if ever there was one. How can you 'be' one without denouncing the other? How can you 'be' both without being neither? For as long as antagonism is the dominant mode through which polemics are expressed, dual commitment will always be received with suspicion, and no matter how rootless the era may be, the intense demand for rootedness will persist. Yet it is between these two polarities that I situate Berger's project in art criticism: between the centrifugal forces that tend towards dispersal and the centripetal movement towards unity. Berger's art criticism takes meaning when seen in this crosscurrent of irreconcilable tensions. His work cuts across a variety of debates and discourses on modernism and modernity. Thus the intention of this chapter is not to plot the chronological development of his art criticism, but to map out the parallelism between his thematic and political concerns against the trajectory of critical theory. The aim is not only to connect these different levels of criticism so that they mutually reflect on and illuminate one another, but also to offer another contribution to the collective language which defines the relationship between art and society.

Berger is probably best known for his role as the writer and presenter of the television series and book *Ways of Seeing*.[1] The influence of this series has been vast. Its success was secured through a provocative and innovative examination of the relationship between art and society. It demystified the ideological links between the discourse of oil painting and the formation of capitalism without relying on 'Marxist' jargon. It analysed the techniques that influence the perception of art rather than reproducing the technical account of progress in mechanical reproduction. It decoded the patriarchal representation of women and property without adopting a patronising and pontificating tone. In short the aim was to debunk preconceptions and to illuminate alternative methods for the interpretation of visual culture. As a book with a mass circulation and a video series which is part of the syllabus of most tertiary courses on the media, *Ways of Seeing* continues to serve as a great pedagogical device. Like most 'successful' critiques part of its critical vocabulary has been assimilated into the popular grammar of contemporary cultural practice. This selective incorporation has not always been commensurate with the intentions of its makers. It is not within my capability to trace out these filiations and influences, and the reason *Ways of Seeing* is not foregrounded in this chapter is that it is my belief that the key ideas had already been established in his earlier essays. To focus too closely on *Ways of Seeing* may also have some negative repercussions. It could give the impression that it marks the pinnacle of Berger's thinking on art and that it announces his position once and for all. Not only has Berger acknowledged its limitations far more profoundly than for instance, Peter Fuller's perverse revisionism has done,[2] but to dwell on this text could obfuscate the continuous questions and the unresolved tensions that dominate Berger's writing on art. Berger intensely opposed any interpretation of art which did not use the work to expand our understanding of the gap between freedom and alienation in everyday life. In his eyes orthodox art history refused to make this connection between the 'life' of the work and the lives of its viewers.

In order to connect art with life, Berger sought to politicise the historical links between the art work and the viewing public, rather than either formalising the aesthetic experience of viewing or reducing the contemporaneity of art to the psycho-biological universals of human experience. Within his every interpretation one can hear the driving force of three axioms: What can I say about this art work that will link it to another experience? How can I make it speak against the silence of alienation? And what metaphors can I draw from this encounter that will serve as a contribution to the unfinished grammar of freedom? Berger's art criticism is best characterised as a form of persistent contemplation of the potential space for creative expression within an era. Despite the shifts in genre and tone throughout his writing career, his commitment to art criticism has been as regular as the prayers of a believer. The continuous passion that drives his fascination with art is its ability to interpret, to order, to give meaning to experience.

If you expect to discover a linear development or a method that tends towards a system in Berger's criticism, then let me warn you from the outset: you will be frustrated. There is no totalising text, no definitive essay, not even a strict code. The presence of Frederick Antal is unmistakable, but the influence is only in the spirit of inquiry not the letter of application. Berger's criticism stands at the crossroads of a number of critical traditions: romanticism, humanism, modernism, realism and Marxism. To his credit he does not seek to define a single meta-discourse that embraces all; he draws from, and comments against, each position strategically. His art criticism is best situated at the intersection of realism and modernism; the subject position that he defines for the artist combines the innovations of the avant-garde and the idealism of the romantic; his philosophical and political commitment emerge from the conjunctions of humanism and Marxism. For some of Berger's critics it is this dualism which undermines the validity of his claims. Either his politics blurs his appreciation of art, or art is no place from which to begin a serious discussion on politics. Both the left and the right have consistently reasserted this split between culture and society whenever Berger has attempted to question it.[3] Yet for Berger, an alliance between romanticism and Marxism is possible because both philosophies ground the concepts of justice, authenticity and freedom on the prior belief in the possibility of an unalienated society.

While the perspectives of romanticism and Marxism are premised on the ubiquity of alienation and the necessity for transcendence from the material conditions of society, their prescribed routes out of alienation are diametrically opposed. Their difference is a consequence of contradictory subject positions which yield differing relationships to time and space. Marxism commands the integration of the artist with the political, whereby the resulting art is not just subordinated to an imminent revolution, but is also an active expression of the revolutionary struggle. Whereas romanticism offers the image of the suffering and misunderstood artist who rejects the distortions on subjectivity imposed by society, and whose critical response is embodied by 'his'[4] apartness from society and 'his' longing for an appointed time and place in which balance will be restored. The starting point for the Marxist is the immediate. The parameters of the struggle are defined by the here and now. Everything or anything of consequence is measured by its presence in the process of struggle, whereas for the romantic, creativity begins with the recognition of an absence. The impulse is motivated by the need to fill the hollow. The romantic sentiment for contestation is primarily nostalgic, albeit a double nostalgia: for the past and the future. Thus the Marxist struggles to identify the ascendant forces within society, while the romantic yearns for the moment when the individual can ascend beyond the struggles of society.

If the combination of Marxism and romanticism is paradoxical, why should it be received with suspicion? Replay the question in reverse and you have the answer: it is suspicious because it is paradoxical. And the problem with paradox is that by its nature it gives an abundance of questions but offers no answers. By complicating standard definitions, it defies absolutes; it suspends familiar decisions within unusual contexts, it undermines the ability to judge with certainty and finality by insisting on contingency or multiplicity.

Rather than leading to a point of resolution from which one can subordinate different positions, a paradox suggests either the forking into multiple positions or an unmappable frontier. Dual commitments are also suspicious because they cast doubt on the very depth of any commitment, by having a foot in both camps duality makes commitment seem 'merely' tactical, and if there is even the possibility that commitment can be revoked then this instability undermines the expectation of assurance and highlights unreliability in moments of adversity. In the times of antagonism and radical transition being in the 'in-between' is very precarious.

The proclamation that truth, authenticity and purity of philosophical ideals resides only on one side of the political divide consistently emerges as the starting point and the stumbling block of the critical debates in which Berger's criticism was situated. Alisdair MacIntyre's review of *Permanent Red* captures this atmosphere of polemicism and antagonism:

It is not the whole truth, but it is the most important part of the truth that the painter in our society has to live and to paint against the society in which he lives, or else go down to defeat. There are two reasons why this is not the whole truth. The first is that there are painters who struggle through and they also are part of our society. That they are so few and that they have to struggle so hard is the negative side of our culture; that even so they win triumphs is its positive side. The second reason is that the artists who fail are not just defeated. For this suggests that they fought against something and lost. Of many this is untrue. From the outset they conformed successfully. They may be defeated, but the name that they are able to give to defeat is 'success'. They are, to use a phrase of Marx, comfortable in their alienation.[5]

In the midst of the Cold War the dominant mode for critical discourse was oppositional thinking. Hence responses to Berger's work were framed by a fundamental belief that credibility could only be gained through committed resistance, that ideologies could find expression through singular voices and that spokespersons occupied mutually exclusive positions.[6]

If these polemical structures provided the arena for contestation, it was also this oppositional discourse which empowered critics. It identified positions to oppose and presented the critic with an object to work with or against. When appraising other people's work, Berger has always resisted any symmetrical equation between intention and meaning; he is also astute to the specific truncations and refractions of the density of experience within any aesthetic or critical representation. Yet this approach has not been reciprocated by his critics; they have tended to simplify the tension within antonymic structures as they have emphasised the combatory mode in his oppositional work. Consequently critical responses are often confined to either eulogies or rebukes.[7]

Berger's claim to 'be' both a Marxist and a romantic is seldom accepted by his critics. Despite the tension between their pronouncements about his texts and their characterisation of him as the embodiment of the radical will, they rarely question his claim that a conjunction between romanticism and Marxism can compensate for the lack in both terms. While Berger finds in romanticism what Marxism represses, and in Marxism what romanticism disavows – an engagement with the social without an abandonment of the personal – and even though he claims that this mixture secures the vitality of these objective categories while also nourishing his subjective demands, his critics would prefer to categorise him as either a Marxist or a romantic.

Rather than examine the juxtaposition of the known features within both terms, critics have invariably interpreted the congruence between the two as a blurring of each, resulting in the 'dreaded' production of a nameless hybrid, something that they would rather dismiss than attempt to grasp. However, between the difficult polarities and the reductive dismissals there must always be a variety of other positions.

I mention these small episodes in the polemics of cultural criticism in order to demonstrate that the other side of the modern compulsion to eliminate ambivalence is not a reckless dissolution within the zone of polysemy but the profound utility of metaphor. Perhaps one of the most stifling consequences of this persistent attempt to drive out ambiguity through rigid classification is the non-recognition that creativity springs from metaphor: the mixing of differences. One might remember Roland Barthes's cautionary rumination on his own early writings; to be caught in an antagonistic opposition is not just regressive but also self-defeating.

> He used to think of the world of language (the logosphere) as a vast and perpetual conflict of paranoias – the only survivors are the systems (fictions, jargons) inventive enough to produce a final figure, the one which brands the adversary with a half-scientific, half-ethical name, a kind of turnstile that permits us simultaneously to describe, to explain, to condemn, to reject, to recuperate the enemy, in a word: to make him pay.[8]

It is more productive to describe Berger's criticism (and writing in

A romantic Marxist

general) as agonistic (both contestant and polemicist). Such a suture allows us to interpret a greater stock of ploys and manoeuvres in his texts. The achievement of the agonist is not to provoke the surrender of the text, to make it submit to another code, or to extract a result, but rather to advance into its own labour.[9] For the agonist the struggle is as continuous as life itself. There is no once and for all battle, no ultimate victory, no essential motivation – just a generalised/plural truth. The agonist does not attack like a mercenary nor stand like a border guard.

This chapter will attempt to explore the role of dualisms in Berger's writing on art by comparing it to Lyotard's and Burger's mapping of the shifting relationship between the artist and society. Having accepted the argument that modernity is a culture driven by rupture and contradiction, I connect Berger's art criticism to these debates on modern aesthetics in order to investigate the imbrication between the politics of belonging and the process of critical writing in modernity. To this purpose Berger's writing not only exemplifies the shuttling dynamism of representation but also cautions us against the perils of imperious resolutions.

While Berger strongly identified with outsiders and exiles, he did not claim their position as his own. The metaphor that he adopts to express his subject position is that of a 'shuttle'. 'Shuttling' between the outsiders and the insiders, he sees himself as performing the task of critically narrating the displacement and tension between insiders and outsiders.[10] Thus the paradox that I wish to examine is bound not only by the disjunctions between romanticism and Marxism, but by the possibility of making a home in modernity. To clarify this paradox in regard to Berger's criticism it is necessary to have a clear understanding of what is implied by modernity and the differences between modernism, romanticism and the avant-garde.

The avant-garde and the levels of engagement

Modernity is not the name for the modern world. Modernity is the name for a particular way of seeing the modern world. It refers to a process for interpreting and organising social change according to the universalising certitudes that emerged from the Enlightenment's conception of rationality. This distinction between the phenomenon and the perception of the modern world has been blurred by two commonly held assumptions: firstly that modernism is the aesthetic articulation of modernity, and secondly the rigid insistence that aesthetics and politics are separate.[11] Modernism can be understood only if it is seen as coeval with the historical transformations that marshalled in modernity. Modernism is a response to the increasing commercialisation of social practices, the disqualification of the sacred in language, and the attending disjunctures between rational and moral structures for the legitimation of action and for the representation of causation. However, modernism does not fulfil what Zygmunt Bauman calls the 'proselytizing mission' of modernity. Modernism does not mirror back the utopian dream of a transparently homogeneous world. In modernist aesthetics the complexities of cultural difference are not transcended according to the universalising code of modernity.[12]

Debates on modernist aesthetics are regularly polarised by a self-defeating opposition between realism and abstraction. To choose one against the other also implies a contrasting representation of the levels of social engagement between the two modes of artistic practice. My aim is not to evaluate the diverging claims concerning the utility of the relationship between form and content in each mode, but rather to suggest that this tension is linked to the broader shifts in the dynamics between aesthetic representation and political engagement. What I want to emphasise is that a consciousness of the relationship between aesthetic production and dominant ideology heightens our awareness of the gaps between various forms of social practice. Not only am I trying to suggest that modern aesthetics doesn't merely reproduce and repeat the desires of modern politics, but furthermore, I am arguing that within each practice there is an ambivalence between meaning and value. Thus the level of inquiry for an understanding of detachment and engagement in modern aesthetics necessarily combines philosophical reflection with political synthesis.

The conceptual recasting of the border between the representation of reality and the discourse of realism is central to two of the key arguments on the legacy of the avant-garde. Firstly, there is Burger's appraisal which is a departure from the deadlock in the famous debate between Adorno and Lukács.[13] Burger argues that the avant-garde's engagement is not measured by its relationship to the alienation within society, but by the change in its relationship to the institution of art. Then there is also Lyotard's celebrated idea that the avant-garde responded to the alienated condition of society not through the attempt to reclaim the organic position, but by attempting to critically utilise both the ascendant forms of abstraction and the new means of interaction.

Lyotard claims that 'Modernity, in whatever age it appears, cannot exist without a shattering of belief and without discovery of the "lack of reality" of reality, together with the invention of other realities'.[14] This puts the modern artist in an invidious position. The shattering of belief does not usher forth greater freedom but implies far broader responsibilities. The responsibilities extend well beyond the frame of their actual production. For if the representation of the totality of reality is illusory, and an aesthetic of beauty which is based on totality and unity is unrealisable, then the aesthetic pursuit in modernity shifts from the beautiful representation of reality to the invention of messages that will simultaneously articulate the process of their formation as well as question the conditions for reception.[15]

In Lyotard's terms, any direct referencing between the artist and the public connotes a classical situation where there is a known public with defined criteria for judging achievements. The romantics attempted to reproduce this schema, but it could only be realised on an imaginary level; consequently the artist was detached from the present public and more concerned with an ideal public in either the future or the past. However, in modernity the artist cannot presuppose either an organic or a detached relationship with society. It demands the obverse position of both the classical and the romantic artist.

> the artistic vanguard knows that it has no readers, no viewers, and no listeners. If, on the other hand, it is saddled with the image of a reader, viewer, or listener, if, in other words, the contour of an addressee is imposed upon it, and this contour filters out the experiments . . . that the vanguard is allowed to make, then it will not be able to do anything. There is an important issue: the problem is not only political, in the usual and simple sense of the term, but it is a problem of how one views history and society.
>
> . . . experimentnal work will have as one of its effects the constitution of a pragmatic situation that did not exist before. It is the message itself, by its form, that will elicit both the one who receives it and the one who sends it. They are able to communicate with each other.[16]

The critical role of the avant-garde in modernity may be further examined through Peter Burger's argument that the avant-garde took this experimentation with language and the scepticism of social institutions one step further.[17] The radical impact of both modernism and the avant-garde was not in the declaration of the end of narratives, or the end of art as an institution, but rather in the beginning of a consciousness of the significance of the techniques and institutions of art.

Burger charts the emergence of the autonomy of art by schematising the process of detachment. The function of art shifts from serving as a sacred object to representing the life of courtly society, and then to the objectification of the self-consciousness of the bourgeoisie. In this last stage, the production of art occurred in a sphere that was beyond the praxis of life.[18] However, the isolation of the romantic artist was contradictory; it was deemed necessary because it protected the fragile purity of genius from being sullified by market forces, whereas it was also taken as evidence of the artist's unswerving dedication to universal truth and this indomitable stance elevated 'him' beyond the fickle and ephemeral desires of the masses. The claim to transcendence, gained through isolation, not only disguised the withdrawal from society but also secured both the autonomy and increased abstraction in art. Since the artist must be distanced from society, 'his' art must also preclude the present. The less art is bound to place, the stronger its claim to timelessness. Hence the critical moment in romantic art is confined to either a recalling of lost purity or the deferring of unification with the truth into the distant future. By definition, the romantic yearning for the end of all negativity can only be expressed through ahistorical abstractions. The retreat from the present is also a bracketing of hope. By holding back from any direct confrontation between art and society, it inflates the role of critical intervention to speculation in possible reconciliations in an unspecified future. Thus any sociological conclusion that can be drawn from romantic work must also neutralise its political intent, for at best it addresses the suffering in society through the sentimental affirmation of individual will or the ultimate triumph of social values.

The distinction between the romantics and the avant-garde is the difference between sentimentalism and ambivalence; isolation and engagement. However, to insist on this difference in mutually exclusive terms would introduce another binary opposition precisely at the point at which it is best to question them. As Burger argues, the break of the avant-garde from the institution of art – because it promoted the 'apartness' of art from the praxis of life – does not imply a total severance from the institution, but 'the destruction of the possibility of positing aesthetic norms as valid ones'.[19]

The avant-garde defined a new type of engagement by developing new organising principles which structured the political into both the form and the content of the work. Political intentions were no longer restricted to the substantive questions in the work, but also directed by the formal definitions. Thus the effect of the work is no longer mediated by the 'message' of the whole, but by the relative autonomy or coexistence of the individual signs. By freeing the parts from their subordination to the whole, the work was emancipated from the ideology of oppression. While falling short of the revolutionising praxis, Burger claims that the avant-garde succeeded in preserving this intent as they defined a new relationship to society.[20]

In Burger's and Lyotard's argument we witness a more complex awareness of the problematic that surrounds the 'apartness' of the avant-garde. The question of exile and integration for the artist in modernity does not simply refer to the distance or proximity from home, nor is it bound to overt forms of political struggle; rather it addresses the changing relationship to the construction of meaning in modern culture. For when the hierarchy of values and norms is as fragmented and as dispersed as it is today, then the role of the artist shifts from offering an enduring and unified worldview, to the construction of new meanings from the emergent fragments. The 'apartness' of the modern artist is not simply precipitated by a need to gain distance in order to see things more clearly, nor is it purely reflective of social division, it is neither merely a methodological nor a political distance that separates the artist from society. In contemporary society these factors are also cross-cut by an instability in the determination of value.

Berger's art criticism

Having laid out the problematics of cultural criticism and offered a generalised account of the relationship between aesthetics and politics in the social theory of modernity, in the last section I will now attempt to evaluate Berger's art criticism. Berger is an active polymath, constantly searching for paradigms and examples which will push or test his own propositions. This quest has invariably led him to compare the role of art criticism with other forms of social critique. In this sense my forays into philosophy and sociology are a continuation of the process that is already intrinsic to his own way of thinking. What I hope to achieve in this section is to identify the vitality and persistence of the themes of exile and home as the axiological co-ordinates to his writing. I will support this claim through a close reading of his texts. The path through his writing that I have chosen begins at the middle – contrasting his representations of Picasso and Niezvestny.

I will contextualise Berger's assessment of Pablo Picasso in *The Success and Failure of Picasso* and the Russian sculptor Ernst Niezvestny in *Art and Revolution* by an outline of the broader co-ordinates of his interpretation of the relationship between art and society.

For Berger there are no ahistorical benchmarks which define the enigma of art. His attention is not directed towards the eternity of art but rather concerned with the relationship between art and the social.[21] Tradition and revolution are the forces and the horizons which are persistently interwoven in Berger's art criticism. He does not perceive the function of tradition as a closed system for the perpetuation of privileges, but as the vital mechanism for the formation of social values, and the stimulus to relational thinking which secures the means for expanding the possibilities of dialogue with the public discourse.

One of the key moments in art history was the Russian Revolution. Berger argues that in the post-revolutionary period artists overcame many of the rigid and exclusive boundaries that separated the specific media from the general public. It was a time when artists

believed in the profound influence that art could have on individual and social development: all believed in the social role of art. Yet their social consciousness was affirmative rather than critical. They saw themselves as already representing the liberated future. This liberation meant the breaking down of all divisions between classes, professions, discipline and previous bureaucratic categories. *Their works were like hinged doors, connecting activity with activity.* Art with engineering; music with painting; poetry with design; fine art with propaganda; photography with typography; diagrams with action; the studio with the street, etc.[22] (emphasis mine)

Berger's faith in the integrity, health and interrelatedness of art and culture at this point in Russia's history is the idealised counterpoint to his despair at the decline and fragmentation of his own culture. The 'other's' integration served to highlight the disintegration of the self.[23]

For Berger, integration means reciprocal identification. A 'successful' relationship between the artist and the public cannot be reduced to a series of one-way dictations or monologues. It demands a mutual exchange of aspirations and self-discovery. And it is *from* this interaction that the question of the responsibility of form and content emerges. Dialogue requires both distance and proximity, difference and similitude. Duality in referencing, that is, the translation between the near and far, and the generalisation from the personal to the public, is the basis for the critical force of the artist's work. The ideal social position for the artist is thus delicately poised between this outward requirement for identification with the other, and the inward demand for the extension of the self. 'Their works were like hinged doors', and so was their social position. The artist as a hinge, connecting and carrying differences, embodies the function of metaphor. The artist as rebel, prophet or exile, is also a metaphor that highlights the ambivalence and the metaphoricity of the artist's perspective and social position.

Failure is the obverse. It is the narrowing of critical attention and social aspiration to the point of abstraction which trivialises the contact with society and reduces dialogue to a self-defeating and narcissistic mythology. For Berger, cubism marked a moment of stunning 'success' whereas surrealism had all the symptoms of 'failure'. The surrealists may have distanced themselves from bourgeois rationality but their critical faculties were blunted by a 'mere' celebration of irrationality. In numerous articles Berger attacked the surrealists for the way they restricted themselves to the 'ghetto' of the personal, for their detachment from social responsibility and, ultimately, for being patronised as eccentrics. Their work lost its shock value, it was used to reinscribe the boundaries of the institutional art world which traditionally profits from mystification and is invariably attracted to tokens which can be taken to represent the bizarre or remote regions of culture and consciousness. The surrealists were subversive only in their use of manners. Their grotesque images did not challenge the border but reconfirmed the gap between the rational and the irrational.[24] Berger perceived their claim of freedom from the known rules of society as equivalent to a servitude to rules which, while being previously unknown, were nevertheless of no social value. Hence their protest against the strictures of bourgeois rationality was but a confirmation of another level of bourgeois irrationality.

The limits of romanticism

The Success and Failure of Picasso is a story of disenchantment. It reveals how the profundity of Picasso's vision which pivoted on the intuitive links between romanticism and Marxism was distorted by the shallowness of metropolitan success and by the myopia of the left. It could be said that Picasso was the first icon of modernity. His work is neither linked to the aspirations of the bourgeoisie of a nation state, nor associated with any imperial court: it stands as the herald to modern metropolitan culture, belonging equally to Paris, London, New York and Barcelona, belonging everywhere but at home nowhere. This is the paradox of modern globalism. Berger sees Picasso's destiny in tragic terms, a tragedy which parallels the structures and horizons of everyday life, and it is his discomfort with this condition which issues to us the challenge to read Picasso's work as an allegory to the pitfalls of modernity.

Berger's most trenchant criticism of Picasso is aimed at the way Picasso adopted the 'romantic attitude' without having a romantic subject with which to identify. Picasso's 'romantic attitude' was rejected, not because of its anachronism but because of Picasso's truncation of romanticism as a critical mode for modernity. Berger acknowledged that throughout his career Picasso was a prolific producer of images; what he disputed was the relationship between his production and their consumption. For if there was an assertion that the social position of the artist would inevitably affect the reception of art, then the judgement concerning the value of Picasso's work would also be framed by a celebration of engagement and an attack on detachment. Picasso's detachment both propelled him into a 'privatised' mythology that celebrated the narcissism of the individual and relied on a negative appropriation of romantic distance: an aloofness that abstracted as it disempowered the critical faculties.

Berger's critique of Picasso's romanticism can be better understood if we distinguish between a critical and a sentimental representation of the past and the other.

As the past can be retrieved only through an interpretive venture, its fictive dimensions are often confined to a regressive nostalgia that revolves around sentimentalism rather than heightening criticism. However, the very process of recollecting the past may be a way of incorporating it into the present. Berger's appreciation of the imbrication between past and present is always closely related to Benjamin's theses on the philosophy of history. Benjamin faced the dialectic between past and present not by seeking the eternal past in the present, but by actively engaging with the unique experience of the past'[25] and opening up the traces of 'memorable things'[26] within the historical amnesia of modernity. Benjamin's philosophy was a direct challenge to the historicist presupposition that the linear representations of the past culminate in universal history. It was also a refutation of evolutionist models which to Benjamin were no more than an apologia for the dominance of particular traditions, and he attacked the determinist schemas that relegated the question of survival for the subordinant cultures to a crude conception of power.[27] Like Nietzsche, who distinguished between three kinds of history – the monumental, the antiquarian and the critical[28] – Benjamin rejected any form of historical investigation which proceeds with the assumption that the past is dead, and that symbols which are shorn of the residues of historical time can at best be reified as they are returned to the present in the form of a commodity. Benjamin's philosophy was not directed towards the celebration of the transmission, or a lament for the loss of putative wholes, but was a method for understanding the relative autonomy and irreconcilability of the parts which migrate across and within various histories. There are no ready-made solutions lurking in the past which prefigure the problems of the present. The past arrives neither intact nor in a passive form. Through the criss-crossing patterns of structuration, the past is constructed as it constructs an interminable agenda of catchment and deferral. It is in this way, Benjamin suggested, that the past is woven into the realisations and choices that a historical role of the present is called upon to resolve.[29]

What differentiates Benjamin's and Berger's vision of the past from a regressive form of nostalgia is the use of the past as an 'active station' that vibrates within the critical manoeuvrings of the present. The return to the past is not motivated by a desire to go outside of time, but is paradoxically, an attempt to address those traces which signal towards the future.[30] The past never appears as a self-contained island that can harbour a blissful retreat; more generally what is significant about the critical vision is that it is characterised by a 'shuttling' process.

It was by this criterion that Berger found value in Picasso's early work. It was Picasso's status as an 'outsider' which validated his self-identification with outcasts, and justified his romantic affiliation with a primitive way of life: this gave him 'special standards with which to criticise what he saw'.[31] But the return to the 'primitive' as an idealised point of comparison in his later work is problematical. 'He first made such a choice as a direct criticism of what he saw around him. An element of criticism still exist ... [but] Picasso's imagination begins to gravitate *naturally* towards the archaic. An attitude, once consciously held, has become a cast of mind'.³² If ambivalence makes possible the process of critical thinking, then this state of mind must be distinguished from the undialectical excavations of the past which merely serve as a means of defusing or displacing the tensions in the present. For once Picasso had been admitted into the 'charmed' circles of Paris, his access to 'other' circles was neither neutral nor impossible, but his forays were checked by the incommensurability of the two circles. Berger argued that in Picasso's later work he subordinated the critical perspective of romanticism into a rhetoric of universal appeasement. The emotions he sought to provoke were numbed and his reference point increasingly depended on a timeless past which abstracts and blurs the questions of conflict.

The idealisation of the past and the other must not be conflated with an identification with the past and the other. Idealisations fix the self and the other in an antagonistic opposition which ultimately neglects or truncates the position of the other, whereas identifications open relationships agonistically and the 'engagement' between the two positions does not demand the defeat of either.³³ While the element of contestation occurs in both, the 'surrender' of the other is not central to the process of identification. The oscillation between self and other in identification does not amount to either the possession of the other or the obsession with the other.³⁴ For Picasso, this difference disappears as he claims to collapse the borderline between self and other:

> I see for others. That is to say I put down on the canvas the sudden visions which force themselves on me. I don't know beforehand what I shall put on the canvas, even less can I decide what colours to use. Whilst I'm working I'm not aware of what I'm painting on the canvas. Each time I begin a picture, I have the feeling of throwing myself into space. I never know whether I'll land on my feet. It's only later that I begin to assess the effect of what I've done.³⁵

By contrasting Picasso with Rousseau, Berger was able to illustrate two 'romantic' applications of the process of self-depiction through self-projection. Berger argued that in both cases this process was motivated by their precarious feelings of exile and their wish for integration with a sympathetic space.³⁶

The amalgam of Picasso's and Rousseau's visions was composed of contradictory and irreconcilable elements. Their identity also oscillated between two refusals: to 'settle' in France, or to return 'home'. In defence of the self and as an attack of the antagonistic other, they both cultivated the exoticism of the inner 'noble savage'. They both insisted on solitude for creativity which in turn was the basis for the expression of the absolute. Yet their romantic beliefs were also a constant source of despair; with each abstraction there was the deepening realisation that they failed to achieve the unity with the idyllic nature, or create the totality to which their convictions predisposed them.

Rousseau and Picasso may sound equally naive and innocent, but Berger insisted on a distinction that redeems Rousseau as it condemns Picasso:

> But here we must make a distinction between innocence as an arm of experience, and innocence as a natural state of being. The former is a social idea which, like the concept of Utopia, is the result of men seeing the possibility of a future which could be better than the corrupt present. Innocence as a natural state of being is by definition changeless. No such thing exists. The theoretical possibility of such a state inspired by Rousseau – but part of his greatness was that he never glossed over or hid the contradiction in his theory. In Picasso's case his belief in a natural state of innocence is a dream in which he only half believes, but which allows him to retreat deeper and deeper back into himself and his strange isolation.[37]

For Berger, the two high points in Picasso's career were the experiments with cubism and the painting of *Guernica*. Berger judged the cubist period a success because Picasso abandoned the solitary romantic position for an intense bonding with Braque and other cubists, whereas in *Guernica* Picasso found a subject which affirmed the critical perspective of the romantic position. Berger also speculated on Picasso's tentative alliance with the French Communist Party as a romantic rescue mission that failed.

At the outset Picasso declared: 'I have never felt freer, never felt more complete. And then I have never been so impatient to find a country again. I have always been an exile, now I am no longer one: whilst waiting for Spain to welcome me back, the French Communist Party have opened their arms to me . . . again I am among my brothers.'[38] Yet this embrace of brothers was not like the cubist years in which each partner used each other to scaffold up to new heights. For Picasso the experiment with the Communist Party was a failure which deepened his sense of exile. And here Berger reminds us that exile is not a static state, where the individual is somehow 'caught' in a dilemma, or 'suspended' in no-man's-land: 'Exile is a state which, in its subjective effects, never stands still: you either feel increasingly exiled as time passes, or increasingly absorbed by your adopted country.'³⁹ Exile is the opposite of integration. While being *in exile* or *at home* are both social experiences, Berger presents them as mutually exclusive states. Exile leads to utter solitude. It is not just the feeling of estrangement of individual from a group, for it requires the individual to be also perceived as a stranger *by* the group. Such an austere definition of exile requires closer examination.

This binary opposition between exile and integration which is redolent of the romantic opposition between hell and utopia, is also implicated in Berger's criterion of success and failure: home is integration through objective engagement and production with social ends, home involves belonging to a sympathetic space and a positive identification with a variety of alter egos.⁴⁰ Exile is isolation with subjective detachment, where at best creativity provides some private compensation but always fails to be incorporated in the subject. Exile becomes like Sartre's conception of Hell in *No Exit*, an abandonment in an antagonistic arena with 'other people'. In this opposition there is neither symmetry nor generative tension, the negative always remains afflicted with destructive and disintegrating impulses. It is afflicted with the anxieties of being 'un-natural', torn by feelings of lack, ruined by a perpetual hunger for its opposite.

By valorising the positive and prevaricating over the negative, Berger repeats the failure of our culture to conceive of a third space between exile and integration. At times he sees exile as a metaphor for the relational mode between detachment and attachment. However, in Picasso's case, exile was always an allegory for the perverse detachments and impotent attachments in modern society.

This judgement on Picasso's exile was complicated by Spain's peculiar relationship to modernity, and Picasso's partial embodiment of 'pre-modern' values.⁴¹ Berger took Ortega y Gasset's description of Picasso as the 'vertical invader', but then reduced this metaphor in order to condemn Picasso.

> He came from Spain through the trap-door of Barcelona on to the stage of Europe. At first he was repulsed. Quite quickly he gained a bridgehead. Finally he became a conqueror. But always, I am convinced, he was conscious of being a vertical invader, always he has subjected what he has seen around him to a comparison with what he brought with him from his own country, from the past.⁴²

Berger saw Picasso's use of the pre-modern not as a vindication of an alterior perspective but as a manipulation of both the fetishisation of the artist as a magician and the modern desire for exoticism.⁴³ He observed that the mysticism in the process by which an object is transformed into art was not just accentuated by parasitic critics who were all too willing to surrender rationality at the foot of his otherworldly genius, but was also dramatised by his own paradoxical and self-aggrandising declarations: 'A painting is a sum of destructions',[44] 'to search means nothing in painting, to find is the thing'.[45]

Berger was fascinated with the spiralling metaphors which wove Picasso's name into a legend. 'You may say that to recognize a name doesn't amount to recognizing a personality. But everything remembered trails and attracts associations'.[46] In the legend of Picasso Berger found a modern myth which, as he later noted, 'has an outward action but no personalized centre'.[47] He wanted to debunk this myth, not because it was premised on fantasy rather than reality but because it offered delusion rather than illumination, consolation instead of instigation, and because it privileged the magician over the prophet. Berger contested the myth of Picasso because, for all its elevation of the artist's status, it leads nevertheless to the decline of the social utility of art.

Berger also drew an analogy between Lorca's account of the duende, 'a kind of undiabolic demon',[48] and the peculiar form of inspiration and obsession with which Picasso worked. The duende differs from the classical muse in that it simultaneously finds strength in the declaration of destruction and the confrontation with death as it issues a challenge against the strictures of life. And in the white heat of instantaneous revolt, 'the duende guarantees art'.[49] However, Berger did not consider the duende as a possible strategy for questioning the oppositions within consciousness and history. He reduced it to a temperamental form of defiance whereby creativity was released in occasional eruptions and thus lacked an affirmative or future-orientated dynamic.

Despite Picasso's own celebration of the 'magical' properties inherent in the artist, Berger was canny enough to perceive his unacknowledged affirmation of the 'modern' oppositions between mind and body; past and present. To Berger, Picasso did not represent the other in modernity, he appropriated and foreclosed the 'other' possibilities. In *Picasso*, the pre-modern was not an enunciation of difference but a confirmation of the homogenising, or what Jean Fisher calls the 'vampiric', tendencies within modernity.

The portrayal of the Russian sculptor Niezvestny in *Art and Revolution* revealed another form of the dynamic between exile and disintegration. Niezvestny oppposed political power, but affirmed the philosophy of socialism: his opposition was thus an embodiment of the principles of hope.⁵⁰ For as long as Niezvestny remained an 'inner exile' in the Soviet Union, as the rebel who upheld the highest principles of society, Berger proclaimed him as a prophet.⁵¹ This form of valorisation stood in stark contrast to the suggestion that Picasso's decline was measured against the level of integration into Parisian high society. For oncė Picasso was detached from his 'pre-modern' past and shunned by the French Communist Party, Berger argued that the critical edge of this 'vertical invader' was blurred as he was forced to retreat deeper into his own subjectivity, the work which ensued then being, at best, sentimental.

From this typology we can see why Picasso was the anti-hero and Niezvestny was the hero. The opposition was even echoed by the symbolism attached to their names; as a counter to the international legend that surrounds Picasso's name, Niezvestny's name literally means 'The Unknown One'.⁵² In contradistinction to Picasso's quasi-mysticism and obsessive narcissism, Niezvestny's work extolled the civic nature of art and challenged the political assumptions of his society.⁵³ Where Picasso used exile as a luxury commodity, Niezvestny's inner exile was the whetstone which sharpened his dissidence.⁵⁴

To clarify Niezvestny's social position Berger distinguished the inner exile from the idiosyncratic non-conformist.⁵⁵ The inner exile did not seek freedom through disavowal, but paradoxically used exemption from the orthodoxy as a strategic intervention which ultimately sought to excavate the unarticulated public conscience.⁵⁶ Mary McCarthy also emphasised the visionary powers and the superior moral authority of internal émigrés:

The internal exiles seem to have made it a principle to behave ... as though by their determination they could oblige the 'as if' to come true ... A better metaphor for internal exile might be purgatory, a place where you wait, like exiles in a foreign land, to go home ... This might be a definition of the internal exile: a man who has taught himself to behave as if he had already crossed a frontier while refusing to leave his home.⁵⁷

Berger described Ernst Niezvestny as a prophet and found in his sculptures a representation of a prophet's body. In Niezvestny's sculpture the body was broken down to interchangeable components with a violent substitution of inner and outer forms. This representation of the body can have a number of conflicting interpretations.

Berger argued that Niezvestny was not concerned with an idealisation of the body but with an 'image of man that celebrates his total nature'.[58] The rupture of boundaries and intrusion of extraneous elements was meant to testify to the limits of human endurance and stretch the poles that define life and death.

Berger quoted from Pushkin to illustrate how bodily transformation is a sign of transcendence.

> A six-winged seraph appeared to me at the crossing of the ways . . . He bent down to my mouth and tore out my tongue, sinful, deceitful and given to idle talk; and with his right hand steeped in blood he inserted the forked tongue of a wise serpent into my benumbed mouth. He clove my breast with a sword, and plucked out my quivering heart, and thrust a coal of live fire into my gaping breast. Like a corpse I lay in the desert. And the voice of God called out to me; 'Arise, O prophet, see and hear, be filled with my Will, go forth over the land and sea, and set the hearts of men on fire with your Word.'[59]

The parallel between the artist and the prophet rests on their demonstration of relational thinking and their ambivalent social position. Both artist and prophet oscillate between attachment and detachment, juxtapose the past with the future 'to bring history to its appointed consummation'.[60] They dream the promises of an era, and speak of the difference between the expedient and the necessary options in history.

Art may testify to a historical despair; however its service is not placation but the enunciation of the endurance that constructs a 'narrow pass across despair'.[61] The quality that Berger sought in an artist's vision, and the position that he ascribed for the artist, is related to their ability to recognise the full dimensions of 'man's proportions'. Like a sexless secular saint, the ideal artist is 'an example of man, and it is his art which exemplifies him'.[62] To realise this paradigmatic being, the artist like the prophet must tread carefully at the borders of non-being. The return is the gift of an era. Seeing the artist as a prophet is another way of intensifying the liminality of the artist's position within society and directing the question of alienation towards the pursuit of totalising truth claims that enlighten the perceptions of emancipation.

Camus argued that, if the role of art is to reveal a different order of cognition, then rebellion is integral to it. For rebellion begins with the desire for the impossible utopia – the metaphysical demand for unity – whereas the struggle reveals the impossibility of capturing unity, yielding in its place a substitute-partial universe.[63]

There is no rebel without a barrier. Similarly, for the artist to take an oppositional stance towards 'society', there must also be a discourse which defines the position of the artist which each artist either rebels against or conforms to. Characterisations of the rebel as an 'asocial' or 'marginal' figure presuppose a distinction between inside and outside, the centre and the periphery, which is untenable. It is more accurate to perceive the processes of rebellion as integral with all the constitutive forces that define identities and tradition within society. If we are to represent the rebel's relationship with society in spatial terms, then it is best to move on from the models which claimed that the rebel is bound to the radix in a concentric manner, or the claim that the rebel refuses the inferior interior for an idealised exterior, and consider a scheme which implicates the rebel in both the multiple processes of defining the parameters of a container and the definitions of the contained possibilities. The destiny of rebellion is therefore not so much towards the 'beyond', but in the 'within', and then not just repetition but re-assemblage.

Rather than the proclamation of a new identity through the inversion of the existing identities, Foucault[64] suggests that transgressions name the excluded and unacknowledged experiences by pushing the boundaries of existing identities to the limit, to a space where the prior closures break down. While rebellion and transgression focus attention towards the ruptures within certainties and the incommensurability of the past and the future within the present, it is only through prophecy, Berger claims, that the artist can find bridges and pathways. The vision that Berger celebrates, as he separates it from 'mere' reformism, is the one which contains the hope of going beyond the continuous rebounding within the prescribed polarities of contestation.

The only inspiration which exists is the intimation of our potential. Inspiration is the mirror image of history: by means of it we can see our past, while turning our back upon it. And it is precisely this which happens at the instant when a piece of music begins. We suddenly become aware of the previous silence at the same moment as our attention is concentrated upon following sequences and resolutions which will contain the desired.[65]

The achievement of cubism was, for Berger, not just the apogee of modernist aesthetics, but also the exceptional moment in Picasso's career where experimentation with the means of representation heightened the powers of revelation. The latent possibilities of the epoch were to be found *in* the artist's expression:

the gifts of an imaginative artist are often outriders of the gifts of his period. Frequently the new abilities and attitudes become recognizable in art and are given a name before their existence in life is appreciated. This is why a love of art which accompanies a fear or rejection of life is so inadequate. It is why ideally there should always be a road open to art even for those to whom the medium, the talent, the activity involved means nothing. Art is the nearest to an oracle that our position as modern scientific men can allow us.[66]

These conclusions have truth as their apex. Berger insists that while truth may not be immediately apparent, it is not mediated by a primordial lie as Picasso suggested when he asserted that 'We know that art is not the truth. Art is a lie enabling us to approach the truth'.[67] Berger was canny enough to reveal Picasso's celebration of the lie as evidence of a romantic ideology which simultaneously detaches social responsibility as it extracts material patronage. However, the options are not just relativism on the one hand, or positivism on the other. One must also consider Adorno's claim that 'Art is magic delivered from the lie of being truth',[68] which recognises the necessity for the quest for truth and totalisation while questioning the fixity of the original and ultimate points of reference in which *a* truth is located.

The role of the critic

From *The Success and Failure of Picasso* and *Art and Revolution* we can gain an accurate understanding of Berger's vision of the artist's position in society and his appreciation of the social value of art. However, if we wish to consider the possibilities for social intervention that are open to an art critic – the process of contestation, assertion and definition, as well as its counterside, the moments of retreat, doubt and reflexiveness – then we must turn to his journalism.[69] From the oscillations within Berger's own position one glimpses both the cultural limits that separate art from politics and the dreams of social justice. In this section I will focus on a theme that has recurred throughout his writing: the relationship between criticism and exile.

In response to the question, what makes Watteau 'The painter of his time', Berger answers:

He revealed in feeling the true transitional nature of the style he worked in. He remained (and was born) outside the social order he painted, but the ambivalence of the mood of his work was a perfect expression of the nature and destiny of that order . . . [in his work] a nostalgia for a past order, partly a premonition of the instability of the present, partly an unknown hope for the future.[70]

If the artist's ambivalent desire for totality and untimeliness is not a disavowal of his or her time but the alterior yet necessary route for the affirmation of truth, and if the question of responsibility in form and content emerges from the reciprocal identification between the artist and the public, then what is the space and function of criticism?

For Berger the role of the critic was not to speak for or against the intentions of the artist but to measure achievement. Criticism was not concerned with promotion or demotion, but with evaluation.

Like the artist, the critic's individual talents are not the crux of success and value: it is the dialectical relationship between imagination, method and subject which yields a representation that stretches the component parts beyond their initial inputs.[71] Thus criticism emerges not just from the identification of tensions and the plotting of oppositional forces, but from the prediction of a new convergence.

Berger argued that the critic must not just appreciate an artist's work but also anticipate the future of art. He insisted that the critic must not look over the shoulders of the artist to discover the truth or totality that is latent in the work, but must strive ahead of the artist. Berger took Charles Baudelaire's famous dictum that 'criticism follows the works of the mind as the shadow follows the body' and reverses it into 'criticism is the shadow that precedes the body'. With this paradoxical metaphor he extended the role of criticism from the engagement with a particular text to a coupling with the promise of social change.

> Criticism only occurs when a hope, or theory of art promises more than the practices of it, when a writer has a vision of art in his mind which no painting, nor poem, nor song, can equal in largeness, generosity, brilliance. In all great criticism one finds the vision of a new state, and yet not a single brick laid towards directly building it.[72]

During the formative years of cubism, Braque noted that he and Picasso worked 'rather like mountaineers roped together',[73] scaling the unknown. This bonded but transgressive allegiance, which had nothing to do with parasitic or sycophantic attachments, served as Berger's paradigm for the artist's and critic's commitment to both their work and their relationship to society.

Berger distinguished between the ideal critic and the fighting critic. The ideal critic was represented in two ways: as assuming either the ahistorical position of objectivity or the positionless relativism of subjectivity. Judgement was crippled in both instances, either through the hollow pontification of a critic who claims the omniscience of God, or by the critic's chameleon-like appreciation of everything according to the intentions of the producer. Berger dismissed the position of the ideal critic because it either trivialises or abstracts the criteria for judgement. The 'impotence' of the sympathetic critic, and the 'rigidity' of the critic who claims a totalising perspective are found equally untenable because they fail to contest the conventional categories in which art and politics are inserted.

In contrast, the fighting critic's stance is neither passive nor external to history. For Berger the critic must insert him/herself into the subject matter. However, each intervention must specify both the material conditions of the work's existence and the possibilities for change that the work presents to the viewer. Thus achievement is neither measured by transcendental categories nor reduced to the mere correlation between the artist's intention and its execution. The fighting critic's task is to form a *relationship* between the political and the aesthetic. In this 'struggle' the fighting critic is both pragmatic and ethical.

The function of criticism is not to provide a scoresheet in the pursuit of absolutes; 'Proper criticism' is less reified, it is always more engaged, more polemical, more committed to a specific historical situation, and is 'more modest'.[74]

'First, you must answer the question: What can art serve here and now? Then you criticize according to whether the works in question serves that purpose or not.'[75]

Think of nothing but the pictures as you stand in front of them. But in the end they will either make you grow or they will make you shrink. And the process of growing is the process of learning to connect. And every extension of a person's awareness is a political fact.[76]

The pursuit of these inter-relationships between social justice and art does not imply that there will be a direct or definitive one-to-one correlation between the image and the idea. Art and criticism are not to be confused with propaganda, which always insists on the univocal expression of reality. Berger argued that the critic's function is to enter into the artist's metaphorical mode, to see how a particular way of seeing things creates a relationship with the world. In *Art and Revolution* Berger concluded that criticism cannot proceed by literal analysis which inevitably abstracts at as it attempts to elucidate it. Such an investigation is ultimately a negation of the impulse which concerns the work that a critic is facing. Literal analysis invariably builds a hedge around the work, excluding what Blanchot calls the necessary 'risk',[77] whereas a 'metaphorical reading' rescues both the potency of art and criticism by emphasising the process of resistance in every critical encounter. Through metaphor the project, which the artist initiated can be extended, affirmed and contextualised as the critic rebounds against it.

If it were the function of criticism to explain and decode the meaning of these works precisely and completely, criticism would amount to no more than sabotage, the destruction of art. Or to put the same proposition in a different way, it would mean that the works in question were not truly prophetic, but were merely an illustration of the already formulated and known.[78]

In other words, the role of the critic is not to repeat the artist's message but to translate the vision of art. Thus it is not the finished product which is of consequence, but the initiation of a form of consciousness which can transform both the means of representation and the 'ways of seeing'. And this reciprocal process is always plural, open-ended: 'No man is single. No action is separate. We merge and change like the clouds. Energy cannot exist without time. We grow and are grown over.'[79] The visionary potential of the artist and the critic is achieved neither by an extrapolation of the present nor via a transmigration into an idealised past; rather, Berger claims, through the apprehension of the unfulfilled expectations that oscillate between the past and the present. For Berger the hope for finding the desired future *within* history was also the means for the critical intervention in the present. By merging the critic's and artist's role with that of a visionary, Berger was attempting to heighten their prophetic function. The importance of this claim rests between the opposed views in the British and Russian culture. The role of the artist as prophet in British cultural debates was considered as a pompous or absurd duty, whereas in the Russian culture, with which Berger strongly identified, the position of the artist or the critic as a prophet was considered as a given. It was no coincidence then, that Berger's claims were perceived as far-fetched and therefore received with either resistance or silence.

Throughout his career as the weekly art critic for *The New Statesman* the critical response to Berger completely by-passed his claim that the failure of the artist to take the position of prophet was an expression of a culture that has lost faith in itself. His critics either attacked or supported his political objectives and, while they questioned the absence or presence of the political with the aesthetic, there was no discussion as to whether or not the cultural base could facilitate such an integration. Declarations that British culture did or did not integrate the arts with public life were in abundance, but there was no examination of if or how it could. Furthermore, Berger's identification with Russian culture,[80] as exemplifying the unified other which provided the counterpoint that sharpened his argument against the insularity and the parochialism of British culture, was never connected to a further claim that a transformation of the political order presupposes particular cultural mechanisms. This silence suggests that Berger's claims were either extraneous to, or already contained within, British culture. For the admission of tension would have implied the recognition of prior exclusion or repression of Berger's claim.

By noting the points at which the reception of Berger's writing was transformed from insignificant rhetoric to intolerable propaganda, we can witness the sites of ethnocentrism and the limits of political tolerance by the art world's establishment. Why is it that when Berger made sweeping comments about the marginalised socialist realists, or unknown European artists, the London art world didn't even hear the pebble drop into their still pond, and when he located the hope for humanist art in the lap of the colonial or post-colonial artist this scarcely caused a ripple? However, the moment Berger criticised Bacon, Picasso and Moore the art world was up in arms, civility was abandoned and defensive prejudices were ushered in to fortify the belief that some artists were 'gods' whose art and genius was a transcendental quality unsullied by the profanity of politics.[81]

When re-reading the essays written for the *New Statesman* and collected in *Permanent Red*, Berger acknowledged that his journalistic writing was formed by an 'attitude of belligerent wariness'.[82] He argued that this explains both the puritanism and the sharpness of his generalisations, but he failed to consider whether or not this 'belligerence', or what he earlier described as his 'perversity',[83] was formed not just by the dictates of the genre, but also by the absence of a space that he was contesting in British culture.

The relationship between exile and art was certainly a recurring motif throughout this period and was in fact one of the central questions in John Berger's first novel, *A Painter of Our Time* (1958). While *Permanent Red* had been described as both personal chronicle and historical document, it is curious to note the relative absence of the haunting interrelationship between exile and art. A supplementary volume could be extracted from this voluminous period in his writing:[84] it might be entitled *Permanent Exiles* and include, for instance, the aticle in which he entwines the conviction of Jewish exiles with the enigma of memory. Here Berger distinguished a particular yearning which blurs the conventional separation of nostalgia from hope; suffering and redemption: 'Jewish nostalgia does not imply the sense of something hopelessly lost, but rather hopelessly desired . . . it is paradoxical – it amounts to nostalgia for the future. Paradise becomes the promised land'. He concluded this article even more ambiguously: 'To assess such a work, if one responds to its impetus as strongly as I do, is difficult'.[85]

What *Permanent Red* also failed to document were the historical debates in which Berger was embroiled. While these debates, with all their inevitable fixations and frustrations, never seemed to undermine either Berger's incisiveness nor his commitment, they did seem to produce essays which showed signs of his exhaustion and disillusionment. There were two particular instances where 'flashpoint' of self-criticism was followed by a departure from his stated position. The essays, which preceded his first temporary leave from the *New Statesman* (1956) and those haunting essays prior to his announcement of leaving Britain and full-time journalism in 1959, did not find a place in *Permanent Red*.

It is also worthwhile considering Berger's claims for the role of the artist and the critic, not only with these essays in mind, but also in conjunction with a number of essays on 'third world' artists in which Berger expressed some of his most affirmative and optimistic comments. Does the failure to further the claims in these essays suggest that they were merely expressions of a rhetorical sympathy bordering on sentimentality, and is their omission from *Permanent Red* another expression of the eurocentrism of British culture?

Identification with other and the contestation against the self as the first step towards departure

Berger's opposition to the powerful figures of the art world was related to his 'intuitive'[86] allegiance with those who struggle against that power. When confronting the works by exiles, struggling British artists, or non-metropolitans, Berger's sympathy for their predicament was predicated not just by a generalised response against the exclusive and divisive structures of the dominant culture, but also because these examples afforded him the space to express his own identity. In another context, Berger argued that this is the paradoxical basis of a storyteller's identity: for it is only when working on something *other* than the self, that a strong sense of identity emerges.[87]

When writing about exiled artists, Berger always redeemed profundity and hope from their sadness and nostalgia.[88] For instance, the tenacity which bordered on obstinacy, and the commitment to work through suffering, that Berger identified in 'Peter Peri' was partly projected into the protagonist of *A Painter of Our Time*.[89]

When reviewing an exhibition of twelve Australian painters he not only found merit in their work but also a lesson to the British artists; they offered a useful and clear demonstration of 'what is meant by a proper "national tradition" '.[90]

As Berger increasingly identified the West as the site of decay crumbling under the weight of its own corrupt materialism, he claimed that the 'sensitive man must turn to the East'.[91] While Berger repeatedly championed Affandi as one of the 'three best painters alive', the fashionable galleries and the other critics remained ignorant of Affandi's 'heroic endurance'.[92]

In these essays Berger represented the non-metropolitans as having achieved the project that the metropolitans aspired to but were unable to grasp. Examples like Affandi were celebrated because, through his integration of the arts with national practices, he also secured the critical tradition through which individuals could extend their claim to social rights. Thus Berger located the space of hope for the future of humanist art in the very place that was popularly perceived as either locked in an archaic past or deprived of any trace of humanism.

However, when examining the products of his own culture, there was a tendency to categorise negatively the mainstream with such a rigidity that it denied them even the possibility of a trace of ambivalence. This was where Berger's 'belligerent wariness' was most evident, and where the binary oppositions were most trenchant. The dominant polarities were abstract expressionism and social realism. Social realism was defined as the art form that was positive, active and organic, and unsurprisingly, abstract expressionism was the opposite; negative, passive and inorganic. In these debates the middle ground seemed to vanish.

Throughout Berger's writing in the 1950s there was not a single positive or sympathetic comment about the mainstream arts. He interpreted their expression of feelings as confused and incoherent, lacking any structure or purpose, deprived of any commitment to a generalised theory. Condemned to an individualism which merely nourished private mythologies, their work 'floundered' between being a description of their own perversions or simply boring.[93] At best, British painting was seen as a 'heresy: an interesting half-truth which threatens the stable but constantly developing main tradition'.[94] All claims to an autonomous art movement were rejected. The central body, to which Britain was an unacknowledged client, was Europe. He argued that the failure to confront this subordinant position has led to critical imbalances, the consequences of which were that

> most English painters and sculptors have had only a second or third hand connection with the main movements of modern European art. As a result their discoveries, instead of stemming from and adding to a tradition, are, on the whole, eccentric in character. What such artists lack in mastery of method, they must make up for by intensity and singularity of vision.[95]

His description of those attending the glamorous galleries reads like a vivid list of pretenders, exploiters and apologists.[96] He attacked the art schools for failing to provide a positive example to their students. He perceived the abandonment of traditions as the licence to wallow in a borderless relativism. Similarly, the Arts Council was rebuked for shirking its responsibilities to establish a centralised authority to which artists can either conform or rebel. In this antagonistic atmosphere any expression of openness was interpreted as a false claim on freedom, and the benign equated with the castrated.[97]

Authenticity and hope were always elsewhere. Success and value were not defined by the self-deluding and narcissistic confines of the art world, but could only be found if the artist and the critic were prepared 'to break through this world to a broader, more ignorant, but finally more human, more grateful, more intelligent'.[98] The latter world was of course the 'real' world: a genuine space in which there was dialogue, as opposed to pontification, evaluation rather than sycophantic praise. In other words, this was the 'vitalised' space of reciprocity which is counter to the ghetto of estrangement. For Berger, estrangement was predicated not only on expulsion or exclusion, but also on the absence of dialogue.

If the visionary function of the critic is in 'connecting activity with activity', then the refusal to relate art to the political is to diminish the parameters of both. Of William Blake, Berger said he 'so much hated what he saw around him that he dreamt to give himself space.'[99] For Berger, consciousness of social rights, like the processes that underwrite aesthetic innovation, can only be heightened through the expansiveness of metaphor; the hinge that connects dissimilars.

While open space is necessary for hope, the acceptance of closures is equated with the expression of despair. And while the 'fighting' critic is looking towards the 'beyond' in order to sharpen the appreciation of contrasts within, the 'ideal' critic double-crosses, denies change while rationalising defeats, consoles victims while flattering victors. In criticism as in politics there are heroes and traitors. However, the problem with the either/or polarisation of truth and falsehood, hope and despair, is not just that between these poles there are always the mediating structures of ideology whose effects have neither a fixed origin nor an inexorable destiny,[100] but also that this opposition is insufficient for measuring value. It tends to condemn or ignore anything that might refuse or elude its own terms. The solution is not to replace certainty with doubt as the motor for critical appreciation, but to admit the interpolation of both.

In *A Painter of Our Time*, the protagonist reflected on the 'perverse' individualism of the artist, and the ambiguous social utility of art. He concluded that the artist does not 'serve' society according to utilitarian or instrumental codes, and that, while the artist's strategy is invariably related to political objectives, this 'relationship' can only be realisable if society is willing to embrace the flexibility, obliqueness and expansiveness of art.

> The dilemma of the artist is unimportant, if you are considering his art. But it can be important if you consider it as an intense reflection of a wider but less obvious dilemma. If we are to continue working at all under capitalism, only two possible attitudes of mind are open to us: we must be either ambitious or arrogant. The humble artist is a man whom we shall only rediscover much later. Today the artist either serves or searches arrogantly alone. Few, of course, of those who serve do so consciously. Simply, they are more frightened of making fools of themselves than they are aware of their true capabilities. The power of fashion is based on the fear of being a fool. The ambitious artist is the man who places his talent on the pedestal of good opinion. And how we all long to be in such a position! There is nothing essentially shameful in it. But everything depends upon the state of contemporary opinion. There are fish that you throw back into the sea as not being worth the catch. And there – in that last sentence – is the other attitude of mind: the arrogant attitude. Bill Neale would say this was a false dilemma that could only be posed by a bourgeois artist frightened of the people. Serve *them*, I can hear him saying, and you'll purge yourself of both ambition and arrogance. But he is wrong. It is in the name and the virtue and the potentiality of the life that the working class can gain for the world, that I am arrogant. All their strength, of which many of them are yet unaware, is reflected in my naivete.[101]

When responding to the works of 'past masters', or to the works of rebels, strangers and exiles in modernity, Berger demonstrated an awareness of this tension between service and transgression, yet the potential for such 'reconciliation' within his own subject position as a critic was at times, especially after protracted and aggressive debates, suggested either negatively or rhetorically.

In 1956 Berger decided that he would stop writing as a regular critic for one year. His last article was called 'Exit and Credo?' and it expressed doubt about the ability to locate the critic's social position: 'The critic is a bastard – in more sense than one. Finally, he has no definite status. He is merely the index of the tension, the relationships between the changes taking place in art and the changes taking place in the ideas and economics of his time.'[102] In 1959, his final year as a critic writing in Britain, Berger again reflected over his past and again questioned the position of the critic. He rejected the omniscient and totalising position of the historian-judge and proffered a radicalised version of the subjective-witness.

> The critic in my view can teach very little about painting as such: for that go to museums and studios. What he can do is to try to reveal and describe causes and consequences, and so be a guide to action.[103]

> Critics aren't gods. And even less spokesmen for history. They are partial, obstinate teachers – without textbooks, and so must use anything they set eyes on to push their lesson home.[104]

In an article titled 'Who Are You?' (11 April 1959), Berger split his voice into two personae – 'B' and '2B': one represents a critic and the other a painter. The staging of these two voices did not extend Berger's earlier statement that it is the critic's task to precede rather than follow the artist, for the two positions are not represented in any parallel relationship. What ensued was not a dialogue that tended toward mutual understanding, but a dramatisation of the distance between the critic and the painter and the antagonisms that displaced the utility of each.[105]

From this perspective we can speculate over the complex reasons that motivated Berger's exit from Britain. It is obvious that he was not banished by some political decree. However, he claimed that his departure was a consequence of both his ambivalent relationship with England and his attraction to France. In England he felt that there were parts of his self which were being denied.[106] And at that time the intellectual figures with whom he identified were Sartre, Camus and Merleau-Ponty.[107]

The personal dynamics that determined his 'voluntary exile' were also related to a broader conception of the social position of the critic. His project as a critic was both monumentally ambitious and destined to frustration. He was not only writing against the grain of British culture, but also demanding fundamental changes concerning the relationship between the public and the arts. In Britain Berger felt doomed to perpetual detachment and marginalisation. What was popularly celebrated as intellectual freedom he perceived as another form of servitude. France promised integration and a culture that took its critics seriously. Throughout Berger yearned for the position that Gramsci described as that of the 'organic intellectual'.

Yet there is a paradox at the centre of this desire. Why does voluntary exile seem both to be a logical step and to offer a solution from the involuntary alienation at home? How will integration be found with the 'other' when it is denied to the self? Is there not the fear that the denials experienced at home will be compounded abroad? And to what extent does the distinction between the centre and the periphery, which embodies the values of success and recognition, not just of an individual but also of the historical consciousness of a whole class, predicate the decision to leave?

Prophecy and critical intimacy

Recent debates which have foregrounded the artist's cultural location should not overlook the correlation between aesthetics and broader political transformations, and the modern forms of migration which have displaced our conventional understanding of representation. Consider, for instance, the problematic of self-definition that arises when the place of origin and the place of work are physically separate. We might immediately question the nature of the linkages that bridge these two places. To generate the momentum of leaving there must be a dialectic of pushes and pulls. The two places cannot be isomorphic. The driving factor might be economic necessity, personal ambition, cultural aspiration, political or religious persecution. It might be a combination of all these factors, but for any of these factors to be translated into a force there must be the attending *interpretation* that the difference between the two places signifies a hierarchisation of space. In modernity the increasing knowledge of the difference *between* other places has generated a symbolic ordering of space which has intensified the attraction to the metropolis. The signs of beckoning are everywhere and the reasons for leaving are not always found in the sociology of migration. To understand the modern condition of exile we also need a semiotics of displacement.

The dispersal of signs across the modern world has punctured the borders that defined the cultural identity of particular places. Images of distant places have crossed many hands. This multiplication of symbolic exchange has done little to undermine the basic opposition between the centre and the periphery; tourism and migration go in different directions: the decision to visit and the decision to leave has a different gravity let alone price. Furthermore, this new global culture has not reduced the popular consciousness into a homogenous mulch. Self-definition proceeds through opposition, making the asymmetrical relationships to power all too apparent. Increased mobility seems to have sharpened the need to know ourselves all the more by defining who is and is not our permissible neighbour, our competitor, our guide.

An understanding of the dynamics of displacement in modernity would not necessarily celebrate the stranger as the critical subject of modernity, but it would utilise the condition of estrangement to consider both the achievements of modern culture and the methodological principles of critical inquiry. From this perspective we might come to a revaluation of the social position of the avant-garde and question the ways that the methodological strategy of critical distance 'enabled' subjects to create a narrative about the crisis they were in. Was critical distance another position within the labyrinthine insecurities of a particular rationality, another expression of a culture's anxieties, rather than the impartial viewpoint from which to articulate the dynamics of transition? Was the avant-garde's oscillation between historical reference points and cultural constituencies a rejection of the fixity of the either/or opposition? Could their advance towards the combinatory dualism of the neither/nor, or both/and, be an expression of a perspective whereby the difference in vantage point twists and entwines the productive interpolation of the 'near' and the 'far'?

In this section I will trace the arguments within literary and cultural criticism which have linked the experience of exile with a critical representation of modernity. Throughout the arguments there is a correlation between estrangement and transcendence. I will bypass those accounts in which the dialectics of exilic vision are stunted by a rhetorical and moralistic set of oppositions. Thus I will attempt to see how the critical and the sentimental voices of exile are distinguished in critical theory. Most theories have inbuilt dispositions which privilege a particular representative as the critical subject of modernity: exiles are played off against expatriates, the post-colonial realist is the counter to the metropolitan modernist. It is not always productive to repeat such allegiances and contestations. I am not trying to insert an excluded other into the dominant discourse. My aim is twofold: to question the epistemological framework for evaluating otherness and prophecy, and to consider the cultural perspective which regulates the degrees of permissible difference in the subject position of social critic. My critique will try to ascertain whether the 'gift' of exile is a consequence of the subtle interplay of difference and intimacy rather than dispassionate detachment. It is the role of metaphor and the cultural dynamics for the social production of truth which are at the centre of this section.

One of the dominant features that literary critics regularly attribute to modernist authors is the distance that they assume vis-à-vis their subject. This utilisation of distance takes on many significant functions. Critics remind us that the 'outsider' author offers a unique position from which to view and evaluate action. Thus authorial position provides the link between place and perspective. Writers' particular way of seeing social interaction is invariably explained by their adjacency, their opposition, or their estrangement from society. On many occasions this correspondence is taken to the extreme whereby there follows the rigid insistence that distanciation is necessary for critical representation. I would like to put a few brakes on this line of arguing, and demonstrate that while the step between the observation of distanciation in literary representation and a sociological comment on the condition of alienation in modern society may seem a short one, it is, nevertheless, filled with contradiction and complexities. Witness for instance, the similarity in the premises to Raymond Williams's and Terry Eagleton's arguments on modernist literature, and yet their conclusions concerning the relationship between exile and the critical representation of modernity are diametrically opposed.

Both Williams and Eagleton are eager to differentiate the logic of appropriation and displacement from that of representation and commitment. They astutely relate the innovative utilisation of opposition and juxtaposition not only to the inherent condition of social division but also to the author's ambivalent cultural location.

However, the moral and political implications that they draw from modernism are significantly different.

Raymond Williams's account of modernism repeats the Lukácsian tendency to reduce the modernists' oscillation to a celebration of detachment, and equates their 'exilic' base with a politically reactionary and psychologically masochistic acceptance of the pervasive estrangement in the metropolis.

Thus the key cultural factor of the modernist shift is the character of the metropolis: in these general conditions, but then, even more decisively, in its direct effect on form. The most important general element of these innovations in form is the fact of immigration to the metropolis, and it cannot too often be emphasised, how many of the major innovators were, in this precise sense, immigrants. At the level of theme, this underlies, in an obvious way, the elements of strangeness and distance, indeed of alienation, which so regularly formed part of the repertory. But the decisive aesthetic effect is at a deeper level. Liberated or breaking from their national or provincial cultures, placed in quite new relations to those other native languages or native visual traditions, and countering meanwhile a novel and dynamic, common environment from which many of the older forms were obviously distant, the artists and writers and thinkers of this phase found the only community available to them; a community of the medium: of their own practices.[108]

The traumatic experience of loss and the search for re-integration once again enters to explain the exiled artist's imaginative processes. Yet here the experience of lack is seen not as being a symptom of the periphery but as a reflection of the more pervasive lack within the centre. The exile's re-vision of language is seen not as the beginning of the formation of a new and radical nexus between identity, history and culture but as the expression of the transformation that undermines the certitudes of traditional social practices and condemns the artist to being the servant and not the critic of modernity.

For Williams the politics of modernism are as pernicious as the politics of modernity. He is not saying that modernism has to be understood in the context of modernity, but rather that the reinscription of their methods and images into the iconography of commercialism, and their central position in the canon, are unequivocal proof of their co-option.[109] Not only did the 'displaced' modernists supplant the 'rooted' realists, but in the process of being integrated into the culture of modernity, their critical faculties were shorn, and their entry into the canon endorsed the centrality of displacement in the culture of modernity.

In Williams's account there is little doubt that the validation of an inorganic relationship to society, coupled with an increasing emphasis on the role of form, was a recipe for mannerism and an abandonment of the critical function of art. Terry Eagleton is less willing to push the argument in this direction. In *Exile and Emigres* Eagleton is prepared to stake a grand claim on the vision that emerges from the motion between the foreign and the familiar as he equates it with the motion between the particular and the general. This guarantees that the 'cultural betweenness' of the modernist is not conflated with the romantic claim for 'apartness'. Nevertheless the destiny and duty for the romantic is transposed upon the modernist. Eagleton imbues the modernist artist with curative and guiding qualities. Eagleton's modernist prophet-visionary seems to possess virtues similar to those expressed by Williams's romantic and realist artist, who is the 'outrider, herald, and witness of social change'.

Eagleton's account proceeds from the assumption that the dynamism of a culture can be measured by the quality of the literature it generates. Literary and cultural mechanisms are linked organically to the dynamism of social transformation. The failure of the former is interpreted as exposing the flaw of the latter. Hence Eagleton's observation that the domination of English literature by foreigners is a paradox that proves the internal decline of English society. Yet the paradox deepens if we ask: For whom does a Pole living in England write? The ambivalence of Conrad, for instance, is not interpreted as affecting the transformation of the artist's relationship to society, but only as an indication of the failure of the indigenous society to produce 'high' culture. Eagleton positions Conrad on the periphery of English culture and focuses on his doubleness to the extent that it questions the stability of English culture. The other cultures remain silent. They are effectively silenced by a framework that constructs the route from the periphery to the centre as a one-way street. An inverse relationship is constructed which recognises the value of the periphery purely as an indicator of the decline of the centre. While Eagleton usefully questions the way the canon selects entrants in order to ignore the problematical material conditions of society, he does not consider how such heterogeneous entrants can possibly question the homogeneity of the canon's cultural claims.

According to Eagleton the value of exiles is that they had a greater sense of vision than the natives. It was the exiles who grasped a totalised view of all the dynamic elements and interactions within society and who projected a transcendental view which could transpose a personal perspective on to a broader historical plane. The exile's superior claim to rationality was based on the ability to fuse the particular with the general and to move sensitively from subjective attachment to objective detachment.

For Eagleton ambivalence is neither an end in itself, nor a dynamic invested with autonomy, but a form of tension which blocks the preferred resoluteness of objectivity. Objectivity must show no trace of its 'ambivalent journey'. The contestation between opposites must be resolved before the artist can claim to have achieved transcendence and totalisation. This was the privilege of foreigners, for they,

> were able to fuse the profoundest inwardness with the specific life of their own times with a capacity to generalize that life into the form of a complete vision. In the best work of those writers, the shape and structure of an entire culture can be elicited, by an alert sensitivity to the general forces and significant movements of their societies, from the focused detail of local and concrete detail . . . to write out of a relationship of intricately detailed intimacy with his society; yet he is also able to grasp that society as a totality, in a way which one might have expected to be genuinely available only to an outsider free of its most immediate pressures . . . able to discover a point of operative distance from the partial interests and allegiances of their own cultures: a point of balance at which inwardness could combine with an essential externality to produce major art.[110]

Eagleton argues that this position was achieved by a form of abstraction which was proceeded by a complex and diffuse relationship of attraction and repulsion, it maintained a firm gaze on the present while also recovering and transforming the myths and legacies marginalised by the dominant culture.[111] In Eagleton's schema, the solution to social crisis lies within the antinomies of society. Art and objectivity emerge from the 'subtle and involuted tensions between the remembered and the real, the potential and the actual, integration and dispossession, exile and involvement'.[112]

In Eagleton's and Williams's account of modernism the question of 'foreignness' is explored primarily on a linguistic level. It is the author's shift in language which is the fundamental dislocation and it is also the author's re-utilisation of the language which announces the possibility of a critical intervention in the culture of modernity. However, within the history of modernism there is another level of 'foreignness' which is in need of theorising. This is related to the phenomenon of cultural dislocation and cultural re-negotiation. This factor has come closer to the centre of the debates on modernism as the mainstream critical discourse has begun to recognise the complicity of dominant western culture with colonialism. This acknowledgement is, however, somewhat conveniently phrased only in the past tense. While there has been a boom industry in the relationship between early modernism and colonialism, there is a relative silence on the relationship between contemporary culture and the legacies of colonialism. Within these debates which have acknowledged the contribution of critics from non-metropolitan spaces there has emerged another set of theoretical presuppositions which demand scrutinising. For instance, when cultural critics contrast metropolitan with (post-) colonial writers, there is a tendency to repeat a series of 'reassuring' but 'disarming' polarities which bypass the complexities of identity in modernity. In this schema, the exiles and (post-) colonial writers are ushered into the academic forum to confirm both the alterity of identity in modernity and the utility of realism.

Mary McCarthy's distinction between 'real' exiles and 'inauthentic' expatriates draws on a paradigm which issues credibility only to those who struggle with the home. Expatriates, who leave without coercion, are systematically condemned by her for being narcissistic, apolitical, decadent and parasitic on the metropolitan economy. In this portrait, Henry James is marked as the pretender. Expatriates are represented like spoilt children who are never satisfied with their life at home – always yearning for the ideal, but never contesting the real. On the other hand, exiles personify the mature conscience and independent character that challenges the rules at home, and, even when evicted, they persist with the aim of redeeming the image of home. McCarthy admits one 'intermediate exile', Joyce, on the grounds that his mission was to 'forge in the smithy of my soul the uncreated conscience of my race'.[113] Both humble and arrogant, the fusing of the particular with the universal, the finding of the self in the social – this is the practice for the artist as prophet.

Andrew Gurr also argues that for the metropolitan modernist expatriation is a journey into solipsism, whereas for the colonial realist exile (which he also confines to the experience of flight after a contestation against a perceived lack in the homeland) becomes a 'positive' space in which the delicate synthesis between estrangement and integration can find aesthetic expression. Gurr repeatedly claims that art requires freedom and distance, and that exile is its most proximate parallel.

the colonial writers found themselves so placed as to uniquely enjoy an enormous freedom from the solipsism which has afflicted the central metropolitan tradition of writing since the end of the nineteenth century. Their need to find an identity not in the solipsistic self but in the idea of home, the colonial island wherever it may be, released them from the first difficulty, of knowing the self; and the consequent emphasis on a psychological identity instead of the ego created the possibility of communication outside the creating self. The very process of identifying the social causes of alienation makes the universal of the particular, the general case from the local island.[114]

For Gurr, exile affords the 'critical distance', in and with which the lost past is redeemed along with the consciousness of stricture in the present. This combination of places and historical experiences constitutes the possibility of transcendence into a more generalised consciousness of home and identity.

The paradox of transcendence proceeding from the double experience of lack is not explored in much detail by Gurr. But, against this sense of lack, the colonial writer is also celebrated as the container of a conscious which the metropolitan has 'lost touch' with: a sense of place and tradition. Yet, in Hegelian terms, Gurr also argues that the articulation of this consciousness can only come from, and even be created by, exile. The colonial writers' oscillation from lack to plenitude deepens the paradox of identity, for any articulation of identity in exile, or exile in identity, will only confirm the double estrangement from identity – in both the homeland and the place of exile. This paradox does not suggest transcendence but rather a restating of this most intimate question.

In part detachment is a reaction against the solipsistic trap of egocentricity. Narcissism and nostalgia alike blur the social identity which the searcher needs for his sense of home and therefore his own identity. Detachment is then the clearest signal the exile can give that he is free. It signals freedom from all attachments but the self-created identity of home. We need not of course deny that in such circumstances detachment is a pose just as freedom is a chimaera in a deterministic universe. Like exile itself it is both traumatic and liberating, a compulsion and a freedom, which traps the writer into solitude and defends him against the distractions of the world. That is the paradox within whose bounds the artist works out the terms of his exile.[115]

Fredric Jameson has also foregrounded the experience of exile in his differentiation between metropolitan and non-metropolitan literature. His schema resembles Gurr's in the sense that it also looks towards the example of the post-colonial author in order to discover solutions or alternative routes from the impasses in metropolitan discourse. However, as Gayatri Spivak observed, there is a 'productive unease' in Jameson's version of this argument.[116] Jameson counters the modernists' surrender of the writer's subject-position by celebrating its affirmation by post-colonial writers.[117] As modernism marks the moment of incommensurability in the First World, the 'National Allegory' in the Third World ushers in a correspondence between the abstract and the concrete. Meanwhile the First World *suffers*:

a radical split between the private and the public, between the poetic and the political, between what we have come to think of as the domain of sexuality and the unconscious and that of the public world of the classes, of the economic, and the secular political power: in other words, Freud versus Marx.[118]

In the Third World, Jameson argues, the narrative is 'invested with a properly libidinal dynamic' and is layered with political dimensions so that 'the story of the private individual's destiny is always an allegory of the embattled situation of the public third-world culture and society'.[119]

Spivak questions this relocation of the burden of responsibility and commitment 'not because the migrant must still consider the question of identity, plurality, roots. But, because fabricating de-centered subjects as the sign of the times is not necessarily this time de-centering the subject'.[120] For just as there is the unrigorous assumption that the 'representation of de-centering [is] de-centering',[121] there is also the assumption that the tropes of opposition lead to the topos of conjuncture. Valorising the radical otherness of an other culture is no solution to the complexities of representing identity. Equally, Hegel's master/servant dialectic is no more acceptable, even if it is the servant who is elevated as the carrier of truth and totality. For as Spivak argues, the representations of the post-colonial other invariaby unstick the possibility of a resolute synthesis emerging from critical distance.[122]

The disinterested and neutral relationship between object and subject is not the structure that unfolds the complexities of identity in modernity. The antinomy between remoteness and proximity which constitutes critical intimacy is the ambivalent space that constantly destabilises both the space from which the writer speaks and the knowledge of the object which the writer represents. This mode for social enquiry is also related to the sociological antinomies of modernity, which I would argue are exile and integration. However, exile and integration are not to be understood as conceptual analogues to the metaphysical opposition between error and truth, for to claim that in modernity the individual is permanently in exile is not equivalent to the assertion that the totality or essence of truth is perpetually beyond reach, but rather the recognition that the ambivalence of the 'other' possibility displaces the territory of truth. In the place of univocal certitudes modernity has substituted writings that, as de Certeau argues, are 'detached from their epiphanic function of representing things'.[123] In modernity, the relevance of discourse is not bound by the opposition between free-floating doubt and codified orders, for its significance is not dependent on the 'reality' it expresses but rather on the 'possibilities' it can generate. In this sense, modernity makes explicit the very metaphoricity of language, for like metaphor, modernity 'moves elusively in the domain of the other'.[124]

Today, as soon as very early childhood is over, the house can never again be a home, as it was in other epochs. This century, for all its wealth and with all its communication systems, is the century of banishment. Eventually perhaps the promise, of which Marx was the great prophet, will be fulfilled, and then the substitute for the shelter of a home will not just be our personal names, but our collective conscious presence in history, and we will live again in the heart of the real. Despite everything, I can imagine it. Meanwhile, we live not just our own lives but the longing of our century.[125]

Modernity is an epoch which undermines stereotypes and other static forms of commonsense. In modernity the strange is always mixed with the familiar. While the experience of estrangement may seem like a historical given, the socio-political preconditions that give estrangement a meaning change. In modernity these changes may appear to occur at a rate that is faster than the ability to name them. Estrangement may be defined as the 'disruptive' discrepancy between the known and the unknown. Yet between these hiatuses there must also be a constant effort at re-grounding. Metaphor is one way of naming the gaps in consciousness, and for Berger the role of the artist was to produce metaphors that named change and thereby heightened the sense of being.

According to Aristotle's often quoted formulation, metaphor is seeing the similarities in differences, the 'thisness' in 'that', and vice versa; thus even as it unites opposites, metaphor is not just the woof and warp of language, but also the ubiquitous path through which we seek meaning, and by which we establish generalisations. If metaphor is the means by which we arrive at understanding, then there are still two possibilities that can emerge: either metaphor facilitates the further insight that all definitions rest on an interminable process of relatedness, or metaphor can be reduced to being; 'merely' the means to another conclusion. Thus the meaning of metaphor splits between a radicalisation of relational thinking and a subordination to essences and totalities. Berger's description of the effect of a mosaic can illustrate the claim that metaphor is only convincing when it merges the edges of its constituent parts and gives a shimmering illusion of a whole: 'It is only when seen from a distance colours are fused and the light is reflected from so many different edges and angles, that the final images seem to destroy their own surface, making it simultaneously more vivid and more ambiguous...'[126] Whereas the following description of the way the cubists responded to changing patterns of perception in modernity illustrates a counter-claim, that metaphor highlights the identity of the part without subordinating meaning to the coherence of a whole: 'the visible, in continual flux, became fugitive. For the Cubists the visible was no longer what confronted the single eye, but the totality of possible views taken from points all round the object (or person) being depicted.'[127]

The relational thinking that Berger advocates must not be equated with any isomorphic reinscription of the whole in the context of the part, nor with what is conventionally described as relativism. Whenever Berger attempts to assess the value of a generalisation he repeats the lessons he learnt from Blake: discovering the intensity of minutiae does not push one away from the dimensions of reality and into a private dream world;[128] the grandeur of an idea is founded on the precision with which actual particulars have been understood.[129]

Whenever Berger describes 'genius' he centres his definition in an oxymoron and then proceeds to show the relatedness of the seemingly incompatible elements of objectivity and subjectivity, the universal and particulars. For example, the tone of Montaigne's voice was one of 'passionate dispassion'. Buffet's success in representing genuine emotion without over-intellectualising was achieved through his 'tense austerity'. Degas's masterpieces are described as having been executed with 'almost ruthless compassion, having been shaped by the conclusive disciplines of art, they yet remain as heroically inconclusive and therefore, in one sense, as ordinary as the life from which they sprang'.[130] Berger shares Anthony Blunt's belief that the greatest works in the individualist period of art were achieved by the most delicate and controlled balance of emotion and reason. For both, Poussin was the master.[131]

Berger argues that every 'great artist' turns 'his' attention to what innocence or ignorance passes by. The act of naming the unnamed faces two directions: by confronting the new in society, and by turning towards that which is denied by language. Stereotypically, the 'great artist' is defined as someone who struggles against material circumstances, social conventions and his own subjectivity, but Berger adds that the critical qualities are generated through a contestation of the social position of the artist and the very language of art. To distinguish between the typical and the exceptional artist, Berger emphasises that the critic must understand the terms of this antagonism.

> To be an exception a painter whose vision had been formed by the tradition, and who had probably studied as an apprentice or student from the age of sixteen, needed to recognize his vision for what it was, and then to separate it from the usage for which it had been developed. Single-handed he had to contest the norms of the art that had formed him. He had to see himself as a painter in a way that denied the seeing of a painter. This meant that he saw himself doing something that nobody else could foresee.[132]

The vision of the exceptional painter is 'the result of a prolonged successful struggle'.[133] The issue of the struggle is not just between the subject matter and the capability of the artist to find a suitable expression; it also arises from the artist's estrangement from 'his' social position and the language of art. In Berger's eyes Rembrandt epitomised the exceptional artist, who in his last self-portrait stood before the institution of art as a stranger: 'He has turned the tradition [of painting] against itself. He has wrested its language away from it. He is an old man. All has gone except a sense of the question of existence, of existence as a question'[134]

The estrangement and ambivalence of the exceptional painter must be understood beyond the position of disagreement with convention, or any form of romantic disavowal. Rebellion does not wholly contain the revelation formed in ambivalence. Furthermore, this process of questioning goes beyond the introduction of a new variation into tradition; it requires a rupture from the norms of the tradition that produced it. In Berger's eyes the paradox of the exceptional painter is that 'he' is both the master and the stranger to tradition and, as Lyotard said of all the work that is modern throughout history, 'it tests hitherto untouched limits of sensibility'.[135] And in my eyes, Berger's criticism serves as a bridge between the common touchstones and the untouched dynamics of language and experience. His writing achieves this enabling function not only by addressing the visible advances within an object, but by relating an artist's method to the ongoing process of giving 'voice' to those impressions which seem both crucial and fragile, those newfound 'feelings' which appear faint, for they have not yet been firmly inscribed in public discourse, but are unmistakably poignant because they lie at the upper edge of everyday experience.

Notes

1   This series was originally broadcast on BBC2 in January 1972; it was subsequently published in *The Listener* and republished as a book. See J. Berger, *Ways of Seeing*, British Broadcasting Corporation and Penguin Books, London 1972.

2   P. Fuller, *Seeing Through Berger*, London, The Claridge Press, 1988.

3   See for instance the critical response to Berger's first novel, *A Painter of Our Time*, which questions the relationship between art and politics. First published in 1958 by Secker and Warburg, it was reissued by Penguin (1965) and by Writers and Readers (1977). Reviewing the book (in *Art Monthly*, no. 4, February 1977). Peter Fuller outlined some of the conspiratorial and incendiary motivations of the critics who attacked the book. It would not be an exaggeration to say that some of this hostility (see review by S. Spender, *The Observer*, 9 November 1958), and the surreptitious withdrawing of the book from the stores by its first publishers, reflected the excesses of the Cold War paranoia.

Paul Ignotus's review (*Encounter*, vol. 65, February 1959) was probably the most contradictory. At first Ignotus argued that the fictional devices were not convincingly executed and then criticised the portrayal of the hero with such a vehemence that his critique could only confirm the plausibility of the convictions in the novel that he so intensely disavowed.

It is interesting to note that while all the sympathetic reviewers claim that Berger's characteisation of the hero is strong and undisturbed by the intensity of his politics, and that Berger succeeds in demystifying reality (*Times Literary Supplement*, no. 28, 1958; Arnold Kettle, *Labour Monthly*, March 1959; E. W. Foell, *Christian Science Monitor*, 18 June 1959; G. R. Clay, *New York Times Book Review*, 8 March 1959), his antipathetic reviewers claim the exact opposite; his characterisation of the hero is false as it buckles under the weight of dogma, and his attempt to fictionalise his prejudices, not only obscures the reality but trivialises the importance of an argument worth pursuing (R. Wollheim, *Spectator*, 14 November 1958; A. Duchene, *Manchester Guardian*, 21 November 1958; R. Guthrie, *Nation*, 18 April 1959). Is it enough just to dismiss this conflict with the shrugging of our subjectivist shoulders and exclaim that one person's decadence is, for some others, an idyll of liberation? A metaphor breaks at least in two ways, as Stephen Spender realised when on another occasion he accused Berger of being a 'foghorn': the following week Berger replied, thanking him for the praise – what could be more useful in the English climate? (*New Statesman*, 11 September 1954).

4   I place 'his' in quotation marks for two reasons: firstly, to draw attention to the fact that the discourse on the romantic artist is predominantly masculinist which no cosmetic alteration of pronouns will significantly affect, and, secondly, to note that this opposition between Marxism and romanticism also relies on a gendered distinction between active and passive. The questioning of these privileges and oppositions will be explored in greater depth in chapter 4.

5   A. MacIntyre, 'The Barricades of Art', *New Statesman*, 29 October 1960.

6   This also applies to the visual arts. As one critic observed, Berger also had a formative influence, as the necessary counterpoint for orientation, on painters who didn't even share a single article of faith with him. See the review of *Permanent Red* by Andrew Forge, 'In Times of Sickness', *Spectator*, 28 October 1960.

Texts invariably relate and draw from other texts, and the critic's task is, in part, to examine these conjunctions and disjunctions. However, the critical appraisal of Berger's texts has not been directed towards their relationship *with* other texts but rather concerned with fixing them *into* a particular position. It is as if critical appraisal is incomplete unless a very specific category can be identified. This is a process of re-housing the text either within a recognisable line of descent or as confirmation of a prescribed social duty. For instance, R. Craig argues that Berger follows Sartre's interpretation of Marx's method: that is, in his fiction Berger defines people not just by their needs and material conditions but also by their struggle against these things (R. Craig, 'Fiction and Freedom: the novels of John Berger', *Dalhousie Review*, vol. 63, 1983 p. 666).

David Caute argued that Berger's irrepressible attraction towards the displaced, disinherited and exiled, and his desire for social change, was part of a Marxist's 'duty' to overcome alienation: 'the nature of all art is an attempt to define and render unnatural the distinction between the actual and the possible, to express the inadequacy of the given state of things, sometimes with horror, sometimes by presenting the desirable ideal' (D. Caute, *Collisions*, London, Quartet Books, 1974, p. 26).

7   In a very sympathetic critique G. Szanto characterises Berger's function as a witness to both the complexity in the world and the failure of a culture to give voice to this diversity. He concludes that Berger's writing exemplifies the redemptive process of naming those experiences that the cultures 'choose' to repress, disavow or forget G. Szanto, 'Oppositional Way Signs: Some Passages with John Berger's History Making, History Unravelling Experiment', *College English*, vol. 40, no. 4, December 1978).

R. A. Mazurek's attraction to Berger's work is also generated by Berger's representation of the 'other' side (R. A. Mazurek, 'Totalization and Contemporary Realism: John Berger's Recent Fiction', *Critique*, spring 1984, p. 134). Both Szanto's and Mazurek's appreciations of Berger's use of the oppositional mode and his representation of the alterior spaces in culture and consciousness can be read as attempts to find in Berger's text a method with which to relocate and resolve the contradictions of the 'self' and the 'real'. In their schemes there is the claim that behind obfuscation there is truth, beyond distortion there is transparency, and that reality begins where ideology ends. Meaning in Berger's texts, like political struggle, is caught between the condition that exists and the truth that can be gained through resistance, but that truth cannot be apprehended merely through the rhetoric of hope.

For an interesting reading which situates Berger's work between a number of other writers who have also questioned the conjunctions and disjunctions between Marxism and humanism, and which reads his work against the 'strains, compromises and incoherences', as well as the 'latent powers and directions' of these debates, see Bruce Robbins, 'Feeling Global: John Berger and Experience', in *Postmoden Politics*, ed. by Jonathon Arac, Manchester, Manchester University Press, 1986. While Robbins's argument highlights the ongoing and unresolved problems of representation in literature, his conclusion repeats the usual declaration that Berger's work can serve as both talisman and guide to radical commitment. Robbins reads Berger's texts as 'a series of preparatory inroads into the obscure, uniquely modern no-man's-land of global experience – not as a reduction but as an expansion of experience, in which sections of the impalpable but determining realm of the international begin to solidify and become sensuously present. Reading Berger, we can recognise that we have not yet learned how to "feel global" ' (p. 151).

It seems that a critical awareness of the problematic of representing experience in 'postmodernity' has not dislodged the author from the romantic position of both witness and herald to modernity. There is also a tendency to conflate the paradigm of the critical subject with the characteristic of hero as rebel. For in each instance the sympathetic critic tends to validate Berger's representation of the other not only by establishing a correspondence between his literary strategies and the philosophical principles of either Marxism or romanticism, but also through the projection of Berger as the *embodiment* of these abstractions.

8   R. Bathes, *The Pleasure of the Text*, New York, Hill and Wang, 1975, p. 28.

9   R. Bathes, *New Critical Essays*, New York, Hill and Wang, 1980, pp. 79, 89.

10   Liminality – that state of 'in-betweenness' where the subject constantly shuttles between one pole and another – has served as the paradigm 'position(s)' for both alterity and objectivity in modernity. The sense of liminality that I am suggesting, which involves a constant process of shuttling between different points, must be differentiated from the anthropological sense of liminality, as a phase of transition that involves the inversion of two more stable but very different points. In A. Van Gennep, *The Rites of Passage*, translated by M. B. Vizeden and G. L. Caffee, London, Routledge and Kegan Paul, 1960, and V. Turner, *The Ritual Process: Structure and Anti-Structure*, Harmondsworth, Pelican, 1974, the liminal zone is the place where the anthropologist or the writer is situated, but this is a privilege of the technology of representation not necessarily equatable with the liminal *rite de passage*, initiation or migration which is an irreversible process. I am in debt to John Hutnyk for this distinction.

11   Even the leading thinkers who have attempted to integrate

aesthetics and politics remain divided over the question of form in art and its implications for understanding the transformations of the modern world. For instance, there remains within the critical discourse on modernity a recurring antagonism between the 'Lukácsian' method for representing reality through a model which links the part to the whole, and an 'Adornian' method which admits that each representation of reality must also confront the irreconcilable gap between the part and the whole.

Jameson confronts the problematical use of opposition by the modernists by asking to what extent they repudiate or reconfirm the very reifications and fetishes that they seek to expose and undermine. For while juxtapositions highlight differences and sharpen the appreciation of existing antagonisms, what is to prevent this method of oppositional thinking from re-entering the system as another means of crisis-management? Has the modernist gone no further than being a producer rather than a critic of the transformations spawned by modernity? See F. Jameson, 'Modernism and its Repressed; or Robbe-Grillet as Anti-Colonialist', in *The Ideologies of Theory*, London, Routledge, 1988, pp. 177–9.

12   The expression of the ambivalence in modernism surfaces through the problematic relationship between the modernist and the other. Stephen Tyler ('On Being Out of Words', *Cultural Anthropology*, vol. 1, no. 2, May 1986) argues that integral with the pride in 'progress' is a lament for what is 'left behind'. This dilemma, once fused with the perception that material achievement can only be gained at the expense of moral decay, inspired a paradoxical celebration of the other as the source of hope and authenticity. 'It is the modernist fable of technology triumphant, of the creativity-in-destruction of the technology of the alphabet, of the rise of the civilization from savagery, and the surpassing of the life-world of commonsense and oral mnemonics by science and technology. [This story of the glory of the eye is also the elegy that tells of loss and alienation, for the price of civilization is the fragmentation of the wholeness of a form of life, and liberation from nature is paid for by alienation in nature]. The kingdom of the liberated, autonomous cognito is a lonely place where others are only ghosts out of a romanticized past, summoned like natives from far off places to justify and legitimize alienation by their outlandish otherness. The difference that is the past is overcome in a utopian future still to come, but surely around the corner' (Tyler, p. 131).

The paradox of modernism was in its sustained belief that it could almost 'have it' both ways. By confining the crisis of rationality in modernity to the textual level, there was the expectation that the incorporation of alternative conditions could compensate for the loss of faith in the hegemonic institution. While salvaging the savage, it was hoped that the modernist would also find salvation.

When facing the immense social changes of their age the modernists did not turn away with incomprehension. They proceeded to contest and distance themselves from the cataclysmic repercussions through a critique of the conventions of language. By disidentifying with the perceived lacunae within 'realism', they hoped to open the space for a redemption which actively incorporated the memories and expectations formed in 'other' languages.

Estrangement propelled them not towards silence but towards a search for counter-representations, the injections of innovations, the grafting of insight from other cultures, the unorthodox mixture of genres within the dominant language; this integration ultimately vitalised an otherwise threatened rationality.

13 Their debate over the political engagement of the avant-garde revolved around the Hegelian opposition of organic and non organic work. Adorno embraced the avant-garde's rejection of the principles of coherence in organic realist work as a necessary expression of the more radical protest against all false reconciliations with what exists, whereas for Lukács, this rejection is both a euphemism for failure and an apologia for a pathological subjectivism which can never surmount its own submission to alienation in modernity.

Brecht and Benjamin however, were far from satisfied with the achievements and the paradigm of realism that Lukács championed. They were generally uncomfortable with his extrapolation of traditional ideology analysis and in particular with the crude application of false consciousness to the realm of aesthetics. They foresaw the radical potential of the method of montage and the utilisation of the new communications technology as a way to redefine the means of representations and the possibilities for addressing the public.

14　J.-F. Lyotard, *The Postmodern Condition*, p. 77.
15　*Ibid*, p. 81.
16　J.-F. Lyotard, *Just Gaming*, p. 10.
17　P. Burger, *Theory of the Avant-Garde*, translated by M. Shaw, Manchester, Manchester University Press, 1984, pp. 155–66.
18　P. Burger, *op. cit.*, pp. 47–54.
19　*Ibid.*, p. 89.
20　*Ibid.*, p. 91.
21　The question of art and ideology has been much debated. Berger's position within these debates is consistent with that of his mentors, Frederick Antal, Ernst Fischer and Max Raphael. While acknowledging the necessity of engagement with the social, Berger always insisted that the aesthetic is never purely a product of the material base. In this respect Berger separates himself from both the determinist claims of Hadjnicolaou, and the alibis for escapism and elitism proferred by the abstract expressionists.
22　J. Berger, *Art and Revolution*, London, Weidenfeld & Nicolson, 1969, p. 37.
23　See also 'Russian Art at the Academy', *New Statesman*, 3 January 1959.
24　See the articles on surrealism in the *New Statesman*, 2 August 1952 and 8 March 1958; also of note is a comparison between Picasso and Cézanne, 3 July 1954.
25　W. Benjamin, *Illuminations*, translated by H. Zohn, London, Fontana/Collins, 1982, p. 264.
26　W. Benjamin, *One Way Street*, translated by E. Jephcott and K. Shorter, London, Verso, 1979, p. 360.
27　See Thesis XVII, p. 264, in *Illuminations*, and essay on E. Fuchs, in

One Way Street, pp. 350–2.

28   F. Nietzsche, *The Use and Abuse of History*, translated by A. Collins, New York, Bobbs–Merrill, p. 12.

29   W. Benjamin, *One Way Street*, p. 362.

30   On Szondi's account of the difference between Proust's and Benjamin's conception of the past, in *On Textual Understanding and Other Essays*, translated by H. Mendelsohn, Manchester, Manchester University Press, 1986, pp. 149–53.

31   J. Berger, *The Success and Failure of Picasso*, p. 40.

32   *Ibid.*, p. 114.

33   On the difference between the antagonistic and the agonistic modes, see J.-F. Lyotard, *Just Gaming*, pp. 104–5.

34   J. Fisher claims that this is the dominant mode for the apprehension of the other in the romantic period. (See *The Myth of Primitivism*, ed. S. Hiller, London, Routledge, 1991).

35   J. Berger, *The Success and Failure of Picasso*, p. 216.

36   Keohane extends this argument by applying it not only to Rousseau's literature but also to his political theory. In Rousseau, the cognisance of the individual's right is gained 'in the ability to move directly from that particularity into a participation in the fused self of the 'public person' that the community consists', N. O. Keohane, 'Political Theory and the Uses of the Self', *The Journal of Politics*, vol. 37, no. 4, November 1975, p. 1001.

37   J. Berger, *The Success and Failure of Picasso*, p. 119.

38   *Ibid.*, p. 173.

39   *Ibid.*, p. 15.

40   Note Berger's comparison of Picasso with Aimé Césaire, pp. 172–3. This is only one of many comparisons with others which serve to illustrate the differences between the committed and the detached artist. On p. 82–8, he contrasts Picasso with Gris to highlight two forms of inner exile; a serious solitude which works to solve theoretical problems and a cynical isolation which merely uses distance to note the ironies and frustrations of external happenings. The pocket of exemption that Berger credits with social value is the former. See also a comparison with De Stael in 'The Island of Appearances', *New Society*, 8 October 1981 and with Zadkine, 'Zadkine's Hands', *New Statesman*, 13 January 1961; with Velásquez, 'Only Connect I', *New Statesman*, 20 February 1960; 'Only Connect II', *New Statesman*, 27 February 1960; with Cézanne, 'The Heroism of Cézanne', *New Statesman*, 3 July 1954. 'Why Picasso?', *New Statesman*, 15 May 1954; 'The Example of Mireille', *New Statesman*, 10 August 1957; 'Rebeyrolle and Picasso', *New Statesman*, 30 June 1956; 'Masters and Decadents', *New Statesman*, 26 July 1952.

41   Berger represents Picasso's relationship between his past (Spain) and his present (France) also within a series of binary oppositions: Spain is the past provincial peripheral, traditional, primitive, static, feudal – the hopeful container of the pre-modern, hence authentic, self; whereas France is the present, metropolitan, central, modern, civilised, changing, capitalist – the despairing stage for the inauthentic other.

42   J. Berger, *The Success and Failure of Picasso*, p. 40.
43   Jameson has also argued that modernism bears structural similarities with, rather than being a symptom of, imperialism. Both entail forms of selective truncation, a system that displaces the dynamic segments into an alien space, creating a dissipation of the indigenous mechanisms for generating meaning. Whether he is describing the process of collage or the economic 'development of under-development', Jameson argues that the juxtapositions and transformations are inevitably aggressive and exploitative, and ultimately, the result of a strategy of negative appropriation (F. Jameson, 'Modernism and Imperialism', p. 11).
44   J. Berger, *The Success and Failure of Picasso*, p. 22.
45   *Ibid.*, p. 30.
46   *Ibid.*, p. 6.
47   Interview between Janine Burke and John Berger, *Art Monthly*, March 1989, no. 124, p. 8.
48   J. Berger, *The Success and Failure of Picasso*, p. 38.
49   *Ibid.*, p. 39.
50   Berger argues that Niezvestny's almost fatal injury was fundamental to both the assurance and conviction of his art and politics. 'Death for him is a starting point rather than an end. It is from death that he measures, instead of toward it' (*Art and Revolution*, p. 98). This, he claims, also explains his fearless confrontation with Khrushchev over the status and meaning of his art ('A Soviet Sculptor', *New Society*, 8 September 1966).
51   J. Berger, *Art and Revolution*, p. 22.
52   *Ibid.*, p. 17.
53   *Ibid.*, p. 70.
54   *Ibid.*, p. 69.
55   J. Berger, 'A Soviet Sculptor II', *New Society*, 15 September 1966.
56   J. Berger, 'A Soviet Sculptor I', *New Society*, 8 September 1966.
57   M. McCarthy, 'Exiles, Expatriates and Internal Emigrés', *The Listener*, 25 November 1971.
58   J. Berger, *Art and Revolution*, p. 113.
59   *Ibid.*
60   Cohen's typology of salvation; with the exception of the necessity of the miracle, accords with Berger's criterion for the emancipatory role of the prophet. See N. Cohen, *The Pursuit of the Millennium*, London, Paladin, 1978, p. 255.
61   J. Berger, *About Looking*, p. 133.
62   J. Berger, *Art and Revolution*, p. 152. In Berger's art criticism all the heroes are men. They are represented as the paradigms of struggle against displacement. 'The function of the hero in art is to inspire the reader or spectator to continue in the same spirit from where he, the hero, leaves off. He must release the spectator's potentiality, for potentiality is the historical force behind nobility. And to do this the hero must be typical of the characters and class who at that time only need to be made aware of their heroic potentiality in order to be able to make their society juster and nobler' (*Permanent Red*, p. 211). And when writing on Affandi, he notes that 'the strength and sensitivity of the good works is not the result of romantic identification but rather of the

endurance of the protagonist' (*New Statesman*, 17 May 1952).

However, it did not appear to have been registered by the collective consciousness of Berger's vision that women were also displaced and that attention to their forms of endurance might also redefine the very fundamentals of heroism. In one instance, Berger identified this issue very succinctly, but instead of turning this into an examination of a wider problematic, he collapsed it into a dismissal: 'The only thing which the paintings of Ethel Walker, Frances Hodgkins and Gwen John, have in common is a quality of quietness; all their works await attention rather than demand it . . . ' (*New Statesman*, 24 May 1952).

Berger's representation of the heroic, rebellious and prophetic artist is caught by the masculinist presuppositions that intertwine the romantic, humanist and Marxist discourse. In my chapter on Berger's novels I will examine in more detail the problematic of the male modernist's representation of women.

63   A. Camus, *The Rebel*, Harmondsworth, Penguin, 1982, p. 219.

64   M. Foucault, *Language, Counter-Memory, Practice*, translated by D. F. Bouchard and S. Simon, Ithaca, Cornell University Press, 1977, p. 34.

65   J. Berger, *The White Bird*, London, Chatto and Windus, 1985, p. 187.

66   J. Berger, *The Success and Failure of Picasso*, p. 202.

67   Quoted in 'Ideal State of Art', *New Statesman*, 8 October 1955.

68   T. W. Adorno, *Minima Moralia*, translated by E. F. N. Jephcott, London, Verso, 1978, p. 222.

69   Berger was the weekly art critic for the *New Statesman* between 1951 and 1959. A selection of these essays was subsequently published under the title *Permanent Red*.

70   J. Berger, *Permanent Red*, London, Methuen, 1960, p. 176.

71   'Style and the Man', *New Statesman*, 31 December 1955.

72   'The Ideal State of Art', *New Statesman*, 8 October 1955.

73   Quoted in J. Berger, *The Success and Failure of Picasso*, p. 73.

74   J. Berger, 'Gods and Critics', *New Statesman*, 6 June 1959.

75   J. Berger, 'This Century', *New Statesman*, 20 June 1959.

76   J. Berger, 'Exit and Credo', *New Statesman*, 29 September 1956.

77   M. Blanchot, *The Space of Literature*, translated by Ann Smock, Lincoln, University of Nebraska Press, 1982, p. 234.

78   J. Berger, *Art and Revolution*, p. 126.

79   J. Berger, 'People in a Fruit Tree', *New Statesman*, 21 November 1959.

80   Three *New Statesman* essays on Soviet art draw out the exceptional case of the role of tradition in Russian society where it serves as an inspiration to life, rather than as a consolation for the lack of life. 'Profile of Moscow', 12 December 1953; 'Soviet Values', 26 December 1953; 'Soviet Aesthetics', 6 February 1954.

81   For Berger's criticism of Bacon, see *New Statesman*, 5 January 1952; and of Moore, see *New Statesman*, 5 November 1955. For an indication of the controversy over the social responsibility of the artist and the integration of the arts in social programmes, see the correspondence section of the *New Statesman*, March–April 1953; March–September 1954; January 1955;

December–January 1956–7.
82   J. Berger, *Permanent Red*, p. 9.
83   'Looking back ... I realise how perverse many of my opinions and evaluations have been. By perverse, however, I only mean unfashionable. I find myself opposed to the general taste of most official bodies ...', *New Statesman*, 10 January 1953.
84   Apart from writing the weekly art criticism for *The New Statesman*, Berger also wrote for *The Evening Standard* and *The Burlington Magazine*.
85   J. Berger, *New Statesman*, 12 December 1953. See also the article on Meninsky and Adler, in *New Statesman*, 15 December 1951.
86   John Berger, interview with Geoff Dyer, 'Ways of Witnessing', *Marxism Today*, December 1984, p. 37.
87   John Berger, interview with Janine Burke, 'Raising Hell and Telling Stories', *Art Monthly*, March 1989, no. 124, p. 4.
In other interviews Berger also discusses the process of projective identification in criticism. He emphasises that the creative function was achieved through 'projecting his imagination' into both the works of other people and also into the way 'their works insert themselves into the moment of history in which they were created or in which the spectator is looking at them' (*The Guardian*, 5 October 1971).
Berger's representation of the storyteller as a witness, which bypasses the conventional distinctions between narrator, narratee and narrative, as it forges a heteronomous relationship with the past is, as Lyotard also observed, a form for transmitting knowledge which the West has repressed: 'even when I was writing on art, it was really a way of story-telling – storytellers lose their identity and are open to the lives of other people. Maybe when you look at their entire output you can see something that really belongs to that one person. But at any one moment it is difficult to see what the job of your life is because you are so aware of what you are lending yourself to. This is perhaps why I use the term "being a witness". One is a witness of others but not of oneself'. 'Ways of Witnessing', *Marxism Today*, December 1984.
88   J. Berger, *Permanent Red*, p. 23.
89   J. Berger, 'Peter Peri', *The Look of Things*, New York, Viking Press, 1971, pp. 61–5. See also *New Statesman*, 3 January 1953.
90   J. Berger, *New Statesman*, 8 August 1953.
91   J. Berger, *New Statesman*, 'Art in Ceylon', 23 January 1954. See also *New Statesman*, 'An Indian Painter', 26 February 1955 and 'For Whom is the East East?', 9 May 1959.
92   J. Berger, *New Statesman*, 'Affandi and other Indonesian Painters', 17 May 1952: 'The Unrecognized', January 1956.
93   J. Berger, *New Statesman*, 'The London Group', 17 February 1951; 'British Painters 1925–1950', 5 May 1951; 'Two British Painters', 16 June 1951; 'Present Painting', 17 November 1951; 'The Limits of Dumbness', 16 July 1955; 'Imaginary Illness', 13 December 1958; 'Tooths and Bones', 22 September 1956.
94   J. Berger, *New Statesman*, 11 August 1951.
95   J. Berger, *New Statesman*, 'Not so modest', 3 May 1958.

96   J. Berger, *Permanent Red*, p. 78; see also 'Round the Market', *New Statesman*, 14 March 1959.
97   J. Berger, *New Statesman*, 15 January 1955.
98   J. Berger, 'Success and Value', *New Statesman*, 5 April 1958.
99   J. Berger, *New Statesman*, 25 October 1958.
100 Berger admitted that much of his analysis was flawed by an underestimation of ideology; see 'Staying Socialist', *New Statesman*, 31 October 1959.
101 J. Berger, *A Painter of Our Time*, p. 109.
102 J. Berger, *New Statesman*, 22 September 1956.
103 J. Berger, 'A Belief in Uniforms', *New Statesman*, 17 January 1959.
104 J. Berger, 'Who Are You?', *New Statesman*, 11 April 1959.
105 After the enunciation of crisis over the utility of criticism, Berger wrote three articles which reconfirmed the epistemological position by which he defined the role of the critic. These articles were republished as the introduction and conclusion to *Permanent Red*.
106 Interview between John Berger and Theo Richmond, 'The Great Escape', *Guardian*, 5 October 1971.
107 Interview between John Berger and Geoff Dyer, 'Ways of Witnessing', *Marxism Today*, December 1984.
108 R. Williams, *The Politics of Modernism*, p. 45.
109 *Ibid.*, p. 34.
110 T. Eagleton, *Exiles and Emigres*, London, Chatto and Windus, 1970, p. 215.
111 *Ibid.*
112 *Ibid.*, p. 18.
113 McCarthy, *op. cit.*, p. 708.
114 A. Gurr, *Writers in Exile: The Identity of Home in Modern Literature*, Brighton, Harvester Press, 1981, p. 139.
115 *Ibid.*, p. 146.
116 Gayatri C. Spivak, 'Reading *The Satanic Verses*', *Third Text*, vol. 11, summer 1990, p. 48.
117 Frederic Jameson, 'Third World Literature in the Era of Multinational Capitalism', *Social Text*, vol. 15, 1986. Aijaz Ahmad replied by arguing that Jameson's attempt to encompass the fecundity and diversity of Third World Literature is empirically and theoretically untenable because it presumes 'that there is a unitary determination which can be identified in its splendid isolation, as the source of all narrativity: the proposition that the 'third world' *is* a singular formation, possessing its own unique, unitary form of determination in the sphere of ideology (nationalism) and cultural production (the national allegory)', (Aijaz Ahmad, 'Jameson's Rhetoric of Otherness and the "National Allegory"', *Social Text*, vol. 17, fall 1987, p. 22). Ahmad's valuable claim, that Jameson's conception of unity and totality is dependent on a prior movement which simultaneously displaces heterogeneity from the margin as it represses difference, is however also presupposing a form of philosophical idealism, and this is most apparent in his moralising over the difference of cultural difference.
118 F. Jameson, *op. cit.*, p. 69.

119 *Ibid.*
120 Spivak, *op. cit.*, p. 48.
121 *Ibid.*
122 *Ibid.*, p. 49.
123 M. de Certeau, *Heterologies*, translated by B. Massumi, Manchester, Manchester University Press, 1986, p. 201.
124 *Ibid.*, p. 203.
125 J. Berger, And Our Faces ..., p. 67.
126 J. Berger, *New Statesman*, 31 May 1952.
127 J. Berger, *Ways of Seeing*, p. 18.
128 J. Berger, *New Statesman*, 23 June 1951.
129 J. Berger, *New Statesman*, 8 December 1951.
130 J. Berger, *New Statesman*, 29 December 1951.
131 See 'Poussin's Order', in *Permanent Red* and the references to Poussin as an artist's role model, pp. 12, 54, 119, 124, 129, 171, in *A Painter of Our Time*.
132 J. Berger, *Ways of Seeing*, p. 110.
133 *Ibid.*
134 *Ibid.*, p. 112.
135 J.-F. Lyotard and J.-L. Thebaud, *Just Gaming*, p. 14.

3

Death of a stranger

> As for exiles
> I think they had
> never found you,
> Peace, more difficult
> to endure!
>
> Sappho

> You won't find a new country, won't find another shore.
> This city will always pursue you.
> You'll walk the same streets, grow old
> in the same neighbourhoods, turn grey in the same houses.
> You'll always end in this city. Don't hope for things elsewhere:
> there's no ship for you, there's no road.
> Now that you've wasted your life here, in this small corner,
> you've destroyed it everywhere in the world.
>
> Cavafy

The pulse of belonging

The logic of the stranger is the story of oscillation. The logic of oscillation is the story of dialectical tension, both creative and destructive. Brecht said that the exile was the best dialectician. Or as Benjamin said of Brecht, 'He is an expert in fresh starts.'[1] This chapter explores the thematic of exile and estrangement in modernity by juxtaposing the representations of the stranger in social theory with Berger's and Mohr's photo-sociological books *A Fortunate Man* and *A Seventh Man*.

Berger's documentary essay *A Fortunate Man* portrays a hero called Sassal whose life was dedicated to affirming the possibilities of living. Sassal's first response to the perception of constraint was to leave. Travelling and working in foreign places taught him that despite the intensity of his service his integration into another culture would always be limited by the fact that he was a stranger. However, he found that this partial form of integration sharpened the quality of his insight into the fundamental questions of social belonging. With this realisation the prospects of return seemed enhanced. The time away had offered him the opportunity to reflect on the ways of working at home. It also enabled him to see himself as a sort of intimate stranger. As a stranger he could touch the real and also reach out towards a possibility that for others was barely imaginable. After Berger had written this story and Mohr had photographed it, this hero committed suicide. His final statement to the living had all the perplexity of a myth. His suicide baffled every word, and confounded every image that had been constructed from 'him' – neither the writer anticipated nor the photographer predicted this conclusion.² After Benjamin's suicide Brecht was to write about his friend's death:

> In the end driven to an impassable frontier
> You, we hear, passed over a passable one.³

Sassal's suicide was not brought on by being forced up against a wall, a border that marked the limits of endurance and exhaustion. His final act was not in response to being blocked between the crashing pressure of inner convictions and outer persecution. On the two sides against which death stood as the only exit was not the ideal and the anti-ideal of politics. For Sassal the twin forces that led to suicide were not between struggle and denial but between desire and promise.

Sassal committed suicide on the threshold of a second marriage. It was a marriage that promised to release him from the perpetual oscillation between restraint and commitment. He was in love, probably for the first time, and there was no room for estrangement. It was a passion without obligation and maybe this is what was utterly unfaceable about it – the very possibility that he was about to be engulfed in a zone that was so close to him. Somehow the markers that could separate him from the other, his beloved, had dissolved. Attraction had burnt distance. Suddenly his entire way of approaching, understanding and naming the other was fading. It was as if this love 'threatened' to extinguish language. And he could not face the intensity, the brilliance, the light of this bliss. Here there was no outside. What irony to be called A Fortunate Man.

Sassal's suicide was as much an expression of the inability to accept what was to come as it was a comment against the sensibility that had directed his previous life. Such a suicide makes us think again about the virtues and cost of being a stranger. The shadow of suicide does not only fall back over the life of Sassal but also leans into a zone of interpretation. It makes us reconsider the stranger's ambivalence.

With Berger's two photo-sociological books at hand - the case study of Sassal in *A Fortunate Man*, and the representation of the migrant in *A Seventh Man* – I will trace Berger's representation of estrangement against the shifting conceptions of the stranger in social and cultural theory. The paradigmatic reference point for such a comparative exercise is Simmel's essay 'The Stranger'. With stunning suggestiveness and precision but also with serious limitations Simmel not only sets out the problematic of the perspective of a stranger but also characterises a form of social relationship that plays a dominant role in modernity. While many subsequent critics have followed Simmel's lead, few have questioned his assumptions let alone attempted to extend his 'brief'.

As a consequence of decolonisation and the pooling of 'cheap labour' to turn the industrial wheels of the West, the contact between natives and strangers has intensified to a degree that was beyond Simmel's imagination. Thus to understand the contemporary context of the stranger we need to go beyond the parameters that were set out by key figures in the sociological tradition. It is no coincidence that the advances that have been proposed in this discourse are also by people, who themselves have also experienced the radical edge of displacement and witnessed the traumas of migration. It is to cultural critics like Edward Said, Wole Soyinka, Gayatri Chakravorty Spivak and Homi Bhabha that I turn not only to add new dimensions to the representation of estrangement but also to rethink the link between the figure of the stranger and the figuration of objectivity. To commence this investigation let me ask the questions of origin and location.

To be a stranger where must one be? In a place that is neither 'here' nor 'there'? But where did the identity of the stranger come from? *From* the departure from the home? *At* the point of arrival in a foreign place? In the journey *between* the here and the there? If the stranger is someone who travels between fixed places, and if there is a defined sense of origin and destiny, and pre-determined certitudes mark the passages of entry and exit, then how do we define this transitional period? Perhaps the identity of the stranger is not coterminous with the person's spatial positioning, but emerges from an unspecifiable temporal instance in which his or her sense of belonging is detached from both the 'here' and the 'there'. Such a recognition may occur before a journey across space. This perception does not presuppose that the stranger is outside society, on the way to another, but rather perceives estrangement within the social. It defines estrangement as an internal condition rather than as a purely external phenomena.

Traditionally exile, alienation, estrangement have been defined against the fixity of home. Home was the metaphor for the centre, in terms of both origin and destiny – the place/time – where meanings and actions folded together, found resolution. But if modernity can be characterised as that phenomenon which has usurped the basis of tradition, and the condition that demands the continuous reinvention of social meaning, then how can we legitimately speak of strangers and natives?

The ambiguity of the stranger's social position needs further scrutiny. Torrance, for instance, argues against the premise of Judaic–Christian myths of origin which suggest that identity is rooted in primal exile. He proposes a counter-story, which implicitly acknowledges that even the myths of origin, which claim to precede the time and space of society, must be embedded and articulated within the social. Estrangement is thus a social rather than pre-social process. Taking the example of Rousseau as rebel or nonconformist intellectual. Torrance suggests that such an oppositional stance against society is still a position that lies within the social. In order to form a ground from which to critique society, the intellectual cannot assume the non-existent position of 'individualistic self-sufficiency'.[4]

Simmel argues that all social relations rebound between the organisational principles of nearness and remoteness. For Simmel, the stranger and the concept of objectivity, which are both conventionally perceived as standing outside or above the social, are not only defined by this principle but are exemplars of it. The voice of objectivity can be expressed only through the stranger because of 'his'[5] ambivalent social position. Simmel begins his famous essay on the stranger with this proposition: 'If wandering is the liberation from every given point in space, and thus the conceptional opposite to fixation at such a point, the sociological form of the 'stranger' presents the unity, as it were, of these two characteristics.'[6] The stranger is not an individual who has been totally divested of any sense of belonging. For Simmel, the stranger is someone who has the *potential* for both wandering and fixation. Located somewhere between the rootless nomad and the rooted member of a group, the stranger is defined as 'the person who comes today and stays tomorrow'.[7]

Since 1908, when Georg Simmel proffered the role of the stranger as the critical position in modernity, in various guises and with selective truncations, this figure has been incorporated as the subject and object of investigation in the sociological tradition. The contemporary sociologist Zygmunt Bauman presents his critique of modernity by emphasising the critical force of the 'stranger'. Combining the Simmelian stranger, with traits drawn from Derridean terms for 'undecidability', he argues that the stranger's ambivalent matrix of socialisation can insert difference precisely at the point when modernity is tethering culture to similitude.[8]

The stranger's social position is neither outside nor 'beyond far and near',[9] but, rather, spatially defined within society. Having come from elsewhere the stranger will always have a foreign past. His sense of belonging cannot be singular and complete in relation to the place in which he stays. He may even 'import' qualities which the group does not possess. But the stranger is not a man without any attachment or involvement with the place in which he is situated. The stranger may not have been part of the group from the beginning, but he is constantly facing it. His relationship to it is defined by being both 'outside it and confronting it'.[10] Appended to the group 'inorganically', the stranger can maintain the synthesis of nearness and remoteness which also secures his position as an organic member.[11]

This perpetual oscillation between inside and outside is what defines the stranger as a member with a difference. However, difference is registered only in terms of a generalised type rather than being distinguished by its own specificity. The pre-existence of this type as an anonymous or multi-purpose category may account for why the stranger is often perceived as lacking identity, but the inadequacy of this category also explains why the stranger's social position is fraught with ambivalence.

The bond between the stranger and the group is at best abstract and contingent. The commonality between the stranger and the member is restricted by the incommensurability between their respective histories. The absence of shared past may even be supplemented by the revelation of common features, but this in turn is a reminder that their experience of a particular event is different. Thus the relationship that is forged between the stranger and the member of the group is so general that it too could in turn be extended beyond the stranger to connect almost anyone. The link that draws the stranger closer to the group also serves to push the stranger outwards. Difference is always the resultant of any found commonality because of

> the extent to which common features are general, they add, to the warmth of the relation founded on them, an element of coolness, a feeling of the contingency of precisely this relation – the connecting forces have lost their specific and centripetal character.[12]

Devoid of political sovereignty, having no irrevocable union with the local traditions, being beyond the protection of the sacred, the destiny of the stranger's social position always remains negotiable. 'The stranger is everywhere a trader.'[13] While Simmel's stranger has come from outside society, he is not regarded as a barbarian, for whom the only relationship would be one of a non-relation. Such an identity would *a priori* exclude him from entry into society, because this identity is precluded from the social. *A* stranger can only form a relationship with society when an internal (social) space exists for *the* stranger.

Either as the emissary of good tidings or as the harbinger of damnation, the stranger's critical force is always related back to his anomalous social position. In Bauman's translation of Simmel's schema, the non-originary inclusion of the stranger seems to open up the underlying presuppositions that construct the social fabric in three ways. Firstly, the stranger's not belonging to society from the beginning not only casts doubt over the depth of his attachment, but also the memory of his arrival makes his presence a negotiable event in history, rather than an inexorable fact of nature. His passage could thus heighten the awareness that all 'natural' rights are not ontological givens but consequences of history. Secondly, the spatial ordering of the world for the construction of moral co-ordinates is also jeopardised by the stranger. The stranger has somehow positioned himself between the position of friend and enemy: 'the stranger disturbs the resonance between physical and psychical distance – he is physically near while remaining spiritually remote.'[14] And finally, the stranger's oscillation between distance and proximity casts a different perspective on social relationships; he can 'view local conditions with an equanimity the native residents can hardly afford'.[15] For the stranger commitment is always bracketed within this peculiar synthesis of involvement and detachment.

The stranger, because he has experienced a displacement of certitude within his own biography, finds himself in the invidious position of unpicking the certitudes of others. The transitions in his biography become a metaphor for the transience in modernity. Where others see transparency, the stranger perceives opaqueness; where others write words assured of their correspondence with things, the stranger reads both in inverted commas. The stranger's stance is not oppositional, as is the rebel who exposes the apparent perversity of society by pointing to its derailment from the social ideals. Reality is not played off against an ideal, for there is no ultimate truth which can either indict the untruths, or redeem them from error. The stranger's perversity has no resting place, no originary point to which he can return.

After placing all the weight of difference on the back of the stranger, Bauman fails to declare who these agents of change may be. Who can qualify as a stranger? Is it the cosmopolitan intellectual, a free-floating trader, the peasant who migrates from Third World village to First World metropolis, or an avant-garde artist? Can all these 'figures' share the name stranger?

This chapter is concerned with the inner and outer dynamics of migration. The process of transgression and renewal is examined through both the imaginary tension between absence and presence and the experiential contradiction between the dream of arrival and the ceaseless journey of exile.

Strangers and others

To evaluate the 'potential' space that is claimed when the figure of the stranger is represented as harbinger, one must also articulate the position of ambivalence within society. It calls for a questioning of the polarities that define inside and outside, and the moral presuppositions of threat and promise implied in every evocation of the beyond.

A commonplace error that occurs when different levels of representation are brought together to address the condition of the periphery and the migrant is the tendency to conflate the positions of stranger, migrant, subaltern, diasporic or other. Clearly there are important differentiations to be made, the periphery is by definition a zone of unstable heterogeneity and disequilibrium. Consequently, the multiple discourses on the stranger cannot be uncritically transferred to address the silence of the other. The stranger is not the other. The social space and the textual tropes that precede and are available for the stranger to manipulate and transform are dependent on the particular cultural structures and psychological predispositions that are at play at any given time and space. Thus to level out the differences through typifications which assume such homogeneity would blunt our understanding of the complex dynamics that facilitate a degree of flexibility at cultural borders and also regulate the permissibility of particular interventions within the social order. In this section I will attempt to sharpen the conceptual tools for differentiating between the position of stranger as diasporic artist and the social position of the stranger as migrant labourer by tracing the various representations of exile in the debates on cultural production.

Addressing a group of fellow exiles, Joseph Brodsky, a Nobel Prize winner for poetry, decided to examine the condition of exile by connecting it with his conviction that 'literature is the only form of moral insurance a society has'.[16]

In this analysis of exile Brodsky offers seven axioms. Firstly, he assigns the life of an exile to the genre of the tragicomic. Secondly, the gain of exile is physical safety – freedom – but with this is the attending loss of identity, the reduction to social insignificance. Thirdly, exile is the ultimate lesson in humility; displaced from specific arenas of contestation, the exile drifts in the infinite hollow of indifference. Fourthly, exile turns the individual inwardly, away from reality, and further into metaphysical dimensions. Abstractions are necessary for interpretation, yet also deadly, in that they compound isolation within an ossifying self-absorption. Fifthly, exile is the displacement of time. Time becomes a defence mechanism. Exile fuses the future with the past and defers the present. This is perceived as a retreat, because the familiar past is perceived as the only safe 'territory'. Sixthly, exile exaggerates and hardens otherness. In desperation the exile holds on tenaciously to the mental values and resources she or he arrives with, and in turn these seem more vital and resonant than the new stimulants that might have otherwise been influential. Thus, stylistically, the exile remains recalcitrant and conservative. Finally, exile accelerates the flight into total isolation 'into the condition in which all one is left with is oneself and one's own language, with nobody and nothing in between'.[17]

Brodsky analyses the condition of exile till it reaches its limit: silence. Perhaps this is where exile begins. He admits that:

exile is due for a further explication; that, famous for its pain, it should also be known for its pain-dulling infiniteness, for its forgetfulness, detachment, indifference, for its terrifying human and inhuman vistas for which we have no yardstick except ourselves.[18]

Brodsky begins his analysis by noting that most accounts of exile tend to sit all too comfortably on the 'banal side of virtue', yet he ends his own by ingesting the uncanny and nameless parts of exile. The myth of the stranger as the receptacle for affirmative creativity is recurrent throughout the discourse on modernity and in the current debates on the cultural and aesthetic practices of individuals from marginalised or post-colonial cultures; the position of the stranger has been re-introduced through the master/slave dialectic. What these arguments have in common is that they all question the conventional opposition between lack and plenitude. Gayatri Chakravorty Spivak, one of the most rigorous critics in these debates, has repeatedly argued that the positions in the master/slave relationship should not be reversed in order to validate, yet again, the dialectic of affirmation.[19] In Ashis Nandy's terms, we must side with the slave not out of sympathy for the material degradation of the slave, but because the slave can include the master into his/her subjectivity without objectification. To favour the oppressed is thus to challenge the rationality that constructs the master and the slave as co-victims by reducing relationships to things.[20] The lesson from the stranger is always objectivity without objectification.

However, less rigorous critics have taken the ethical and cultural vision of exiles either to valorise the romantic value of detachment or to vindicate the rhetoric of affirmation. Both forms of argument attempt to claim that the asocial voice of an exile can both echo the forgotten conscience and articulate the repressed potential within society. Susan Sontag suggests that for the artist who always holds society in contempt, and who has 'demonstrated that he possessed genius and exercised genius', exile is a kind of success, and that the 'craving for silence is to be, in still a further sense, superior to everyone else'.[21]

The romantics proceed with the politely offensive assumption that insight into the human condition is intensified by withdrawing from intimacy and working with retrospection and distance. Somehow Joyce's strategy for escaping the oppressive features of language, nationality and religion by recourse to silence, exile and cunning has been interpreted a little too literally. Hence the popular belief that the ideal position for the artist is not within society but outside of it, in exile. Harry Levin's essay 'Literature and Exile', which surveys the terrain from Ovid to Pasternak, systematically emphasises such points as an artist ought to be a man without a country' (Flaubert).[22]

In the romantic representation of exile, detachment is transformed through a reconfiguration of loss and gain, whereby distance in space becomes distance from time. This equation can reveal a credit because it presupposes that aesthetic contemplation and moral integrity involve a withdrawal from the 'infantile neuroses' and 'regressive prejudices' of society. Thus, the detachment of romantic exile is far from being a condition of terminal silence and privation but rather the profound guarantor of individualism, a vocation for healing moral wounds, and the necessary recourse for social justice or, in Levin's words, the poet's perpetual ostracism is also the 'final triumph of independence over conformity'.[23]

In similar tones George Steiner defines the writer 'as a guest, as a human being whose job is to stay vulnerable to the manifold strange presences, who must keep the doors of his momentary lodgings open to all winds'.[24] If, as Steiner poetically notes, the writer's subjectivity is like a house with lockless doors, this complements his argument that the horizons of language are renewed precisely as its borders are transgressed, and, if his observation that in this century the best writers are those who have been 'linguistically unhoused' extends his description of their method as 'dialectical hesitance',[25] then his characterisation of modern literature as 'extraterritorial' must surely lead us to its relative rather than universal, to its historical rather than transcendental, value. Nevertheless, Steiner bypasses these problematical paradoxes by drawing hope from the axiom that the intensity of suffering will also fuel the artist's creativity:

> it seems proper that those who create art in a civilization of quasi-barbarism which has made so many homeless, which has torn up languages and peoples by the root, should themselves be poets unhoused and wanderers across language. Eccentric, aloof, nostalgic, deliberately untimely . . .[26]

Simply reversing the roles, whereby the losers rather than the winners are elevated as the 'spokesmen' of modernity, is another way of glossing over the very rationality of rupture which connects them both as co-victims. This rupture is sidestepped by Steiner the moment he looks up towards the celestial zones and away from terrestrial realities. The 'extra' leap is rationalised in the name of the transcendental – the timeless, the placeless – whereby exiled artists transform particular discontinuities back into abstract continuity.

In both the modernist and the postmodernist debates on the role of exile in emergent aesthetic practices there are arguments which assign the experience of exile to the negative position within the dialectics of affirmation. Both arguments claim that the very condition of exile – the departure from the homeland and, on arrival, the contact with the foreign land – heightens the creative processes of transformation. Juxtapositions of the old and the new; comparisons between the past and the present; oppositions with origin and destiny lead the modernist artist to the claim of transcendental unity, whereas for the postmodernist they reveal new hybrid forms of identity. Zuzana M. Pick, for instance, argues that 'the subjectivity of exile is constantly re-inventing itself in a labouring process of decantation' and this alerts her to the 'manner in which exile fosters a multi-layered awareness of the elements that constitute inter-national identities'.[27] For Pick the positivity that emerges from the position of exile proceeds from a series of paradoxes. Loss of the origin leads to the multiple representation of origins. Fragmentation of identity, rather than facilitating the subordination of the exile into the existing structures, strengthens a dialogical integration whereby the exile uses the criss-crossing trajectory of history to affirm and extend the histories of re-location. Detachment from the homeland, and the sense of not fully belonging to the place of arrival, lead the exile to a questioning of the certitudes that define identity. This principle is extended into the continuous process of re-mapping all the formal configurations that define social relationships. Marginality thus serves to challenge the hegemonic structures as the exile attempts to incorporate himself into these structures along with his alien experiences. This process of cross-cultural borrowing vitalises the foundations of both cultures as it admits to a selective permeability at their borders. Finally by displacing the fixity between words and things, exile produces a decentred language, thereby demanding that cultural identities should replay the primal mirror stage of identification which Lacan depicted as the struggle of diversity against containment. With all these 'gains' in mind, Pick concludes that 'the landscape of exile is saturated by a discordant expressiveness ... heralds the poetic re-territorialization of an imaginary that struggles against the perplexities of displacement'.[28] Thus the exiled artist is far from homeless, but housed in the international, cross-cultural zone. Rather than lacking an identity, the exiled artist produces a surplus of identities.

    Here we can see a peculiar parallel between George Steiner's 'modernist' advance of the redemptive role of language and Zuzana M. Pick's unrigorous alignment of the perspectival vision of exile with the 'postmodern' retreat into the plenitude of language. Pick highlights those characteristics which intersect with the axioms of postmodern identity. Such a convergence between the levels of experience in exile and the postmodernist decentring of the self in language needs much more elaboration before it can be proclaimed so confidently. While many postmodern critics are quick to discard the modernist rhetoric of universalism, they nevertheless introduce the exile's perspectivism to perform the same function, that is to *resolve* the aporias of displacement. This paradoxical conjunction between modernism and postmodernism through the rhetoric of affirmation is also evident in Michael Fischer's essay 'Ethnicity and the Post-Modern Art of Memory'.[29]

Fischer argues that attention to the perspective of marginalised and counter-hegemonic cultural groups will simultaneously ascribe positive value to their aesthetic production and reinvigorate the process of cross-cultural exchange. The consequence is both the legitimisation of the historical specificity of particular groups and the enhancing of pluralism within the broader social context. It is another equation which, by transferring the value of displaced ethnicity from a negative, enclosed and static sense of self to a positive, open and multiple sense of self,[30] guarantees that cultural renewal is gained through cultural transgression.

It is the inter-references, the interweaving of cultural threads from different arenas, that give ethnicity its phoenix-like capacities for reinvigoration and reinspiration. To kill this play between cultures, between realities, is to kill a reservoir that sustains and renews humane attitudes.

In the modern, technological, secular world, ethnicity has become a puzzling quest to those afflicted by it. But rather than establishing a sense of exclusivity or separation, resolutions of contemporary ethnicity tend toward a pluralistic universalism, a textured sense of being American ... [31]

There are, however, structural problems within the liberal schematisation of tolerance that not only circumvent such neat conjunctions between ethnic diversity and pluralism but also necessitate an objectification of 'marginal identities' for the benefit of the 'dominant identity'. In regard to such a problematic, Fischer's argument shifts attention away from the structural dynamics which foreclose or selectively appropriate the possibilities for cultural exchange, by highlighting the potency and visionary quality of the 'voices' on the margins, and by assuming that their 'bifocal' perspective will be sufficient to *challenge* the hegemonic orthodoxies. This seems a problematic basis upon which to define the politics of emergence for counter-hegemonic groups, for it fails to explain *how* the artist's work articulates both an affirmative ethnicity and a critique of post-industrial society.[32]

Gayatri Spivak has declared that in the discourse on post-coloniality the precise status of the artist as a representative is dislodged from its metropolitan definitions,[33] and Paul Gilroy has observed that the very tension between representation as depiction and representation as delegation or substitution is constitutive of the dynamic that defines the social position of the diasporic artist who confronts the racial and political disjunctures in the British nation-state.[34] Gilroy proposes the term 'Popular Modernism' in order to embrace the black artist's dual function as 'both "defenders and critics of modernism" but mindful of their historical obligation to interrogate the dubious legacies of occidental modernity premised on the exclusion of blacks'[35] and also to part company with the postmodernist orthodoxy which deals 'with the problem of the subject exclusively in terms of its formation rather than through the fundamental issues of agency, action, reason and rationality inherent in considering the relationship between master and slave'.[36] Gilroy emphasizes that the validation of the critical vision of the diasporic artist is not measured through intuitive prefiguration or an untimely convergence with the philosophical abstractions of western philosophy, but through the entry of 'autonomous and self-validating non-European traditions' into the 'institutionalized Western world of art'.[37]

In a somewhat reductive reply to Paul Gilroy's representation of the relationship between aesthetic creativity, political authority and personal experience, Kobena Mercer claims that Gilroy repeats rather than subverts the binarisms that define the racist and anti-racist rationality. To displace the polarities of essentialist claims, Mercer directs his attention not into 'the anterior depths of the soul' but towards the inscriptions by the subject on the surface of language. His appreciation of the specificity of the diasporic subjectivity is based on Bakhtin's 'dialogic imagination' and asserts that these principles are echoed by the practices of the artists themselves:

> I would suggest that, insofar, as we need a general theoretical framework for black art and cultural criticism, it can be derived from a critical dialogue with the aesthetic principles, such as collage and bricolage, that are already at work in the works themselves. This does not imply an 'alternative' to the conception of a hybridized diaspora culture, but merely the proposal that we should avoid making foundationalist claims for metaphorical vocabularies.[38]

One of the most significant contributors to the debates on the correlation between the experience of displacement and the radicalised attention to the question of language and identity is Homi Bhabha. While focusing on the process of power and identification in colonial discourse Bhabha developed key concepts which he has also brought to bear on an understanding of the construction of national and cultural identities that are coeval with modernity.

Bhabha's elaboration of the four key concepts – fetish, stereotype, mimicry and splitting – is not a validation of the pathos arising from the gap between the acquired and the desired identity, but a demonstration of the crisis of signification within the 'double time' and 'contested space' of modern culture. In his first essay Bhabha proposed that we should consider the construction of colonial discourse as 'a complex articulation of the tropes of fetishism'.[39] This proposal was subsequently elaborated through a closer study of the role of stereotype which he argues is a 'form of knowledge and identification that vacillates between what is already "in place", already known, and something that must be repeated'.[40] Similarly, mimicry is not just an example of imitation but serves as a metaphor for the 'excess' and 'slippage' that 'becomes transformed into an uncertainty which fixes the colonial subject as a "partial presence". By "partial" I mean both "incomplete" and "virtual" '.[41] Consequently it is the elusive and mercurial space between image and identification, between mask and identity, which Bhabha suggests creates a crisis in the schematisation of authority as it displaces the unitarian system of identity, 'where the self apprehends itself: it is always the split screen of the self and its doubling, the hybrid'.[42]

Drawing from Fanon's statement that the 'colonial subject is always overdetermined from without', Bhabha argues that alienation is positioned in all the configurations of identity. Identity is no more but no less than a constant process of negotiation between image and fantasy, in which there is no pre-alienated self which can be redeemed, but rather the 'Otherness of the Self' is what is 'inscribed in the perverse palimpsest of colonial identity'.[43] The condition of the colonial subject explicitly opens up the splitting within the processual forms of imaging an identity, and to extend an understanding of both this condition, and these two part identities which imbricate the self in the other, Bhabha adopts the psychoanalytic concept of identification.

In a later essay he clarifies his position, that is, his intervention into the psychological, anthropological and philosophical discourses which presuppose the stability of the ego:

> The postmodern perspective insists that the question of identity can never be seen 'beyond representation', as a psychological problem of personality or even an ethical problem of personhood. . . . We are no longer confronted with an ontological problem of being but with a discursive strategy of the 'moment' of interrogation; a moment in which the demand for identification becomes, primarily, a response to other questions of signification and desire, culture and politics. . . . it is the priority (and play) of the signifier that reveals the Third Space of absence or lack or doubling (not depth) which is the very principle of discourse.[44]

The non-equivalence between image and identity is also the key theme in his exploration of cultural difference in the discourse of the nation.[45]

When examining the discourse on the creative production of displaced individuals, I have tried to shift attention away from some celebration of their 'privileged' position as spokespersons of the ruptures in modernity, and attempted to direct attention towards the tensions in the very representation of identity in modernity. My aim is to focus not on the *problem* of identity in exile, but on the exilic *problematic* of identity in modernity. Thus in this chapter I contrasted the critics who have confused this problematic, by reducing the function of the dialectic to a rhetoric for affirmation, with the work by post-colonial critics who have heightened our attention to the tensions in identity and representation by questioning the metropolitan definitions for both estrangement and self-determination. To understand the condition of estrangement and alienation requires a deeper interrogation of the borderline between the inside and outside, the indigenous and the foreign. These oppositions need to be questioned both in temporal and in spatial terms. For the oscillation between 'here' and 'there', or the dual trajectory from 'in' to 'out', does not diminish alienation for the benefit of self-awareness but, rather, alienation is, as Gayatri Spivak notes, also a process of separation which is 'irreducible in any act of consciousness'.[46]

In Berger's work the stranger is a recurring figure. The two 'sociological' books in which the stranger is foregrounded are *A Fortunate Man* and *A Seventh Man*. These books address experiences which are worlds apart. In *A Fortunate Man*,[47] the doctor is an intellectual, for whom every experience of displacement heightens the process of inquiry. He not only overcomes but gains from each crisis. In *A Seventh Man*,[48] Berger charts the utter displacement of the peasantry within the global process of modernisation and industrialisation. The migrants knew that the journey from the village to the city was a gamble but none counted on the fact that the dice were already loaded; hence for Berger their story is a tragedy without redemption, because it was a swindle from the outset.

The welcome stranger

A Fortunate Man is a portrait of a doctor called Sassal who worked both critically and compassionately in an English village. Sassal is seen as both English and the stranger who has arrived from elsewhere. He is the stranger who does not subscribe to the prejudices and the local common sense, but who can also understand the culture of the village and respect the foresters as individuals. He acts as if part of his duty as doctor is to scrutinise their social predicament in order to show that the range of possibilities for self-realisation can be expanded by re-thinking the assumptions of everyday life. By taking the position of a stranger the path to altruism and self-sacrifice becomes more open. To emphasise the difference and the interdependence between the foresters and the doctor, Berger also represents two opposing modes of thinking: open and closed. The foresters, who for generations have been settled with the belief that the patterns of the world are essentially static, embody the former, whereas the doctor – whose own personal displacements have distanced him from the position of actor and brought him closer to the position of witness, and because he is constantly and consciously probing at the borders of the unconventional – embraces the open thinking, which perpetually extends itself. Sassal achieved this dual function not only through his professional expertise but by offering an image of the possible self that does not amount to an external threat, but an image of the foresters' own unarticulated potential: the side which is repressed by their social conventions. Sassal is the foresters' other in so far as he mirrors and magnifies the unrealised and unnamed parts of their buried selves. While Simmel argues that the stranger's consciousness is neither a *tabula rasa* nor overdetermined by 'accidental dislocations and emphases',[49] Berger similarly represents Sassal's critical consciousness by juxtaposing it with the strictures of the villagers' common sense. Berger represents their common sense as being premised on the belief that the realm of the actual is static and that the desired alternative is eternally distanced rather than bridged by inquiry. Consequently, the role of questioning is confined to the short term, or it is employed rhetorically to emphasise the futility and absurdity of future change. Thus, common sense is a form of habitual thinking which can never push beyond certain limits. It is as much a consolation as it is an explanation, a constant search for repetition within conventions. Berger opposes it to the process of critical inquiry and emancipation by equating it with a Marxist conception of the ideologies that subordinate the culturally deprived. Hence he argues that while perpetuating an obdurate form of passivity and endurance, common sense is also constantly being contradicted by the actions of even those who uphold it:

[For] ... it represents only a part — and often a small part – of their character. These same people say or do many things which are an affront to their own common-sense. And when they justify something by saying 'It's only common-sense', this is frequently an apology for denying or betraying some of their deepest feelings or instincts.[50]

By challenging common sense, Sassal challenges the notion that the present is irrevocable and that the past is homogeneous. His purpose is to widen the horizons of both. Through a mixture of both impulsive behaviour and intellectual thought, Sassal's example re-defines the villagers' expectations as it transgresses the conventions according to which a man of his authority is meant to act. By naming the unnamed experiences he serves as a mirror which their culture failed to provide.[51] He allows them to see their other selves. Sassal could be described as the welcome stranger, who comes to redeem by noting the limitations in self-realisation: 'his license is to challenge the prisoner in every one of his listeners'.[52] Thus Berger's portrait of Sassal is also a projection of the foresters' potential space.

Simmel's stranger also utilises estrangement to facilitate the process of oscillation between fixed positions. The stranger is as much informed by these positions as he is a reformer of them. This mobility, whose authority rests on the perpetuation of comparative judgement, has a perplexing symmetry. While difference is expressed in its every judgement, this difference also assumes a prior and shared code. Simmel's stranger can only perceive the particular differences between societies because he invokes a general condition which is the constituency of the social.[53] What ultimately secures a position for the stranger in society is that he can be seen as a 'speaker' for the fundament of the social. The stranger, while detached from the particular affiliations within a society, is nevertheless re-rooted into the symbolic values and core ideals of the social. Simmel finds in the stranger not just an embodiment of the transitions in modernity, but also by 'virtue' of these displacements he is able to utilise both a bifocal vision and a mode of metaphorical thinking which is the precondition of objectivity.

Berger represents Sassal's critical consciousness as a consequence of his experience. The formative experiences can be characterised under the headings of rebellion, crisis and redemption. With each successive phase Berger demonstrates that Sassal's attachment to place and the form of his knowledge is redefined through his relationship with others. Sassal's journey away from, and back to, his country of origin is also a journey towards a critical participation within the place of belonging. It is a journey which begins with the rejection of the self, which simultaneously inspires or is inspired by an advance towards an idealised other. However, the realisation soon follows that such relationships with the other are, at best, short-lived and circumscribed by unsurpassable boundaries, so that the return back to the self is inevitable. But to return to the self, while retaining the knowledge formed by these displacements, is consequently not to return to a self which is identical to the one before departure. To differentiate adjustment from assimilation there must be the attending search for a 'new' critical space within the original place of belonging. This position will redeem the experiences formed during the journey as it extends the possibilities of 'journeying' within the place of return.

Rebellion and departure

Rebellion's altruism is fuelled by the dual process of rejection and acceptance. The dismissal of the self is matched by an elevation of the self through a positive identification with the idealised other. Sassal's need to leave England is a symptom of a rebellion against his perception of England as a place of decline and decay. The contradictions between his personal aspirations and the example of his elders reflects a generalised perception of failure within the homeland. Hence his rejection of the 'boredom and complacency of middle-class life ashore in England'[14] is motivated by a desire to be buried in an idealised service which would resolve the contradictions of his own identity by raising his own moral stature beyond the opportunism and hypocrisy of others.

The first positive example that was offered to Sassal was the figure of the Master-Mariner in Conrad's novels:

> Yet in this offered poetry there was nothing unmanly or effete: on the contrary, the only men who could face the unimaginable were tough, controlled, taciturn and outwardly ordinary. The quality which Conrad constantly warns against is at the same time the very quality to which he appeals: the quality of imagination. It is almost as though the sea is the symbol of this contradiction. It is to the imagination that the sea appeals: but to face the sea in its unimaginable fury, to meet its own challenge, imagination must be abandoned, for it leads to self-isolation and fear.[15]

The challenges of the sea are marked between the promise of safe delivery into known harbours, the wayward lures of the winds and undercurrents, and the ultimate threat of being engulfed by them. These ambivalent images are also a metaphor for self-realisation through sexual arousal and consummation with an unknown other. And, during the Second World War, Sassal found a partial confirmation of his desire to be subsumed within a higher moral service and an opportunity to forget his past, as he inserted himself into the struggle for Greek Independence. The foreign place thus served as the arena in which his own unrealised self could be aroused and find consummation.

He had proved his skill to himself and his ability to take decisions. With this proof came the conviction that those who lived simply, those who were dependent upon him, possessed qualities and a secret of living that he lacked. Thus whilst having authority over them, he could feel he was serving them.[16]

Return and crisis

With his return home, Sassal considered himself adrift, set further apart. 'Safe thinking was now like settling down ashore.'[17] He resisted this in preference for open thought, bridging the familiar and the foreign, through the process of translation. He could, in this way, investigate that condition 'which no previous explanation will actually fit'.[18] Having rejected common sense because it presupposed the denial of the other and foreclosed the perception of the unusual, Sassal also realised that the certitudes that guided his observation of the other presupposed the denial of imagination with his own self. At this stage Sassal underwent a crisis which Berger could only compare to the solitary trek of the shaman, which the Zulus call the *inyanga*, where the search for reason pushes him deeper into the realm of unreason, tearing the harmony of the self until it becomes a 'house of dreams'.[19] Sassal surfaced from this crisis with the realisation 'that imagination had to be lived with on every level: his own imagination first – because otherwise this could distort his observation – and the imagination of his patients'.[60]

Redemption and identification

'With the "foresters" he seems like a foreigner who has become, by request, the clerk of their records.'[61] Returning to his homeland, Sassal had to face the limitations of 'imaginative distance'. The restrictive fantasy of abstract attachment with the other could not be sustained in the village. Sassal had to forge a new internal relationship which combined intimacy and critical scrutiny. It is in this process that Berger argues that Sassal finds redemption, both for himself and for the villagers. Sassal becomes the benign stranger who offers hope, not because he carries a message of salvation from beyond, but rather through the example of his service which constantly reveals that redemption lies within. Perhaps this is why the foresters trust this stranger – seeing that the external disparities between him and them also represent their own inner potential. The other thus pays a peculiar homage to the self, by being both its atavistic container and the irascible spur to self-identification:

> He does more than treat them when they are ill; he is the objective witness of their lives . . . He keeps the records so that, from time to time, they can consult them themselves . . . He represents their objective (as opposed to subjective) memory, because he represents their lost possibility of understanding and relating to the outside world, and because he also represents some of what they know they cannot think.[62]

Sassal is more than a witness to the memories that the foresters have deposited with him for their safe keeping; he is also a medium through which these articulated memories merge with their unspoken desires in order to find a form that can break the silence that binds their hopes and fears. Sassal is the stranger who holds together both the past and future of the village, his example containing both the enactment and the aspiration of their ideals.

His position as 'clerk of the records' not only means that, more than any other man, he knows the continuing history of the area; it also attributes to him the power to comprehend and realize for the community. To some extent he thinks and speaks what the community feels and incoherently knows. To some extent he is the growing force (albeit very slowly) of their self-consciousness.[63]

When Berger says that 'He [Sassal] cures others to cure himself', he is in fact making Sassal say to the 'foresters': 'I am thou'.

This crossing and blurring of boundaries between the known and the unknown within the many selves of Sassal and the selves of the 'foresters' echoes the method that Berger ascribes to the storyteller. As a novelist, Berger defined his own task as 'trying to define and express something which has not been defined and expressed before . . . If there is something I have half perceived I feel it necessary to turn it into prose and make it therefore part of our consciousness.'[64] For Sassal, to give a name to a condition is to clarify the patients' fears and hopes, and to outline the path of the living. Naming involves separating one set of possibilities from the realm of infinity, distinguishing the possible from the impossible. In *And Our Faces, My Heart, Brief as Photos*, Berger describes the storyteller as 'Death's Secretary'. Like the doctor, the storyteller functions as the intermediary between the living and the dead, forming a bridge between estrangement and solidarity.

Where does this quest for naming the unknown lead to? Psychoanalysis reminds us that even the most future oriented forms of naming can be seen as evidence of the persistence of the past. Since 'objects of nostalgia lived on in the unconscious because of an inability in an identificatory process. . . . every identification is motivated by the wish to find a substitute for lost gratification.'[65] Berger's representation of Sassal in *A Fortunate Man* is as the enlightened stranger whose social position is somewhere between a surrogate for the foresters' history and a prophet for their future. Yet there is one profoundly ironic and disturbing event that occurred after the book was written – the suicide of Sassal. This conclusion must surely put every heroic principle in question.

The final passage of *A Seventh Man* is a dialogue between a migrant who has returned to his village and his younger cousin who dreams of leaving. Asked about the speed with which city people drive their cars, the migrant replies: 'Not as fast as us. You know how we say of a man that he comes back before he goes?'[66]

The returned migrant is speaking of the *stasis* amidst the dynamism of the metropolis. In the city of change, people seem to stand still. But then what could be said of the migrant's journey, one step forward, two steps back?

How many fantasies are punctured by this paradox? In *A Seventh Man* Berger has attempted to follow the migrant's journey. But what

Death of a stranger

is the destiny of Berger's own journey? Where has Berger arrived in order to end his book with the words: 'To be homeless is to be nameless. He. The existence of a migrant worker.'[67]

In an earlier and self-reflective passage Berger says:

> To try to understand the experience of another it is necessary to dismantle the world as seen from one's own place within it, and to reassemble it as seen from his. For example, to understand a given choice another makes, one must face in imagination the lack of choices which may confront and deny him. . . . The world has to be dismantled and re-assembled in order to be able to grasp, however clumsily, the experience of another. To talk of entering the other's subjectivity is misleading. The subjectivity of another does not simply constitute a different interior attitude to the same exterior facts. The constellation of facts, of which he is the centre, is different.[68]

This method of seeing the other, after stripping the subjective position of the self and through the vicarious identification with the other's subjective position, is qualified by Berger when he also admits the necessity of questioning the objective world in which both the self and the other are located:

> To see the experience of another, one must do more than dismantle and reassemble the world with him at its centre. One must interrogate his situation to learn about that part of his experience which derives from the historical moment. What is being done to him, even with his own complicity, under the cover of normalcy? Is what is being done to him new?[69]

This additional critical position no doubt re-introduces the subjectivity of the self, but Berger does not draw out these implications any further. He holds on to the claim that the true contents of norms are 'fully exposed' only when brought up against the position to which they are opposed.

When two strangers meet

In as much as displacement has become the central feature of modernity, the migrant has become the symbol of modernity.

What has happened within him is not distinct from what happens within millions of others who are not migrant workers. It is simply more extreme. He experiences suddenly as an individual, as a man who believes he is choosing his own life, what the industrial consumer societies have experienced gradually through generations without the effort of choosing. He lives the content of our institutions: they transform him violently. They do not need to transform us. We are already within them.[70]

There is some solidarity to be found in the commonality of suffering. As Berger concludes in *A Seventh Man*, the migrant and the native are both co-victims of modernity: the mechanics of oppression which are projected upon the body of the migrant are a manifestation of the violence introjected by the native. Yet my concern at this stage is not to extend the homologies between the migrant's and the native's experience but to consider the migrant's status as a stranger. When *A Fortunate Man* and *A Seventh Man* are juxtaposed, two different archetypes for the stranger are syphoned off.

The stranger in *A Fortunate Man* embodies the 'enlightenment' which is formed through an awareness of the incommensurable processes of journeying. This form of journeying consists of two mutually distinct, yet inseparable, paths: the journey of departure and the journey of arrival. The stranger's vision is enlightened, not because he has transcended his origins but because travelling has revealed the chiasmus within the certitudes of belonging. In the process of apprehending the novel complexities of arrival, and the refusal to erase the history for departure, the stranger questions the fullness or the truncation to meaning that informs others of their belonging. The ambiguity in the stranger's origin is overcome once he can be seen as serving as an impartial guide, like a messenger whose message has echoes of both the 'near and far' or as the 'clerk of the records', who is in the constant process of receiving and delivering, the stranger begins to express the unarticulated history of the group and thus becomes, in Simmel's words, 'inorganically appended to the group'. The stranger was not written into the history of the group, but by being the hand that rewrites it, he includes himself in the process of redefining their identity. The stranger helps the members to rereremember and re-imagine themselves, his liminality serves as the potential space toward which they can both acknowledge his presence and confront an absence within their habitual consciousness. The stranger thus shifts the borderline between the possible and the impossible selves, offering an unthreatening example of how the external can be incorporated within the internal. For the stranger in *A Fortunate Man* wisdom lies in knowing that the truth is as forked and as partial as the multiple paths of a journey, and that like a metaphor a journey is the consequence of the process of connecting different paths. Journeys without destinies are journeys for origins. And this traveller is not just a stranger but a shaman.

While the enlightened stranger uses his severances from the place of origin, to find new links and re-think the relationship of identity, there is another stranger for whom severance does not open up a new space for identity, but condemns the stranger deeper into the abyss of incommensurability between departure and arrival. The strangers in *A Seventh Man* are peasants who left their villages to become manual workers in the metropolis of a foreign country. This stranger embodies the suffering of loss and despair. It is a tragedy without redemption. Having lost his language and lacking the resources to acquire another, he is precluded from entering the social context of the other in any meaningful way. The stranger endures like a hero but finds no reward, not even the salvation of martyrdom. His journey began with the assumption that the money attained would bring salvation. Yet not only did the amount acquired fall short of the amount expected, and not only could he not return as the hero he fantasised himself as, but the very possibility of returning is put into doubt. His personal displacement was part of a wider rupture of social conditions. The stranger in *A Seventh Man* is caught in a double loss: he has lost his village and failed to gain the metropolis. The tragedy is the realisation that the return to the village was not the end of the journey. And to stay in the metropolis requires a reconciliation to a severance that was never anticipated: staying demanded redefining time and space, creating new maps and moving out of the past.

Separating the two archetypes of the stranger – the shaman and the migrant – is an asymmetrical cluster of political, economic and cultural privileges. Factors that would distinguish the tenure of their social position include: the contrasting availability of routes for safe return; the pre-existence of links that partly bridge the distance between some strangers and natives: and the disproportionate relationships of dependency that legitimises the stranger's claim for staying in terms of the native's needs. But most fundamentally, the contrast to their status and their social position is defined by language. Sassal utilises displacement to transform his knowledge, whereas the migrant becomes an automaton as the displacements render him mute.

The authority of language is revealed not only by the recognition of a lack at the point of arrival, but also by the language in which the journey was envisaged. Language in general is the process of reconciliation and compromise, it is the alliance of dissimilars, the constant forging of new links. 'The word in language is half someone else's. It becomes "one's" own only when . . . the speaker appropriates it, adopting it to his own semantic and expressive intention.'[71] The stranger in *A Fortunate Man* embodies this 'dialogic imagination', for he not only knows the language of the natives, but also probes at the borders of representation as he questions its presuppositions. As he challenges the foresters' common sense, he extends and affirms the recuperative and redemptive role of language. The stranger in *A Seventh Man*, however, is mostly silent. The stranger is a migrant who on arrival is reduced to an automaton. After work he dreams of returning to his humanity – his homeland – his language.

Antigone Kefala, a Greek-Australian poet, commences her first collection of poetry with the most enduring line:

> In dreams beings the journey.[72]

Arrival is measured largely by the ability to imagine the other: to imagine the time and space of transition is to imagine a new position for the self. How did the migrant in *A Seventh Man* imagine the journey from the village to the metropolis?

Crossing borders and the relationship to place

What does the migrant hope to see on arrival, and is the reason for leaving buried in these open-ended expectations?

The road leads out of the village across the plain or through the hill. After a few kilometres the village is out of sight the sky continues over the land. He is far more aware of the phenomenon of the horizon than most city dwellers. Yet it is openness that the metropolis represents for him. Within that openness is opportunity to earn a living; to have enough money to act . . .

The migrant wants to live. It is not poverty alone that forces him to emigrate. Through his own individual effort he tries to achieve the dynamism that is lacking in the situation into which he was born.[73]

Berger represents the pre-migratory hopes of the migrant through a combination of the generalised desire to find the opportunity to make a new beginning and the particular impressions gathered from stories by those who have returned from the metropolis. These stories, with all their conspiratorial tones and optimistic hues, may in themselves kindle the desire for departure by heightening the opposition between plenitude and lack. Narratives of conquest often form the springboard into the unknown by simultaneously blurring the privations within struggle, and inflating the force of heroic will. But to what extent do they actually prepare the migrant for the journey? For, if money is

Death of a stranger

both the temptation to and the opportunity for a new life, and the returned migrant is the example of the hero, what will serve as the map that helps the migrant to direct his epic journey away from tragedy? From Berger's perspective it appears that the migrant does not imagine the contents of the metropolis as vividly as he desires to cross a border. It is as if success at the border will also guarantee the continuous passage beyond, and hence the migrant has deferred the necessity of imagining any further.

The journey in *A Seventh Man* is not a story of affirmation; it reveals the limits of the migrant's sense of arrival through the incommensurability between their past and present. The text in *A Seventh Man* is continuously juxtaposed by Jean Mohr's stunning portraits of transition: images of disbelief and excitement; pain and waiting; wonder and nostalgia. The migrant's gaze is always slightly pointing up, looking far and forward. For instance, on the seventh visual page there is a photograph of a man standing on the scaffolding of a building site.[74] His head, with cap firmly in place, is tilting backwards – a proud smile and a cunning wink join into one expression as he raises his chest. With one hand touching his chin, and the other firmly gripping his hammer there is the instantaneous gesture of bewilderment and resilience. He is being photographed from below. He embraces the acknowledgement that the photographer is offering, but he remains uncertain of the purpose. His expression struggles to contain all the generalised possibilities of being without the full recognition of belonging. The pattern on his jumper forms a pattern of starflakes – there is no room for symbolism here, just protection, like his steel capped boots. His pockets are a pouch for his tools – a ruler, some nails . . . Behind him is the wooden structure that he has constructed; it is the mould for the concrete that is about to be poured. Could he be a 'typical' worker? Below the photograph is the caption: 'migrant workers now appear indispensable to Europe's economy. What was initially a temporary expedient has become something close to a permanent necessity.'[75] A permanent necessity without the claim to permanence. The migrant's grip is restricted to the scaffolding. There are no photographs in this book which show the migrants inside the public buildings that they built. They are photographed only outdoors, in factories, by the roadside; and after work, in their private barracks, or at the railway station.

In this scenario, the borders between the peasants' village and the metropolis are no longer a question of geography but the political frontiers that mark the possibility of success and failure. Crossing a border is entering a new realm: 'the frontier is simply where he is liable to be stopped and his intention to leave thwarted. On the far side of the frontier, when he has crossed it, he becomes a migrant worker.'[76] The rites of entry are a matter of power. The migrant cannot enter the metropolis unless he has passed tests and permission is granted. His passivity and subordinance in this confrontation with authority is most poignantly expressed at the point in which he awaits the results. Berger compares the expression on the men's faces to the 'expression of a father waiting outside whilst his child is being born. Here he awaits his own new life'.[77] Yet the expectations are asymmetrical. The migrant wants to be born again, but the host only wants an automaton: 'machine-minders, sweepers, diggers, cement-mixers, cleaners, drillers etc. This is the significance of temporary migration. To re-become a man (husband, father, citizen, patriot) a migrant has to return home. The home he left because it held no future for him.'[78]

How is the city imagined? At first the city is the place where wages are fixed, things are bought, money is saved, cars are driven, new clothes are worn, food is plentiful – all because there are many hours to be worked. The city is also imagined as a place with secrets concerning women who are the objects of pornography and prostitution, men whose authority is unquestionable, buildings which are forbidden and distances which are immeasurable.[79] Berger represents the city as an enigma which the migrants can imagine only inadequately. The city is a secret which they will only partially know. The city is a place of ambivalence. The city is the dynamic discontinuity of the 'new' future as opposed to the static continuity of the 'old' past in the village.

In Berger's representation of the migrant's perception of the metropolis there is no preceding image which has the potency to shape subsequent impressions. The migrant's preconceptions are formed through a generalised mixture of hopes and fears whose very generality embraces a totality that is nevertheless some distance from touching reality. The point of arrival unequivocally announces the shocking distance between these dusky desires and the stark realities. Berger attempts to relay this shock through a series of observations which assume the migrant's eye:

> It is the clothes of the few civilians which are startling. And more than their clothes, their expressions. They look as though they are not using their eyes, and yet they walk quickly . . .

Once more he is under the grey cloud-coloured wall like a television screen on which bright images flicker, and from which new unfamiliar sounds are emitted. The wall will divide and they will enter time . . .

The silence is his. Whatever they are saying, he, with the silent sounds in his head, is going to nod . . .

By looking at each other, they realize how dishevelled and rough they have become in comparison with the strangers who are dealing with them. But equally this is a reminder of their achievement. They have crossed the frontier . . .

Arriving alone, the shock of the birth of his new life is immediate. He calls upon each year of his manhood in order not to panic. In a group it is easier . . .

Everything looks new . . . The newness of the substance of things combines with the incomprehensibility of the language . . .

Around the exit men were talking in his own language. The words of it are like foliage re-appearing on a tree after winter.[80]

But between these last two observations Berger curiously inserts a quotation from Joyce's *Ulysses*. Without quotation marks it almost goes by unnoticed, it reads *like* a list of drudgeries and urban monotonies. But its rhythm defies its contents. Its assertiveness and control demonstrates that this is not the voice of a migrant for whom things are almost totally incomprehensible. By inserting this quotation Berger reveals the distance between the authorial 'I' and the migrant's 'eye'. Berger announces that he is not the migrant, he is an author whose task it is to give a form to the experience of another. This position, however, is not open to the migrant. The migrant's greatest difficulty is precisely this act of distinguishing between the inputs, putting things in order, and giving form to an otherwise meaningless list. As Berger reminds us, the migrant fails to evaluate exchanges properly because to him the codes of honour and ethics have been displaced by the anonymity of the inhabitants and the homogeneity of the city. Berger juxtaposes the migrant's perception of the city with that of his village by foregrounding the presence of altruism as the means of establishing the comprehensibility of social values and the identity of neighbours.

But sometimes something happens on an ordinary day in a village which never happens in a city. (Revolution or siege may confer this possibility upon the city.) A man or woman acts altruistically. A spontaneous action, quite uncalculated. A protest against an injustice suffered by somebody else. An offer which is really a sacrifice. And this action provokes an echo from where? The sky? The fields? Ancestors? The village tower? The echo is inaudible but it completes the act. The one who acts feels it, and some who witness the action feel it too. In the metropolis no action can be completed in this way.[81]

The villages from which the migrants have come, and the metropolis in which they work, stand as opposites from which no reconciliation can be drawn. Berger reproduces the structure of the migrant's journey as an unreconciled tragedy, a doomed odyssey. The migrant is cheated from both sides. He neither gains the metropolis nor wins back the village. He belongs *in* the between. He is most at home on the voyage to his imagined home. Such departures from time and place have precluded a return.

The final return is mythic. It gives meaning to what might otherwise be meaningless. It is larger than life. It is the stuff of longing and prayers. But it is also mythic in the sense that, as imagined it never happens. There is no final return . . .

The village now respects him as a man of different experience. He has seen and received and achieved things which they have not . . . He is interpreter . . . They seize upon them . . . Gradually he is stripped . . . The village behaves like a beggared king . . . If he questions its judgement too openly [he will be] condemned as an agitator . . . An assured place for him no longer exists in his village.[82]

Berger confronts the predicament of the migrant without the illusion that privation leads to progress. Migration is not a sacrifice but a swindle. What the migrant lacks in *A Seventh Man* is language. Without language the migrant is less than a stranger. But where does Berger stand?

In a dream the dreamer wills, act, reacts, speaks, and yet submits to the unfolding of a story which he scarcely influences. The dream happens to him. Afterwards he may ask another to interpret it. But sometimes a dreamer tries to break his dream by deliberately waking himself up. This book represents such an intention within a dream which the subject of the book and each of us is dreaming.[83]

Through his representation of the migrant, it is Berger who becomes the stranger. He is neither the suffering migrant nor the oppressive host. He understands the mechanisms of oppression and has empathy for the victim. Yet in writing their history, whose suffering is redeemed? The central character(s) in *A Seventh Man* is 'He'. The migrant's anonymity speaks again of his silence, as it also ushers Berger in as the stranger. 'He is interpreter.' Without a single identifiable stranger for Berger to project his identity into, Berger becomes the stranger who has introjected the identity of all the migrants. Like his version of Sassal, Berger has become the vessel that articulates the migrants' unarticulated language.

Lacking a language for the other

To open up this process of projection and introjection in Berger's representation of the migrant's journey, I will turn to Schutz's essay 'The Stranger'.[84] By focusing on the interaction between strangers and members, Schutz gives an account of the limitations to habitual schemas for interpreting others. These exchanges parallel the encounters that Berger represents in *A Seventh Man*, and also draw attention to the complexities of language in defining the social position of strangers and members.

Schutz does not distinguish the difference of knowledge between a member and a stranger in terms of perfect and imperfect knowledge. He stresses that a member of a group acts and thinks in the world in a way that is (1) incoherent, (2) only partially clear, and (3) contradictory.[85] Yet despite, or even because of, these shortcomings, the member's vision is deemed sufficient to fulfil the routine goals and expectations of everyday life. The member has, or knows how to get, the knowledge that is required in order to conduct him/herself in the ways that are considered appropriate, and can with unquestionable ease express him/herself in an understandable manner. For this system of exchanges to be operative, the members take for granted the preexistence of

> trustworthy *recipes* for interpreting the social world and for handling things and men in order to obtain the best results in every situation with a minimum of effort by avoiding undesirable consequences ... Thus it is the function of the cultural pattern to eliminate troublesome inquiries by offering ready-made directions for use, to replace truth hard to attain by comfortable truisms, and to substitute the self-explanatory for the questionable.[86]

It is by virtue of the member's fluent exchanges within their habitual systems that the overriding opposition of plentiude and lack returns as the primary basis from which the relationship between the member and the stranger is characterised. The mutual knowledge that governs the actions and interpretations between members is defined by a system of 'recipes' which serve both as 'a scheme of expression and for interpretation'.[87] By defining actions within a typified schema, the 'recipes' issue the members with the appropriate bearings to locate their social position and realm of influence. The members use the recipes to reassure themselves of their centrality in this signifying schema. Lacking such a 'recipe', the stranger is at first unable to interpret the signs that demarcate social positions and consequently feels displaced.

Schutz claims that the validity of these recipes presupposes four factors: the homogeneity and continuity of social structures; the reliability of transmitted knowledge; the ability to anticipate and control, to a limited degree, the general nature of events that members are destined to encounter; and that the recipes are accepted and applied in the public domain as well as the private sphere. These are the certitudes that govern the 'thinking as usual' the absence of any one of these certitudes is sufficient to initiate a 'crisis' in the schemas of expression and interpretation. Yet the stranger can take *none* of these certitudes for granted. By not being attached to the historical traditions in which these certitudes were formed, the stranger inevitably questions their assumptions. The stranger is placed in the no-man's-land between certitudes, between the punctured certitudes of the past and the incomprehensible certitudes of the present. Lack is thus the primary characteristic of the stranger and, for Schutz, what the stranger is fundamentally lacking is history.

Graves and reminiscences can neither be transferred nor conquered. The stranger, therefore, approaches the other group as a newcomer in the true meaning of the term. At best he may be willing and able to share the present and the future with the approached group in vivid and immediate experience: under all circumstances, however, he remains excluded from such experience of its past. Seen from the point of view of the approached group, he is a man without history.[88]

The stranger's first response in interpreting the new social group is via a transposition of the assumptions that were implanted in the old social group. Schutz argues that such a transferral of cultural recipes is predestined to failure for three reasons. Firstly, the very attempt to interpret the social group implies a form of participation that is absent from these assumptions. The approach to the new group must also acknowledge the distance from the old group, and thus lifts the stranger out of the previous state of detachment. This change of position requires another type of knowledge. Secondly, the strangers' new approach also affects their perspective. As new details emerge through the increased process of identification, the stranger is forced to alter preconceived objectifications, and to restate them in terms of the new encounter. Thirdly, there is the realisation of the limitations of the stranger's preconceived image of foreign groups. Schutz concludes that stereotypes of foreigners that were formed in isolation may cast an opinion on the putative characteristics of the foreigner, but they do not serve as a guide for interaction or dialogue.

Consequently, the schema of interpretation refers to members of the foreign group merely as objects of this interpretation, but not beyond it, as addressees of possible acts emanating from the outcome of the interpretive procedure and not as subjects of anticipated reactions toward those acts. Hence, this kind of knowledge is, so to speak, insulated; it can neither be verified nor falsified by responses of the members of the foreign group. The latter, therefore, consider this knowledge – by a kind of 'looking-glass' effect – as both irresponsive and irresponsible and complain of its prejudices, bias and misunderstandings.[89]

The stranger's crisis is not just on the level of being misinformed about a particular group, but rather that the general schema which was formed in the old group is invalidated by the encounter with the new group. Pointing to this generalised depravation of a schema for orientation, Schutz once again defines the stranger in the position of lack.

The stranger, however, has to face the fact that he lacks any status as a member of the social group he is about to join and is therefore unable to get a starting point to take his bearings. He finds himself a border case outside the territory covered by the scheme of orientation current within the group. He is, therefore, no longer permitted to consider himself as the centre of his social environment.[90]

Once the tensions of the dislocation have also opened up the fissures within the interpretative schema, the last remaining option for resilience is through translation. The stranger must constantly translate the new impressions in terms of general cultural patterns of the old group. In practice every instance of translation, in as much as it finds coincidence, also repeats the fundamental possibility of dissidence. The stranger is therefore most struck by the 'miss and fit' relationship of language, constantly reminded of the discrepancy between names, values and things. The gap between the stranger and the member is thus reinforced even when the stranger has become competent in comprehending and exercising the formal rules of a group. There still remains the informal associations that are embedded in key terms, the untranslatable fringes that surround phrases, the several connotations that hang on every word, the private forms of idiom which can conceal specific codes and secrets, and the very plethora in manner with which gestures can be expressed and interpreted. This knowledge can be gained only with intimacy and experience – the very conditions which the stranger lacks.

The confrontation between a stranger and a member exposes the limitations of both schemas for interpretation. Schutz emphasises the process of translation as the key to the stranger's negotiation of a new social position, because it is through this process that the dialectic between severances and links is established. However, translation presupposes the potential space for a dialogue between the old and the new. The migrant in *A Seventh Man* does not express this potential for survival. He seems destined to misunderstanding and his marginal position is confirmed by his perception of the 'opaqueness of words'.

When he crossed the frontier every word spoken or written was meaningless to him. At first he tried to guess what words meant. Most of the words addressed to him were instructions or orders. If he guessed wrong he was in trouble. So he learnt it was safer not to guess. He treated the sounds of the unknown language as if they were silence.

To break through his silence.

He learnt twenty words of the new language. But, to his amazement at first their meaning changed when he spoke them. He asked for coffee. What the word coffee signified to the barman was that he was asking for coffee in a bar where he should not be asking for coffee. He learnt girl. What the word girl meant, when he used it, was that he was a randy dog.[91]

The migrant labourer that Berger describes would not even qualify as a stranger in Schutz's schema. For while Schutz differentiates between the member and the stranger in terms of the degree of knowledge in the linguistic and cultural conventions that regulate social interaction, his schema also presupposes that such differences are mutually translatable. Schutz is conscious that this exchange is often blocked by the pre-existence of stereotypes. Thus for the dialogue between the stranger and the native to commence, both must perceive a possible benefit from their exchange. But where does this presumption of attraction or desire for dialogue originate? Schutz's schema relates only to those encounters where the stranger is capable of translating his past with his present in a way that is to the mutual benefit of both the stranger and the native. The stranger's position in society is precariously situated on the positive translatability between the two tenses and spaces that govern his identity. Whereas for the migrant labourer, his identity is confined to economic productivity, beyond the work-place he has no function, that is why 'He' is nameless. Any attempt to translate his desire for recognition in other zones is precluded. This comparison identifies a crucial limitation in Schutz's schema, and in so far as this essay has played an influential role in the formation of sociology as a discipline for understanding modernity it also reveals the conceptual paucity for understanding the social interaction between strangers and natives.

Death of a stranger

Another approach to these questions can be found by following the figure of the stranger in Siegfried Kracauer's writings. Kracauer represents the stranger on two occasions; firstly in his analysis of identity and homelessness in the detective novel, and secondly in his philosophy of history.

In Kracauer's early writings the stranger is not an impartial witness, but rather the belated detective. Kracauer defines the detective's primary task as the re-thinking of the causes and the course of everyday events, to turn events inside out in search for a clue that might explain a mystery. The confrontation with the mystery in social reality is what makes the experience of the detective analogous to that of a stranger. Being late arrivals both are distanced from the spontaneous assumptions with which native members grasp the 'ordinary' meanings. Both the stranger and the detective confront reality with one eye turned towards that which is seemingly incomprehensible – not because they are cut off from higher meanings, but rather because their perception is particularly attuned to the contradictory and the fragmentary within the layers of social meanings. For Kracauer, truth is always hidden elsewhere. The detective must look for the meaning that lies just below the surface of things, and seeing beyond the artifice of ideology is a penetrative procedure, it involves unveiling a different order. Kracauer's study of the detective novel is indebted to Lukács's concepts of reification and transcendental homelessness as the central keys for the analysis of the novel.[92] While Kracauer extends Lukács's insights as he develops the elements of estrangement in social reality, his detective escapes neither the misogynist presupposition of the genre nor the pitfalls of Lukács's idealism. Not entirely dissimilar, but far more a evocative metaphor for the investigation as an encounter with the other, is Kracauer's re-casting of the stranger as an historian.

In his philosophy of history Kracauer positions the investigator in an ambivalent zone that lies betwixt the realities of others. The historian is situated 'in the near vacuum of extra-territoriality'. Kracauer's essay 'The Historian's Journey'[93] begins with a passage from Proust's *Remembrance of Things Past*, where Marcel considers the moment prior to meeting his beloved grandmother and cherishes the image that he nurtured via an old photograph and the idealising chambers of memory. However, when Marcel meets his grandmother the contradiction between the idealised image and the immediate contact produces an estranging effect.

Expectations have criss-crossed each other, fantasies superimposed with reality.

Sometimes life itself produces such palimpsests. I am thinking of the exile who as an adult person has been forced to leave his country or has left it of his own free will. As he settles elsewhere, all those loyalties, expectations, and aspirations that comprise so large a part of his being are automatically cut off from their roots. His life history is disrupted, his 'natural' self relegated to the background of his mind. To be sure, his inevitable efforts to meet the challenges of an alien environment will affect his outlook, his whole mental make-up. But since the self he was continues to smoulder beneath the person he is about to become, his identity is bound to be in a state of flux; and the odds are that he will never fully belong to the community to which he now belongs. (Nor will its members readily think of him as one of theirs.) In fact, he has ceased to 'belong'. Where then does he live? In the near-vacuum of extra-territoriality, the very no-man's-land which Marcel entered when he first caught sight of his grandmother. The exile's true mode of existence is that of the stranger. So he may look at his previous existence with the eyes of one 'who does not belong to the house'. And just as he is free to step outside the culture which was his own, he is sufficiently uncommitted to get inside the minds of the foreign people in whose midst he is living.[94]

Marcel's estrangement was the consequence of the contradiction between images; those expected and those received. However, with the displacement of a fixed image comes the revelation of multiple identities, and it is this process, which opens the subjectivity of both the observer and the observed, that Kracauer suggests is the exemplary method for the historian. For Kracauer it is the historian's displacement from a fixed social position which will open the boundaries of the self so that it can be inscribed by all the variant forms of the other. Thus the historian must work in a liminal zone, and live like an exile whose 'mode of existence is that of a stranger'.

Kracauer's staging of the historian as a stranger is partly borrowed from the social type that Schutz described in his essay 'The Stranger'.[95] Schutz also emphasised the role of estrangement in order to differentiate the methodology of sociology from 'mere' common-sense observation. He suggested that for a sociologist to maintain a critical position, he must be situated midway between being a stranger and being a member. This midway social position is also echoed in the methodological principles that Schutz outlines. He claims that the sociologist operates on three levels. Firstly the sociologist sets out to study the 'typical situation in which a stranger finds himself in his attempt to interpret the cultural pattern of a social group which he approaches'.[96] Secondly he claims that the sociologist's function is to work as an impartial observer who

> intentionally refrains from participating in the network of plans, means-and-ends relations, motives and chasms, hopes and fears, which the actor within the social world uses for interpreting his experiences of it; as a scientist he tries to observe, describe, classify the social world as clearly as possible in well-ordered terms in accordance with the scientific ideals of coherence, consistency and analytical consequence.[97]

Thirdly, by positioning the sociologist's schema between the 'knowledge of acquaintance' that the members accrue and the 'knowledge about' which the stranger acquires, Schutz can both assert the necessity of estrangement for objectivity, and substantiate his claim that it is the sociologist who acts as an intermediary – the 'mentor' who can 'make them wise to things'.[98] The sociologist is thus proclaimed as being able to hold together two diametrically opposed points: estrangement and solidarity.

Yet to validate this position for the sociologist, Schutz has to bring the stranger back 'inside'. The stranger is not the other; as in Simmel's definition the stranger is not 'beyond near and far'. The stranger is always the insider who, while not sharing the history of the group in which he is situated, can nevertheless relate to the group's historical consciousness. Like Simmel, Schutz excludes 'relationships between individuals and groups of different levels of civilization'.[99] For the sociologist to retain the right of the intermediary, the estrangement between the stranger and the member must not preclude the potential for solidarity. To achieve this relationship it presumes that an alternative social space exists that is adjacent to the existent forms of social solidarity. Not just the liminal zone which the stranger knows as a gap between the certitudes left behind in the homeland, and the certitudes which are present in the new homeland, but also a liminal zone for the member – a space in which the stranger is recognised and which facilitates a re-negotiation of identity for both. About this latter zone Schutz has nothing to say, he presumes that it is the stranger who is singularly in limbo, and thus the 'burden' or the possibility for adjustment is one-sided. By narrowing the terms of estrangement Schutz seems to be securing the reciprocity between the stranger and member only in univocal terms. It becomes the stranger's duty to stand partly outside and partly inside and mirror back the boundaries and orientation of the group, in the process, offering an image that is otherwise unavailable to those who are positioned within.

The stranger's freedom from local prejudice and the particular attunement to the incoherence and contradictions within the cultural pattern is not a product of the superior knowledge that was formed in the previous social group, but a consequence of having been in a liminal state and surfaced with the need to acquire 'full knowledge of the elements of the approached cultural pattern'.[100] The traumatic severance from a local cultural pattern coupled with the loss of the 'recipes' which defined a general orientation, has taught the stranger that there is no single set of rules which can secure a standardised pattern of exchange and interaction.

Therefore, the stranger discerns, frequently with a grievous clear-sightedness, the rising of a crisis which may menace the whole foundation of the 'relatively natural conception of the world', while all those symptoms pass unnoticed by the members of the in-group, who rely on the continuance of their customary way of life.[101]

Schutz's sociologist who is neither a stranger nor a member, but able to comprehend both estrangement and solidarity, is of course above the pitfalls of the binary oppositions by which he defines the stranger and the member.

Schutz claims that it is the stranger's refusal to accept the cultural pattern of the new group as an unproblematic and protective enclosure that explains why the stranger has earned the dual characterisation of ambivalence and objectivity. The doubtful loyalty of the stranger emerges from the undecidability between the past and the present. This initial state of detachment is for Schutz a necessary one, but in order for assimilation (which is what he means by social adjustment) to take place, this state is at best seen as a transitional one. For if it is prolonged it can have only negative effects: 'The stranger remains . . . a cultural hybrid on the verge of two different patterns of group life, not knowing to which of them he belongs'. Presuming the primacy of fixed location in order to define belonging, this state of *in between* is not seen as viable in itself, nor is it seen more generally as a statement of generalised cultural transformations. Schutz focuses instead more narrowly on the process of personal adaptation. By putting all the onus of orientation on the individual he reinforces the opposition between members and strangers as one between presence and absence, plenitude and lack. Without history, excluded from the centre of social hierarchy, caught between the gaps and the excesses of language, the stranger's position is not just precariously hanging in the margin, but defined in opposition to the historical presence, social self-assurance and linguistic fluency of the member. The stranger's lack and insecurity stand in contrast to the member's plenitude and certitude.

Schutz does not use the example of the stranger to investigate the condition of homelessness, but rather he defines it as the external position *from* which instructive insight can be gained into the 'homely' life. The multiple realities of homelessness are subordinated within a framework which singularly draws attention to the conformity with the patterns and parameters of the home. Thus the claim that the stranger has insights which are of significance is dependent on the condition that the stranger regains a home. Without a home, it is presumed that the stranger has no history, language or identity.

Where Schutz differs from Simmel is not just in the limited range of individuals that can even qualify as strangers (as pointed out in an earlier section, this severely restricts the contemporary application of his schema) but in the gravitational pull toward the assimilation of the stranger into the native's home. Like Simmel he noted that the stranger's identity is sustained by an ambivalent tension and is received with ambivalence. The dual qualities of the stranger emerge from his dubious and inorganic social location, on the one hand his freedom from local convention generates insight, and on the other it creates suspicion. Schutz preferred to resolve this ambivalence by choosing the 'ideal' clarity of social integration over the 'incongruity' of cultural difference. This compromise which flattens the position and perspective of the stranger is rejected by Simmel. Schutz foreclosed the subtle dynamics between 'near' and 'far' because he assumed that there is a limit to how long natives can tolerate a stranger as *the* stranger. Furthermore he assumed that the social order tended toward integration and uniformity and that the strangers are obliged to yield to this pressure.

Kracauer's correlation between estrangement and historical investigation also diverges from Schutz's analysis at the very point in which Schutz proclaims a closure. While Schutz is critical of the stranger's ambivalence and inserts the sociologist as the figure who finds resolution, Kracauer embraces those very values which are seen as dubious and threatening. Kracauer's historian is destined to hover in the stranger's liminality. 'It is only in this state of self-effacement, or homelessness, that the historian can commune with the material of his concern.'[102]

The difference between Schutz and Kracauer is the relationship that is attributed to difference. While Schutz defines the stranger as someone who through an oscillation between different positions arrives at a unique position within the new group, Kracauer presents the stranger as someone who embraces different positions and thus remains at the margins of both groups. Kracauer's stranger holds together the dualities and antinomies of identities in a more affirmative mode, keeping both positions open rather than demanding the resolution of one over the other, claiming that these very opposites intensify subjectivity to the point that it transcends itself.[103] While Schutz argued that the stranger's critical faculties were only of significance at the point in which the stranger left the liminal zone and approached the new group, Kracauer does not seem to suggest that this approach in itself signifies a departure from the liminal zone. Kracauer's historian enters into the stranger's liminality in order to establish the necessary distance that alerts himself to the pitfalls of participant observation, avoiding a total empathy with the object of inquiry and heightening sensitivity to the significance of things which are otherwise passed off as random or arbitrary. Kracauer insists that 'there are limits to self-effacement', and the surrender of the self that he is recommending is always a strategic projection of the self into the other to such a degree that it does not endanger the constitution of the self. Thus 'self-effacement begets self-expression'.[104] Or, to rephrase this paradox, estrangement begets liberation. The historian is estranged precisely for the purposes of realising the broader horizons of being, a tantalising fantasy of self-affirmation which includes a hypostasisation of negation at its border: 'What is required of the historian is not merely his "*whole* inner man" as he happens to be, but a self which has expanded in the wake of its near-extinction.'[105] The historian's temporal and spatial positioning is also compared to the stranger's ambivalent duplicity. By asserting that the stranger's task for understanding the new in the present involves a simultaneous suspension and recollection of different pasts whose discontinuity displace the continuity of location upon which identity can be fixed, Kracauer is also calling the historian to embark on a similar journey through which consciousness will be formed by the superimposition of fragmentary and discontinuous historical moments.[106]

To fulfil this vision Kracauer insisted on the historian's 'chronological anonymity' – not that his location should be unknown, but that it should exist in the combination of locations.

> The impact of the historian's journey on his mental build further invalidates the commonplace assumption that he is the son of his time. Actually he is the son of at least two times – his own and the time he is investigating. His mind is in a measure unlocalizable: it perambulates without a fixed abode.[107]

Tragedy without redemption

Kracauer's and Simmel's methods resist the tendency toward the disavowal of the stranger's incongruity that Schutz's schema prescribes. However, to enter deeper into the zone of oscillation and disjuncture that Berger describes in *A Seventh Man* it is better to take Wole Soyinka as guide and interpreter.

For Wole Soyinka the tragic hero attacks the violence of displacement primarily by resisting the force that imposes silence.

The Promethean instinct of rebellion channels anguish into a creative purpose which releases man from a totally destructive despair, releasing from him the most energetic, deeply combative inventions, without usurping the territory of the infernal gulf, bridges it with visionary hopes.[108]

What is the 'infernal gulf' that the hero must cross? How does he 'bridge it with visionary hopes'? Can the migrant engage in this 'creative' battle? Or does he embody the condition of defeat that the tragic hero must rebel against? In *A Seventh Man*, the migrant's suffering is muffled by a silence that doesn't even affirm his existence beyond economic utility, and it is this silence which chokes him in solitude.

Soyinka argues that the loss in tragedy is never something abstract or remote, it must be integral with the self. Tragedy speaks of the severance of the self from that which is its essence. Tragedy is a confrontation with the ruptures in the certitudes upon which the origins are founded. Its most poignant expression is found in the experience of 'uprooting, wandering and settling'.[109] Thus the 'infernal gulf' is the gap between identity and non-identity.

The weightiest burden of severance is that of each from self, not of godhead from mankind, and the most perilous aspect of god's journey is that in which the deity must truly undergo the experience of transition. It is a look into the very heart of the phenomena. To fashion a bridge across it was not only Ogun's task but his very nature, and he had first to experience, to surrender his individuation once again ... to the fragmenting process; to be reabsorbed within universal Oneness, the Unconscious, the deep black whirlpool of mythopoetic forces, to immerse himself thoroughly within it, understand its nature and yet by the combative value of the will to rescue and re-assemble himself and emerge wiser, powerful from the draught of cosmic secrets, organising the mystic and the technical forces of earth and cosmos, to forge a bridge for his companions.[110]

There is no hero in *A Seventh Man*. The migrant does not bridge his spatial and temporal displacements, he ricochets between an idealised future and a past that is continuously re-imagined: 'In his imagination every migrant worker is in transit. He remembers the past: he anticipates the future: his aims and recollections make his thoughts a train between the two.'[111]

Soyinka defines this transitional time and space as the fourth stage. He argues that it is from this 'omni-directional' void that tragedy finds its archetypal images. Tragedy exists 'neither in the evocation of the past nor the future', tragedy is not in the acknowledgement of ancestors, the living or the unborn, but in the representation of the 'no-man's-land of transition'.[112] The fourth stage is the representation of the 'immeasurable gulf' that comes between the temporal definitions of identity. It is the representation of the experience of 'dispersion and re-assemblage in racial coming-into-being'.[113] The migrant in *A Seventh Man* also confronts these chasms within identity, he too is shuttling between the tenses, but the reconciliations that he forges are only as expedient as the forgetfulness and the dulling of the senses that repetitive manual labour allows.

The only present reality for the migrant is work and the fatigue which follows it. Leisure becomes alien to him because it forces him to remember how far away he is from everything that he still believes to be his real life. Beyond the present of work and his own exertion, the rest of his life is reduced to a series of fixed images relating to past and future, to his values and hopes. These images are the landmarks of his life, but they remain static; they do not develop... As soon as he stops working, he is haunted by static images. The images are static in themselves and yet they are shifting in a terrible way. He has the impression that his own image and those of his previous life are hurtling through space, like stars travelling in different directions, so that the distance between them is always increasing and becoming greater. From this impression work is the only relief.[114]

Berger juxtaposes the migrant's perception of time with the normal perception of time. In normal time the continuity between the tenses affirms the stability of identity and sustains the belief which Erikson expressed as 'that the self I was yesterday will also be the self I am tomorrow'. Berger represents the dimensions of normal time as a circle that surrounds the self.

Within the circle the past exists in the form of buried and freestanding memories, the future in the form of fears and hopes; the present enters as it occurs and, immediately, the past and the future relate to it. The three form an amalgam which is expressed in the intentionality of the person's actions at that moment. Such intentionality is informed by the past, it exists in the present, and it is directed towards a future. But for the amalgam to be formed,

Death of a stranger

the elements constituting the past and future of his life's time need to be free and unfixed.[115]

The continuity between the tenses and the resultant amalgam can be undermined through instances of irreparable loss. To explore this time of loss, Berger draws analogies between the time of migration and the time of sacrifice, imprisonment and bereavement.

The comparison between the time in migration and imprisonment is based on the similar combination of the loss of the past and the anticipation for the future which forms a block against the present. This comparison also emphasises that for the migrant and the prisoner, the silence which contains the nostalgia to rejoin their beloved in the future is also a marker of the violence of separation in the present.[116] A comparison with the time of sacrifice is also made but rejected because it has limited value in terms of envisaging the deferral of the present. A sacrifice which involves an offering to the future presupposes not just the continuity of social values that are embedded within broader forms of tradition, but sacrifice also provides the social mechanism through which an individual's action is recognised, received and confirmed. This acknowledgement is what the migrant lacks. For even among fellow migrants, with whom he may share the same space, he still does not share the same present.

> They come closest together when they talk about the past. To keep faith with his decision, each man has to picture his own individual future of acknowledgement to himself . . . To construct the picture he goes back to the past. What is characteristic of the migrant worker is not that he sacrifices the present for the future, but that his condition is such that the value of his present sacrifice is denied. This is why his condition resembles imprisonment.[117]

However, the migrant's experience of time is ultimately compared to the bereaved because both are characterised by their need to live again a part of life that is now lost. The compulsion to return is the predominant metaphor for the characterisation of the migrant's time.

If he could re-live it as he originally lived it, he would be able to experience the still open possibilities of the life now ended. But when the bereaved return to the past, they can never entirely forget what has prompted their return; they go back to the past to foretell a death. The past is robbed of its future, which is now the present. To the extent that the bereaved wants to go on sharing the past life of the dead person, his own past becomes fixed. It is then as though the elements of the past line the circumference of the circle, and the future elements withdraw, losing all immediacy.[118]

Freud also argued that the loss of one's country may produce either mourning or melancholia, depending on the 'pathological disposition' of the person.[119] For Freud mourning is the difficult but normal reaction to loss, which when completed leaves the ego free and uninhibited again. However, in melancholia, the loss is also accompanied by a radical disturbance to the individual's self-regard and its

> distinguishing mental features are a profoundly painful dejection, cessation of interest in the outside world, loss of the capacity of love, inhibition of all activity, and a lowering of the self-regarding feelings to a degree that finds utterance in self-reproaches and self-revilings, and culminates in a delusional expectation of punishment.[120]

Berger does not mobilise Freud's distinction between the normal and the pathological, but his account of bereavement, as an attempt to approximate the time of migration seems to incorporate the characteristics of *both* mourning and melancholia. Furthermore, the bereavement Berger represents is not the consequence of the pathological disposition of the individual but the inevitable consequence of the institutionalised conditions to which the migrants are subjected. Berger reads the migrant's bereavement as a symptom of cultural inversions and the abnormality of time in migration.

For the bereaved the 'past acts as a wall',[121] preventing the admission of the present, subordinating the conception of the future to its terms. Only after bereavement passes will the fixity of this relationship be unblocked.

Returning to Soyinka's portrayal of the heroic artist, we can see that tragedy is not simply about loss, but about the cleaving of the gap within identity. It is by entering this position that the proportions of other stages can be measured. Thus, for Soyinka the fourth stage is both a topos and a trope, both a place and a way for being and non-being. The fourth stage is where estrangement defines self-realisation. Thus the redemption that Soyinka proffers is limited to the 'super man' will of the artist.

> Will is the paradoxical truth of destructiveness and creativeness in acting man. Only one who has himself undergone the experience of disintegration, whose spirit has been tested and whose psychic resources laid under stress by the forces most inimical to individual assertion, only he can understand and be the force of fusion between the two contradictions. The resulting sensibility is also the sensibility of the artist, and he is a profound artist only to the degree to which he comprehends and expresses this principle of destruction and re-creation.[122]

When mediated through the hero's will refusal becomes an affirmative expression. And dignity is maintained in the resistance against the subordination of this will. Soyinka's paradoxical portrait of the hero echoes Nietzsche's representation of the wanderer. The subjectivity of the hero and the wanderer share the same indomitable will. It is this will which refuses solidarity and commits them to estrangement within society, and it is this will which finds within estrangement all the idealised social values that society has forsaken. For Nietzsche estrangement is neither a retrogressive step, nor the lack of solidarity, but the progressive step beyond solidarity.

Nietzsche reverses and displaces the conventional opposition between the stranger and the member, not by claiming the position of estrangement as the embodiment of plenitude, but by asserting that the stranger embraces a broader cultural sensibility and rejects any exclusivist obligation to national identity.

The Europeans are becoming more similar to each other; they become more and more detached from the conditions under which races originate that are tied to some climate or class; they become increasingly independent of any *determinate* milieu that would like to inscribe itself for centuries in body and soul with the same demands. Thus an essentially supranational and nomadic type of man is gradually coming up, a type that possesses physiologically speaking a maximum of the art and power of adaptation as its typical distinction.[123]

We who are homeless are too manifold and mixed racially and in our descent, being 'modern men' . . . We are . . . – *good Europeans*, the heirs of Europe, the rich, the oversupplied, but also overly-obligated heirs of thousands of years of European spirit.[124]

With refusal the 'wanderer' is beyond solidarity, but refusal does not constitute detachment. For with this refusal the agency of the stranger is affirmed as it commits itself to the half-way line of affirmation and negation *in* solidarity.

One must have liberated oneself from many things that oppress, inhibit, hold down, and make heavy precisely us Europeans today. The human being of such a beyond who wants to behold the supreme measures of value of his time must first of all 'overcome' this time in himself – this is the test of his strength – and consequently not only his time but also his prior aversion and contradiction *against* this time, his suffering from this time, his un-timeliness, his *romanticism*.[125]

What Nietzsche rebels against is the containment of identity within the categories that truncate subjectivity and its creative contradictions, categories that would, for instance, deny the self the authority to rebel against itself. The phenomenon that Nietzsche most vehemently sought to attack for its imposition of a unitarian identity was nationalism. As he saw it, the perversity of its logic was not just its fixation with a particular representation of origins, but its transposition of this private form of narcissism into cultural chauvinism.[126]

Nietzsche's representation of the 'wanderer' is an attempt to portray a counter-player whose primary characteristic of resilience is a consequence of a clearsightedness. Nietzsche's wanderer uses traditions, rather than being abused by the monolith of a history that confines players to the stereotypes formed by prejudice, deception, pathos and hypocrisy.[127] To preclude any singular association with history, all senses of belonging have to be constantly displaced into the future. 'We children of the future, how *could* we be at home in this today? We feel disfavour for all ideals that might lead one to feel at home in this fragile, broken time of transition . . .'[128] Nietzsche no doubt would see himself as an exemplary 'wanderer', and, as Derrida has noted, this theme of displacement combined with plenitude in the preface to *Ecce Homo* is not a straightforward equivocation over lineage:

> His own identity – the one he means to declare and which, being so out of proportion with his contemporaries, has nothing to do with what they know by this name, behind his name or rather his homonym, Friedrich Nietzsche – the identity he lays claim to here is not his right of contract drawn up with his contemporaries. It has passed to him through the unheard-of contract he has drawn up with himself.[129]

In *Ecce Homo* Nietzsche consistently contradicts himself and of course says that he contradicts himself, he is at never at one with himself – constantly rebounding off other points, never settling for a resolution, without at least suggesting another point from which it could be broken. In order to keep the ability to renounce alive, his identity must always be double and neutral:

> The fortunateness of my existence, its uniqueness perhaps, lies in its fatality: to express it in the form of a riddle, as my father I have already died, as my mother I still live and grow old. This twofold origin, as it were from the highest and lowest rung of the ladder of life, at once *decadent* and *beginning* – this if anything explains the neutrality, that freedom from party in relation to the total problem of life which perhaps distinguishes me. I have subtler sense of signs of ascent and decline than any man has ever had. I am the teacher *par excellence* in this matter – I know both, I am both.[130]

Thus Nietzsche chooses for himself an identity which will refuse any fixed identifications, or as Derrida observed 'he advances behind masks or pseudonyms without proper names'.[131]

Nietzsche embraced estrangement as a precondition for critical consciousness. These processes of juxtaposing traditions and histories, mobilising the ruses of identity, oscillating between the particular and the general – the seeing of things from a distance in order to see them anew – are the hallmarks of a critical perspective within modernity.

The wanderer speaks – If one would like to see our European morality for once as it looks from a distance, and if one would like to measure it against other moralities, past and future, then one has to proceed like a wanderer who wants to know how high the towers in a town are: he leaves the town.[132]

Conclusion: the truth of strangers

The last entry in Simmel's diary reads: 'I know that I shall die without intellectual heirs, and that is as it should be. My legacy will be like cash, distributed to many heirs, each transforming his part according to his nature – a use which will no longer reveal its indebtedness to this heritage.'[133] This critical mixture of self-effacement with self-aggrandisement is the destiny and the origin of the stranger. Like cash, the example of the stranger serves as the *lingua franca* which mediates the exchanges between two subjects with opposed interests. However, like cash the stranger's exteriority presupposes a correspondence with internal markers. There can be no sedimentary traces of otherness. Simmel's stranger does not seem bound by historical boundaries, he exists in the 'immediate presentness' of modernity.

Although insisting that the stranger's objectivity is not a consequence of detachment, Simmel must nevertheless selectively truncate the subjectivity of the stranger, before the specific and positive interaction between the stranger and the group can begin to resemble his own image of the oscillating pattern of engagement for the inquiring mind. When a name bears a stigma, anonymity may prove to be a strategic way around the encrusted obstacles of petty prejudice, but both the universal availability of this position and its supposed neutrality in terms of critical investigation need far deeper scrutiny. Marx alerted us to the fact that social mobility is not necessarily social liberation, it could simply mean vulnerability to exploitation. Berger's *A Seventh Man* not only testifies to Marx's observation, but also suggests that the unity of identity for Simmel's stranger is precariously dependent on the coincidence of two diametrically opposed principles: nearness and remoteness. The failure of this synthesis would no doubt result in utter displacement, and the conventional criticism that is directed at this perspective is that its overriding tendency is not towards an engagement with reality, but towards an aestheticisation and an abstraction from reality and a retreat into the interior.[134] This criticism is, however, far from an adequate response to the complexities raised by Simmel's work.

To say that Simmel's value is limited to aesthetics is to reproduce the caesura between art and politics. Simmel's stranger bears a direct relationship to Baudelaire's *flâneur* because both figures embody the author's ambivalence towards modernity. In Baudelaire's words:

it is an immense joy to set up house in the heart of the multitude, amid the ebb and flow of movement, in the midst of the fugitive and the infinite. To be away from the home and yet to feel oneself everywhere at home; to see the world, to be at the centre of the world, and yet to remain hidden from the world... The spectator is a *prince* who everywhere rejoices in his incognito.[135]

Anonymity enhances the *flâneur's* agency at the precise moment in which he conflates the dialectic between choice and distance afforded by travel with the more generalised claim for clarity of vision. And furthermore, the subjectivity of the *flâneur* is not threatened by the confrontation with the foreign, because the foreign represents the space which the *flâneur* wishes to inhabit. This mission to estrangement has thus begun with an inoculation against the foreign.[136]

The *flâneur*, the stranger, the gambler, the artist are all types which were valorised by the early sociologists of modernity. They were transgressive figures whose liminality directed attention away from the 'flatness of reified existence',[137] and offered examples of the dislocative potentials that lurk within the margin. What Simmel, Benjamin, Nietzsche and Kracauer foresaw was that with the advent of modernity the margin was to displace the centre. Their response was twofold and contradictory: to identify types in which the emancipatory values could be projected, and to reproduce the tensions and the diversity of the margin within the form of their writing.

Simmel's use of aphorisms, paradoxes and antinomies was not merely a stylistic device. Dualisms permeate his work in a fundamental sense. For Simmel, perspectivism implies a constant distanciation of time and space; thought and object; it restrains engagement and commitment, while maintaining both the critical distance and the anonymity of the writer as witness, rather than as an intervening agent. Even his mode of essay- writing facilitates a relational way of examining phenomena.

Simmel's essay 'The Stranger' has been misread in two ways; firstly its significance has been limited to the sociology of deviance and marginality,[138] and secondly it has been used as the theoretical frame which can redeem Simmel from his own deviance and marginality within the academy.[139] In both cases critics have failed to recognise it as a metaphor for a new critical perspective in modernity. It was an exemplary essay because it articulates with stunning elegance and precision the contradictions implicit in the hankerings of metropolitan modernism.

By foregrounding the figure of the stranger we can see how Simmel participates in what Spivak calls 'tropological deconstruction',[140] he shows 'that the basis of a truth claim is no more than a trope'. But in this process he has not escaped the problems of truth claims, and we should not be blind to the processes in which the stranger (like other types eulogised by modernists) is objectified, how representations also participate in the appropriation of alterity. For the logic of making counter-claims for truth repeats the very structures and practices that it contests, as it invariably truncates the subjectivity of others in order to pass them off as the idealised type, which in this case is the stranger. Or to quote Spivak once again: 'the other must always be constituted by way of consolidating the self'.[141]

Notes

1   The principle of 'beginning again', Benjamin argued, is both the distinguishing mark of the dialectician, and the axiom for the theatre of emigration: 'The theatre of emigration must start again at the beginning; not just its stage, but also its plays must be built anew.' W. Benjamin, 'The Country Where it is Forbidden to Mention the Proletariat', *Understanding Brecht*, translated by Anna Bostock, London, Verso, 1988, p. 37.

2   In the television production of *Another Way of Telling*, John Berger and Jean Mohr pondered over this question, implying that the intimacy gained by having worked so close to Sassal should have revealed some foresight into his future.

3   B. Brecht, *Poems* 1913–1956, ed. J. Willett and R. Manheim, London, Methuen, 1976, p. 363.

4   J. Torrance, *Estrangement, Alienation and Exploitation*, London, Macmillan, 1977, p. 17. On the confusion between alienation, estrangement and objectification, and the various renderings of *Aufhebung* as 'abolition',

'annulment', 'suspension', and 'transcendence', see R. C. Tucker, *The Marx–Engels Reader*, New York, W. W. Norton, 1978, pp. xli–xlii.

5   Janet Wolff has shown the sexual bias in Simmel's notion of the stranger and the modernist's notion of the *flâneur*. See 'The Invisible *Flâneuse*: Women and the Literature of Modernity'. *Theory Culture & Society*, vol. 2, no. 3, 1985. It should also be noted that when I identify the stranger through the male pronoun it is because I am referring to a typification that has already presumed masculinity. When addressing the construction of the figure of the stranger in social theory it is almost exclusively a masculinist zone.

6   G. Simmel, 'The Stranger', in K. H. Wolff, ed., *The Sociology of Georg Simmel*, New York, Free Press, 1950, p. 402.

7   *Ibid.*

8   Z. Bauman: 'Modernity and Ambivalence', in M. Featherstone (ed.), *Global Culture*, London, Sage, 1990, p. 148.

9   G. Simmel, *op. cit.*, p. 402.

10   *Ibid.*, p. 403.

11   *Ibid.*, p. 408.

12   *Ibid.*, p. 406.

13   *Ibid.*, p. 403.

14   Z. Bauman, *op. cit.*, p. 150.

15   *Ibid.*

16   J. Brodsky. 'The Condition We Call Exile', *The New York Review*, 21 January 1988, p. 16.

17   *Ibid.*, p. 19.

18   *Ibid.*, p. 20.

19   G. C. Spivak, 'Explanation and Culture: Marginalia', *In Other Worlds*, New York, Methuen, 1987. The differences and oppositions that are mobilised in colonial practice and scrutinised by colonial discourse do not tend towards either negation or reconciliation. Spivak focuses our attention not towards the seemless syncretism in colonial space but rather to the constant production of fissures and supplements. Her analysis provokes the conventional narratives of domination and resistance by breaking with the binary models which polarised the moments of subjugation and rebellion.

20   A. Nandy, *The Intimate Enemy*, Delhi, Oxford University Press, 1983.

21   S. Sontag, *Styles of Radical Will*, New York, Delta, 1981, p. 6.

22   H. Levin, 'Literature and Exile', *Refractions*, New York, Oxford University Press, 1966, p. 74.

23   *Ibid.*, p. 81.

24   G. Steiner, *Extraterritorial*, London, Faber and Faber, 1972, p. 27.

25   *Ibid.*, p. viii.

26   *Ibid.*, p. 11.

27   Zuzana M. Pick, 'The Dialectical Wanderings of Exile', *Screen*, vol. 30, no. 4, autumn 1989, p. 48.

28   *Ibid.*, p. 64.

29   J. Clifford and G. E. Marcus (eds.), *Writing Culture: The Poetics and Politics of Ethnography*, Berkeley, University of California Press, 1986.

30   *Ibid.*, pp. 195–6.

31   *Ibid.*, p. 230.

32   Ibid., p. 198.
33   G. C. Spivak, 'Reading *The Satanic Verses*', p. 41.
34   P. Gilroy, 'Cruciality and the Frog's Perspective', *Third Text*, no. 5, winter 1988/9, p. 39.
35   Ibid., p. 38.
36   Ibid., p. 40.
37   Ibid., p. 39.
38   K. Mercer, 'Black Art and the Burden of Representation', *Third Text*, no. 10, spring 1990, p. 76.
39   H. K. Bhabha, 'Difference, Discrimination, and the Discourse of Colonialism', in F. Barker et al. (ed.) *The Politics of Theory*, Colchester, University of Essex, 1983, p. 204.
40   H. K. Bhabha, 'The Other Question', *Screen*, vol. 24, December 1983, p. 18.
41   H. K. Bhabha, 'Of Man and Mimicry: The Ambivalence of Colonial Discourse', *October*, vol. 28, spring 1984, p. 127.
42   H. K. Bhabha, 'Signs Taken for Wonders: Questions of Ambivalence and Authority under a Tree Outside Delhi, May 1817', *Critical Inquiry*, vol. 12, autumn 1985, p. 148.
43   H. K. Bhabha, 'What Does The Black Man Want?', *New Formations*, no. 1, spring, 1987, p. 119.
44   H. K. Bhabha, 'Interrogating Identity', *Identity*, London, Institute of Contemporary Arts, Documents, no. 6, 1987, pp. 6–7.
45   For a more detailed analysis of Bhabha's essays see my 'Reading DissemiNation', *Millennium*, vol. 20, no. 3 Winter 1991.
46   G. C. Spivak, *In Other Worlds*, p. 200.
47   J. Berger, *A Fortunate Man: The Story of a Country Doctor* (with Jean Mohr), Harmondsworth, Allen Lane, 1967.
48   J. Berger, *A Seventh Man* (with Jean Mohr and Sven Blomberg), Harmondsworth, Penguin, 1975.
49   Simmel, *op. cit.*, p. 404.
50   *A Fortunate Man*, p. 108.
51   Ibid., p. 99.
52   Ibid., p. 108.
53   Simmel, *op. cit.*, p. 402.
54   *A Fortunate Man*, p. 52.
55   Ibid.
56   Ibid., p. 54.
57   Ibid., p. 62.
58   Ibid.
59   Ibid., p. 61.
60   Ibid., p. 57.
61   Ibid., p. 89.
62   Ibid., p. 109.
63   Ibid., p. 111.
64   J. Berger, *The Times* (London), 22 November 1972.
65   H. Kaplan, 'The Psychopathology of Nostalgia', *The Psychoanalytic Review*, vol. 74, no. 4, winter 1987, p. 468.

66 J. Berger, *A Seventh Man*, p. 225.
67 *Ibid.*, p. 229.
68 *Ibid.*, pp. 92–4.
69 *Ibid.*, p. 104.
70 *Ibid.*, p. 197.
71 M. Bakhtin, *The Dialogic Imagination*, Austin, University of Texas Press, 1981, p. 293.
72 A. Kefala, *The Alien*, St Lucia, Makar, 1973, p. 5.
73 J. Berger, *A Seventh Man*, p. 28 and p. 32.
74 *Ibid.*, p. 18.
75 *Ibid.*
76 *Ibid.*, p. 43.
77 *Ibid.*, p. 57.
78 *Ibid.*, p. 58.
79 *Ibid.*, p. 29.
80 *Ibid.*, pp. 66–8.
81 *Ibid.*, p. 90.
82 *Ibid.*, pp. 216–20.
83 *Ibid.*, p. 7.
84 A. Schutz, *Collected Papers*, vol. II, The Hague, Martinus Nijhoff, 1964.
85 *Ibid.*, p. 93.
86 *Ibid.*, p. 95.
87 *Ibid.*
88 *Ibid.*, p. 97.
89 *Ibid.*, p. 98.
90 *Ibid.*, p. 99.
91 J. Berger, *A Seventh Man*, p. 118.
92 D. Frisby, *Fragments of Modernity*, Cambridge, Polity, 1985, pp. 117–34.
93 S. Kracauer, *History, The Last Things Before the Last*, New York, Oxford University Press.
94 *Ibid.*, p. 83.
95 A. Schutz, *op. cit.*
96 *Ibid.*, p. 91.
97 *Ibid.*, p. 92.
98 *Ibid.*, p. 119.
99 *Ibid.*, p. 91.
100 *Ibid.*, p. 104.
101 *Ibid.*
102 Kracauer, *op. cit.*, p. 84.
103 *Ibid.*, p. 103.
104 *Ibid.*, p. 92.
105 *Ibid.*
106 See also D. N. Radowick, 'The Last Things Before the Last: Kracauer and History', *New German Critique*, no. 41, spring–summer 1987.
107 Kracauer, *op. cit.*, p. 93. Martin Jay also noted that Kracauer's profound sense of marginality was twice born; it began with his own bodily

disfigurement – his very appearance inspired contorted, cross-cultural, hybrid images that defied any unified identity; and the experience of exile which heightened his fascination with the condition of extra-territoriality, as it also sharpened his polemic against the conventional categories of contextualisation and finitude in social inquiry. M. Jay, *Permanent Exiles: Essays on the Intellectual Migration from Germany to America*, New York, Columbia University Press, 1985.
108 W. Soyinka, *Art, Dialogue & Outrage*, Ibadan, New Horn Press, 1988, p. 25.
109 *Ibid.*, p. 34.
110 *Ibid.*, p. 29.
111 J. Berger, *A Seventh Man*, p. 64.
112 Soyinka, *op. cit.*, p. 27.
113 *Ibid.*, p. 34.
114 J. Berger, *A Seventh Man*, p. 171.
115 *Ibid.*, p. 176.
116 *Ibid.*, p. 178.
117 *Ibid.*, p. 188.
118 *Ibid.*, p. 177. Schutz also makes a sentimental mention of this analogy between the time of migration and the time of bereavement. However by leaving it underdeveloped he reinforces his characterisation of the increasing negativity of a stranger's experience as he argues that for the migrant the sense of immediacy is overwhelmed by static memories. Developments are frozen. What was once unique and thriving becomes typical and deformed, and the other is no longer accessible as a whole but remains fragmentary. See Schutz, *op. cit.*, p. 112.
119 S. Freud, *On Metapsychology: The Theory of Psychoanalysis*, translated by J. Strachey, Harmondsworth, Penguin, 1984, p. 252.
120 *Ibid.*
121 J. Berger, *A Seventh Man*, p. 178.
122 W. Soyinka, *op. cit.*, p. 27.
123 F. Nietzsche, *Beyond Good and Evil*, translated by W. Kaufmann, New York, Vintage, 1966, p. 176.
124 F. Nietzsche, *The Gay Science*, translated by W. Kaufmann, New York, Vintage, 1974, p. 340.
125 *Ibid.*, p. 343.
126 *Ibid.*, p. 339.
127 F. Nietzsche, *The Use and Abuse of History*, translated by A. Collin, Indianapolis, The Library of Liberal Arts, 1957.
128 F. Nietzsche, *The Gay Science*, p. 338.
129 J. Derrida, *The Ear of the Other*, New York, Schoken, 1958, p. 8.
130 F. Nietzsche, *Ecce Homo*, translated by R. J. Hollingdale, Harmondsworth, Penguin, p. 38.
131 Derrida, *op. cit.*, p. 7.
132 F. Nietzsche, *The Gay Science*, p. 342.
133 G. Simmel, *On Individuality and Social Forms*, Chicago, Chicago University Press, 1971, p. x.
134 D. Frisby, *Sociological Impression: A Reassessment of Georg Simmel's*

Social Theory, London, Heinemann, 1981. D. N. Levine, 'The Structure of Simmel's Social Thought', in K. H. Wolff (ed.), *Essays on Sociology, Philosophy & Aesthetics: George Simmel*, New York Free Press, 1965.

135 C. Baudelaire, *The Painter of Modern Life and Other Essays*, London, Phaidon, 1964, p. 9.

136 These observations are supported by Spivak's more systematic analysis of the correlation between homoerotic fantasies and the foreclosure of the other's subjectivity. In regard to Baudelaire's poetry and the rhetorical strategies for projecting images of the self and the other she concludes that 'the poet-speaker retains a syntactically impregnable house and a rhetorically enigmatic subjectivity . . . not only the power but even the self-undermining of the man may be operated by the troping of the woman'. See Gayatri Chakravorty Spivak, 'Imperialism and Sexual Difference', *The Oxford Literary Review*, vol. 8, nos 1–2, 1986, p. 228.

137 D. Frisby, *Fragments of Modernity*, p. 67.

138 See Lewis Coser, 'The Stranger in the Academy', *Georg Simmel*, Englewood Cliffs, Prentice-Hall, 1965.

139 In one of the more noteworthy accounts of this controversy, Lewis Coser conflates the difference between a stranger and a rebel by drawing an artificial borderline between the academy and the public. 'The pressures on his role set exerted by these role partners led to appropriate modifications of self-definitions and to appropriate role appropriate . . . [As in his analysis of the stranger] . . . He was inorganically appended to the academy, yet he was an organic member of the group. He could afford to maintain such a difficult marginal role because he found support and encouragement among his nonacademic listeners' (Coser, p. 36). Coser fails to realise that if the individual who challenges the conventional roles has not come from beyond the boundaries of the group, then this individual is a rebel, not a stranger. The rebel can challenge the radix in two ways; either by showing the contradiction between particular and general rules, or by trying to expand the parameters of the radix to a more permissive level. The rebel need not wish to subvert the fundaments of the radix, and the rebel's vision is not necessarily formed through primary experiences which are alien to the group. For the rebel, the rigidity of structure leads to non-conformity, but transgressions are recuperated back to the radix as evidence of innovation or grander vision. The stranger, however, does not start from within, he or she does not move to the periphery and return in order to instruct the centre of its waywardness, unlike the rebel who is always firmly bound to the radix, the stranger having come from elsewhere is by definition excluded from the centre.

140 Spivak, *op. cit.*, p. 225.

141 *Ibid.*, p. 229.

4

Under the silken sky

Home is bordered by exile and exile is limited by home
The romantic tradition of exile emphasises that identity was either suspended or cauterised by the separation from the homeland. On the other side of this lament is the claim that the true essence of identity exists only in the past. That once upon a time, and prior to the traumatic separation from the homeland, the mythical unity of an unalienated identity actually roamed free with nature. The integrity of this myth rests on the assumption not just that identity was unrepressed, but that it was not even conscious of estrangement arising within identity. Exile stands as the exact counterpoint, it is the commencement of the consciousness of estrangement in identity. Exile puts that prior state of unalienated nature in quotation marks. If exile is that point at which a gap is opened between resemblances and identities, then exile is also used to announce the point beyond – the place in which the gap can be imagined as reconciled. Before and after exile there is the imagined bonding of resemblances and identities. Before and after exile it is assumed that there was and there will be a home.

But when and where does exile begin? Juliet Mitchell observed that Freud's theory revolves around the question of the past. For Freud the conscious past begins after the repression of Oedipal wishes by the castration complex destroying with it the fantasy of an eternally satisfying relationship with the mother.[1] Homi Bhabha has noted that in Lacan the enunciation of this gap arrives with the entry into language. Exile replays, as it serves as the metaphor for this primal but forgotten trauma. The exile's arrival into an/other language, an/other symbolic (one that is foreign from the mother-tongue/country) accentuates the incommensurability between resemblances and identities.² This primal exile is perhaps one of the most fundamental metaphors with which the more generalised and pervasive experience of estrangement in modernity has been articulated. Both the past and self-identity 'begin' with the separation from the mother-tongue/country and the discontent with the law of the father: 'He lies with his head between her legs . . . Everything here is re-enactment, everything here is return. Home is the return to where distance did not yet count'.³ What I want to argue is that it is counter productive to determine or yearn for any singular locus of identity. The meaning of exile is that once it disrupts the embeddedness of the self-image with identity, once the self-image has become a palimpsest of other-images, then the originary identity is displaced by a constant series of negations. Affirmation of a fixed identity can never return without the shadow of denial. Consequently, we need to radicalise our understanding of identity in modernity by acknowledging the ubiquity of rupture.

The term exile is used not only to demarcate that geo-political passage out of a place of origin and towards an uncertain place beyond the familiar horizons, but to signify the more generalised passages in the psycho-social domain which involve a fundamental questioning of what might be called the innate points of reference. I link exile to the phenomenon of modernity in order to characterise the ruptures and transitions intrinsic to it.

The absence of mutuality is the fundamental starting point in Berger's novels. The consciousness of this absence is not deemed as something inevitable but as the commencement of another quest. But what is Berger searching for, and how is the contestation against the absence of mutuality lined with a desire for something else? This quest for mutuality is framed within the dialectics of exile and integration, which, in turn, is examined through the representations of crises in male identity and the ambivalent identifications with the male other and woman. Both the male other and woman are the metaphors through which and with which this crisis is articulated.

Berger's identification with the male other is not an idealisation. While the marginalised other is invoked to proffer an initiative and a maturity that stands in contrast to the impotence and narcissism of the dominant self, his identifications never lose track of the distance between the other and the self. Berger constantly positions his authorial self between the two, like 'a shuttle on a loom: repeatedly it approaches and withdraws, closes in and takes its distance'.⁴ Through the repeated oscillations between closeness to and distance from the other, an intimacy emerges. Meaning is formed as in the act of metaphor, through the combination and mobilisation of dissimilars. Both the position and the metaphor of the male other provide the ground and the edge that make Berger's writing possible.

The position of woman in this crisis and her role in Berger's writing is even more complicated. In Berger's novels women are never central characters, but *woman* is the central subject. Woman bears the brunt of both male cynicism and sentimentality. Woman is blamed for and called upon to rescue man from his loss of certitude. Through the dreams, hopes and sexual desires of his male protagonists, Berger begins a journey into the unknown. These journeys, which may be precipitated by voluntary or involuntary displacements of the self, invariably construct woman as their horizon. Yet the protagonists never find a homely end.

As Freud observed, this ambivalence towards the maternal space is defined by the omnipotence of the mother – for she can either provide or renege the maternal love – and the contest between the son and the father for this love: 'a mother's importance, unique, without parallel, established unalterably for a whole lifetime as the first and strongest love-object and as the prototype of all later love-relations'.[5] Woman thus dominates man's desire, man both resents this domination and is confined to it.

While the term misogyny needs to be inserted into the configurations of modernity in order to focus on the crucial role of sexualised ambivalence that attends exile, I do not want to confine my analysis to an exercise in corrective interpretation. The politics of blaming, which man mastered with every fantasy of woman, must not be recycled. Rather than tallying up stereotypes, attention needs to be directed to the discursive and heterogeneous process that produces identities.

Misogyny implies that identities exist like fixed targets, and while there are characters who express outright misogyny it is clear that this isn't even half the story: there are both antagonisms and agonisms, and what eventually emerges and is exemplified in Berger's novel G[6] is what Alice Jardine has named *gynesis* – the putting of women into discourse,[7] or what Gayatri Spivak calls the 'double displacement' of woman, whereby the gesture with which man secures the taking of woman as a model for the unknowable also displaces the figure of woman twofold in discourse.[8]

The configurations that interweave the exile of man with the certitudes that grounded his identity and the figuring of woman in modern discourse can be situated on three levels; firstly these intersections are related to an ambivalent stereotyping of women – oscillating between misogyny and idealisation; secondly, the anxieties over the loss of male identity also figure woman through uncanny and nostalgic manifestations; and finally, the search for new identities which affirms a desire for the other and actively confronts the unknown produces a critical reappraisal of the limits and horizons of self-identity. These configurations will be examined by following the representation of exile and woman in Berger's novels.

A Painter of Our Time

Berger's first novel[9] set out to explore the themes that were to preoccupy him throughout his writing career. The relationship between the artist and society that is scrutinised here is framed by the ongoing examination of the ontological question of exile and integration in modernity. The protagonist is Janos, a painter and a revolutionary who for most of the novel is in exile. The novel, set in 1956, begins with the narrator, John, announcing that Janos has mysteriously vanished. John, who considers himself to be Janos's best friend, is stunned. While wandering through Janos's abandoned studio, he stumbles upon a diary. The story unfolds as we read Janos's reflections which are sporadically supplemented by John's comments. Through the diary we learn about Janos's thoughts on art and politics, get a glimpse of his relationship with his wife Diana and his fellow exile Max, and most importantly it reveals his undying but utterly private relationship with his old friend Laszlo; a poet and a revolutionary who stayed in Hungary, and whose execution precipitated Janos's return.

Pervasive estrangement

The condition of Janos's exile in England is the misery of being surrounded with a hostile and superficial milieu. His colleagues at the art school in which he teaches are mostly self-serving, secretive and defensive,[10] the gallery directors and critics are of course suave but stupid slaves of fashion,[11] even the horrible weather is a hindrance to this 'realist' painter: 'It is this fog that makes me feel most a foreigner.

I hate it so much . . . I rage against it – like it was an injustice, like something that's been done to my eyes by the English'.[12] The only person Janos has any sympathy for is someone who also stands outside the hegemonic discourse of metropolitan culture – his neighbour, an unlikely butcher whose 'Sunday portraits' while being naive and provincial possess a glimmer of 'real' sensuality. Throughout his diary England is constantly compared to his homeland. The past in Hungary is imbued with all the qualities of organic unity, moral and social integrity, and every recollection is brought forward only to reinforce the condemnation of England as intrinsically fragmented, abstract and hypocritical. The integration of politics and art, which Berger rather problematically portrays as the only form of real experience, is positioned as either a figment in Janos's memory or a faint hope in the imminence of revolution in his distant homeland. It appears that estrangement does not threaten Janos's sense of self-worth. He considers himself too strong for consolation, the only emotional nourishment he demands is the ability to wander through the city and to wonder about its inhabitants. Contact and engagement do not seem essential, in fact his estrangement seems to enhance the sharpness of his observations, and paradoxically fuels his fantasy of self-reliance.

The primacy of exile in identity

The fundamental exile is of course the originary one – the exile from the homeland. The primacy of exile is related by Janos on two levels; firstly he suggests that the loss of his homeland also marks the consciousness of his dependence on it for his identity – this echoes Freud's theory that identity begins after the traumatic separation from the mother and the repression of the castration complex. However, there is also the further suggestion that the English natives have forgotten this trauma and so remain unconscious of the antagonistic delineations of their own identity. Thus it is the exile's loss of nationality that not only affirms his nationalism but grounds his sense of belonging:

Civil war usually begins after national defeat. The English have forgotten what it is to experience either. From this comes their assumption that a person's nationality is the primary fact about him – coming even before sex, let alone class or political beliefs. I never fully realized that I was Hungarian until I came to England.[13]

Not one but two exiles

The stated counterpoint to Janos's exile is his friend Max: a permanent refugee who literally holds his identity in reserve, protecting it by proclaiming in advance that, his every performance in the present is only half-hearted, a shadow of what he was, or a mere hint of what he could be. Yet for Janos exile without recommencement is atrophy. He rejects the position of exile which entails an outright refusal to participate in the present.

There is a time when every refugee lives in a no-man's land. He must. Yet his mind is not there. It is backwards in regret, forwards in fear or hope. But Max has camped there in no-man's-land now for twenty years. The way he has made it cosy with his nonchalance, his charm, and his hand-made shoes, strikes many, I suppose, as heroic. In fact, it is detestable. He has no sense of duty or responsibility towards anything except his past, which has now become nothing but his pride. A refugee is nothing until he ceases to be one. Max has tried to turn it into an honourable profession. Consequently he has become the most parochial man I know...

I have fought in myself against everything that he has become: right from the beginning, because after there is no one place where you can begin to fight. Every time that I have arrived in a new city or a new country, I have been tempted to establish myself – in my own eyes at least – with the memory of what little security, prestige, achievement I had won in the last place... And always I have resisted this. I have not denied my past, ... But I have clung to the idea of the present being a culmination. . . . .

You arrive somewhere alone. And then you want to take out your memories, which are also dreams, and hang them round your room – like pictures. And between each picture you think of placing an imaginary mirror with your own face in it. That is how you furnish a room with the past. . . . But I have preferred . . . to walk the new streets. The staring eyes of those who have noticed me – an obvious foreigner – have challenged me, and I have always accepted that challenge. . . . The process of learning is the process of constantly beginning again . . .

We cannot be Virgin Marys. Yet when the world is very rough it is easier to be a spinster and only dream and judge. How many spinster artists and spinster intellectuals there are today![14]

Resistance to regression

Janos's identity is thus formed in the reaction against the permanence of loss which calcifies the identity of a permanent refugee, and also a reaction against the presuming wholeness of identity that empowers the locals' challenging eyes. For Janos, identity is in the oscillation between the poles of negation and affirmation. Unlike the English, whose life isn't scarred by a series of traumatic ruptures, Janos sees his identity as constituted by the very succession of beginnings. His sense of purpose is built anew and upon the culmination of each stage – the end of one life marks the beginning of another. Janos thus sees his identity as the patchwork of multiple exiles.

Exile and the paradox of representation

A Painter of Our Time reveals two forms of displacement – identity and representation – both of which are premised on a splitting of time. While demonstrating that exile invariably displaces identity, Berger also shows that the splitting is necessary for the conjunctions of representation. Both the paintings of the exiled artist and the story told by the native narrator presuppose the deferral of the present, and work towards the idealised merger between past and future. In this portrait of the artist as an exile, Berger is also simultaneously investigating the necessity of exile in art, and the primacy of alienation in representation.

Through the diaries of Janos, Berger reflects on the paradoxes of art and exile. The basis to both art and exile is contradictory, staked between the twin poles of nostalgia and utopia; art calls for the integration between image and object, a unity which can only occur *in* utopia, whereas exile reveals that this demand can only be expressed *through* nostalgia. For as long as authenticity is premised on the intersection of utopian conjunctions, and the form of nostalgia, the enunciation of banishment from authentic lived experience but also the yearning for it, then this configuration of the utopian and the nostalgic will remain unrequited. Nostalgia does not erase the gaps between the desired image and the idealised object, but it begins within the reinscription of this gap: 'Nostalgia is the repetition that mourns the inauthenticity of all repetition and denies the repetition's capacity to form identity'.[15] Nostalgia is the enunciation of the absence of utopia, the separation of the image from its object. For if utopia is expressed only by nostalgia then utopia will always remain a point beyond the horizon of representation, eluding the very demand of representation. Janos's diary is preoccupied with the paradoxical nexus between art and exile, and the identification of the artist's position in society. He concludes: art cannot be used to preserve experience, art is born from the compulsion to find in a lost object a significance that can bear on both the past and the future; and art emerges in between the disavowal of the absence of the originary experience and the designation of its transcendental presence.[16] Thus the nexus between art and exile, between nostalgia and utopia, arises between the contradictions of the originary experience and its mediated representation. Against the claim that any lived experience possesses a reality that is not negotiable, that it cannot be transferred across to a mediated language, is the secondary claim, that mediated language can offer a structure within which insight into, and translation of, the lived experience can occur. Janos insists that it is through the merger between past and future that the sense of the present is heightened, but this claim also comes perilously close to bypassing the present altogether.

When Janos claims that the artist during work 'straddles time',[17] he is expressing that specific yearning for a union with both object and its representation. It is here that his nostalgia, in both its past and future orientations, takes root and finds routes, culminating in his gigantic work *The Games*. This great work is to be his ultimate reaction against the introversion of the reified and insular variety of nostalgia, but also an expression of his own desire for transcendence, the unity of subject with form. This last work must in every sense be larger than life, its expanse is the opening of the absent dialogue, a defiance of the limited parameters of the existing culture.[18] In contradistinction to the gigantic is the miniature, and implicit within this form is a retreat into a private, silent and purified nostalgia. The miniature is an escape from, rather than a contestation with the boundaries of the present. It is a fragile attempt to reconstruct and contain the uncontaminated memories of the past. There is no desire to capture the past with the intention of projecting it into the future. The miniature as opposed to the gigantic marks a singular return to the past as if it were possible to live in a timeless utopia.

Max epitomises the exile who is singularly obsessed with his past. For Janos such a retreat not only involves a truncation of identity and a regression in time, but is also a rereat that admits no escape. It is an unconditional surrender. Janos does his best to resist this and construct for himself a counter-position. While he admits that he has been 'cut off' from the time and place where his identity was organically integrated into the vital dynamics of the present, exile has not precluded the ability to 'look forward'.

Could it be shown that Janos's need to dismiss Max's nostalgia is also related to a repression of his own nostalgia, that his very aspirations for the new and future self are also rooted in the past, that the proximity between his aspirations and the image offered by Max threatens the mirroring effect of Janos's possible future self thus compelling him to withdraw the comparisons all the more vehemently? For as the narrator observes, Janos is too strong to be nostalgic, but nevertheless he is haunted by the exile from the place where his identity can stand for what it *is*. In order to work, Janos must also have grounds for hope: this is why the central figure in his diary is Laszlo, for the memories of Laszlo mark the possibilities of both the heroic past and an idealised future. The loss of the homeland becomes a threat to Janos's identity only at the point when Laszlo is executed. Janos can admit defeat in the past but refuses to abdicate his future. For Janos, exile does not mark a new beginning as his diary proclaims, but it is a strategic retreat. Janos uses his exile in England as the space in which he can gain exemption from the present. Hence Janos's counter-position is similar to Max's in that it is also premised on a relative disavowal of the present. For neither Janos nor Max demonstrates an active engagement with the present. While Max regresses into the past, Janos lives in that nameless state which constantly juggles the past in one hand and the future in the other. Neither of them fully embodies the idea that identity can begin only with exile. Janos accepts the proposition that the dialectics of identity are synonymous with the dialectics of exile – that a new identity is formed as it is separated from that which it is not. But the possibility of living through this process is precluded not by his conscious strategy but by his unconscious desires. Identity and non-identity remain in a binary opposition that mutually excludes the homeland from the place of exile.

Another no-man's-land as nostalgia returns

Janos's perpetual distance from both England and Hungary casts a shadow over any neat reconciliation between the two. When thinking of an English landscape he remembers a place in Hungary where he and his friend Laszlo lost their virginity. From this juxtaposition between place and memory a reverie is enacted that restages the arrivals and departures that traversed and shaped his identity. While thinking of the women they made love with, he says: 'They fled the country in 1919. No more is known. We were a generation of unfinished stories. But we did tell them to one another'.[19] If the past is an unfinished story, which nevertheless had both a speaker and a listener, the present not only has no listener but is also a story without a beginning, let alone a middle or an end. Janos's declaration that his new life in each country is the repetition of the act of beginning again is not followed up with a story that will express such a beginning, it is followed only by earnest declarations that fight against his own solitude as much as anything else. His place remains ambiguous and he appears unaffected by the other political struggles.[20] While Max seems to have submerged beneath experience, Janos remains above it, for as he notes: 'Max is the opposite side of my coin'.[21] And the coin of this exile has two sides; detachment and exemption.

Detachment and exemption

Berger insists on a differentiation amongst the two forms of exile: detachment and exemption. As in the difference between Brancusi and Picasso,[22] the difference between Janos's and Max's exile is in their relationship to work. Janos's exemption is directly related to his work – to pursue his work he builds a fortress of solitude: 'In the past I recognized myself in the critical events in which I took part. But now for ten years in this secluded and fortunate country my life has been eventless... Such a state of affairs, however, leads to a loss of a proper sense of time'.[23] In contradistinction, Max's refusal to work is his defensive fortress: it protects his self-image as it limits the admission of the present in such a way that it will either console him for the pains of exile or will confirm the 'superiority' of his past. Janos exempts himself from the horizontal surface of social engagement in order to investigate further the formal complexities within the vertical planes of his work. In contradistinction Max's detachment has sealed off the past, preserved it in a frame that can testify to loss and pre-empts any further engagement. Neither strategy will suffice in the long run: Janos cannot autonomously generate the purpose and context that will give his work meaning, and Max will never escape his suffering by simply making a lifeless spectacle of exile.

The loss of Laszlo and the loss of time and hope

The protective enclosure of Janos's exemption fractures as he learns of Laszlo's execution. If the 'other side' – the repulsive side – of Janos's coin is personified by Max, then the attracting and virtuous side is personified by Laszlo. It was with Laszlo that Janos's journey began. And if there is a reason for the existence of the diary, it is not to explain himself to John or Diana, but to Laszlo. It is to Laszlo that his private dreams, his reflections on aesthetics and politics are addressed; Laszlo is the imagined listener for his unfinished stories, and this absent addressee explains why John feels that Janos is so elusive. It reveals the side of Janos that John yearned to know and claim, as it also discloses the unbridgeable distance between them. John thought that he was Janos's 'intimate'[24] but it is Laszlo who eternally occupies this position. John will remain a relative stranger – an Englishman.

The death of Laszlo precipitates a crisis for Janos. For the first time he feels utterly dislocated, without bearings, anomic.[25] Eventually Laszlo's ghost merges with Janos's guilt and destroys time. At one point the entry to his diary reads 'GOD KNOWS THE DATE. The roses are finished. I painted them for Laszlo's rehabilitation'.[26] The next entry in Janos's diary is about the relationship between time and exile. Janos reflects on the centrality of time to measure achievement and the danger of exile is that it disrupts these markings. The execution of Laszlo threatens to sever Janos from his past and future. Laszlo was the personification of his hope and as he once told John, 'Take the future away from a man, and you have done something worse than killing him'.[27] Hence the contradiction implicit in his letter to John: he returns to Hungary not just to avenge the nostalgia/ghosts of the past but also for the sake of his future: 'And I chose my direction long past. Those who are not like I was will chose the same as I did. I go now to tell my mistake to those who are like I was'.[28]

The silence of Janos is the space for John

This binary opposition between past and present which gives Janos's homeland the upper hand in determining the real not only serves to legitimise the dismissal of the symbolic order in the land of exile, but also puts the sympathetic natives in an ambivalent position. Both John and Diana are doubly displaced. They are kept in the convenient margin which will support but not interfere with the central 'text' of Janos's life. Janos tolerates them because they are the only ones who try to understand and defend him. He shows, however, scant interest in their desires. He demonstrates little attachment to anything apart from his work. When he decides to leave England and return to Hungary he offers a vague and retrospective explanation and takes nothing with him.

Janos's silence is crucial in understanding his haunting presence in John's consciousness. It is this silence which opens the space for John's wishful identification and fans his willing subordination to Janos's artistic genius and political commitment. It is through the identification with the other's exile that the self's ambivalence towards the home can find a more sustained critique. This identification can be intensified only if the other merely provides a generalised frame into which the self's projection can be ushered in without having to contest the specificity of the other. Janos's reticence over his past struggles and his present exile works as the necessary gap which ventilates John's hopes for self-realisation. The peculiarity of this logic is that it doesn't conform to the general economy where the appropriation of the other is also the feminisation of the other. In this case the other is not appropriated, the exile assumes the privileged position of the dominant male and it is the native who is 'feminised' into the subordinate position of lack. This conscientious Englishman proceeds by identifying with a condition that he will never possess. The English are thus precluded from the real as the exile is repositioned as the steadfast pillar of authenticity and certitude. When John returns to the studio his grief for the loss of a friend is stronger than any grief expressed by Janos for the loss of his homeland. Without Janos, John seems exiled from both the present and the possibility of an idealised future:

All the old life had gone . . . The whole place was very quiet, as if I were hearing an accumulated absence of sound . . . The wheel of the etching press over in the alcove looked as permanently stationary as a mill wheel whose stream has long dried up. . . . On to everything else in the studio except the paintings I was able to project my own feeling of confusion and loss. In their own way the paintings were as independent as the sky on a day of national tragedy.[29]

The marriage of ambivalence

By defining Janos as the arbiter of the 'real' John and Diana have abdicated their homes as the place of the 'real', without being able to claim a place in 'his' reality. He leaves for Hungary, but what are they left with? They remain trapped in the conventional 'feminine' circle of simultaneous affirmation and denial. Their loyalty to Janos not only confines them to the position of lack, through their idealisation of the plenitude in his position, but also pre-empts any possible bonding, for they have already undermined their own potential for self-realisation. In the absence of any mutuality it is easy to see how Janos's passions are fused with his politics; Janos's sense of virility and commitment leaves him with no other option but to terminate this paradoxical series of dependencies with an outright and uncontested rejection. Diana's and Janos's marriage was the union of opposites:

> She had never been hungry... interrogated,... smuggled over a frontier,... cut-off. Whereas Janos was entirely cut-off.... If Janos married her, she would be included in all that his exile meant. And then, exiled with him, she would be able to fight for them both in the country where her privileged birth gave her certain advantages, which as exiles they would certainly need.[30]

Diana saw in Janos the opportunity for a principled basis to justify her own revolt against the indulgent and ineffectual lifestyle of her upbringing. While she sought an active collaboration his attraction was not gauged in terms of active struggle with the exterior world.[31] His need for salvation was an interior one, a strategic retreat. Diana did not grant meaning and permanence to his life through an active engagement with the principles that defined his past, but rather stood as a 'sentinel at either end of a phase of his life'; like a firm but passive border she contained as she separated his past and his future, she was the reminder of both 'as it were, by omission'.[32] If Janos's last request to Diana is to find Max (a rather demeaning comment against Diana's own initiative, an arrogant claim indicating that he even has the foresight to find her a substitute), for Max 'was a real refugee and Diana could rescue him from his failure',[33] what is John left with? He is left to his own devices, forced to unshackle his own dependency, and Janos's last words to him are: 'Trust your imagination a little more'.[34]

The departure marks the wall between the exile and the native

The insurmountable distance between the exile and the native is most explicitly played out in the relationship between Janos and the narrator, John. John informs the reader that he thought he and Janos were intimates. Yet the contents of the diary and the narrative structure reveal the opposite. As a figure in Janos's diary John remains peripheral, and as a narrator of the story John is far from omniscient, he subordinates his role to that of merely supplementing the diaries with information that contextualises Janos's abstract reflections. The narrator plays a passive and supportive role, yet the story that emerges is that such support offered in the past failed to bring him as close to Janos as he desired. This narrative structure which doubles Janos's distance from John confirms the absence of mutuality between the local and the exile.[35]

Janos is set at a distance in order for Berger to express further his perceptions of the limitations and contradictions in English culture. However, we do not see England through the estranged eyes of an exile, but rather with the alienated eyes of a local who looks up at an exile and from there looks down at his culture. For Berger, this 'Platonic' bonding also sexualises his perception of England: England is a woman not worth loving because she will never understand your pain.

Love for the other is withheld either in order to pre-empt the pain of not finding reciprocity or from the fear of being unable to sustain such love. The austerity that Berger is contesting is the failure of the English to recognise the resonance and the atavism of the other's pain and love. To probe the limits of these emotional and cultural parameters, Berger consistently identifies with the plight of exiles but distances himself from the traumas of the English. Referring to the experiences from which he drew to form the character of Janos, Berger said:

> It so happened that more than half of the artists I knew, mostly older than myself, were refugees from fascism . . . I lived in a circle of refugees and there was a kind of complicity and understanding between us, despite our different experiences. These people had survived because of England . . . But there was something that distanced them from the English and made them feel foreign. I knew what it was. The English refusal to recognise pain. For the refugees, pain was inevitable, even a spur to creativity. It was what we had in common.[36]

Distorted bodies and multiple identity

In Berger's subsequent novel *The Foot of Clive* the repression of pain is inextricably bound to misogyny. The physical proximity of the characters in this novel belies the vast emotional distances that they must cross before any mutuality can arise. The novel is primarily an exploration into the psychological and cultural boundaries that preclude mutuality. These boundaries are most apparent not just through the pretence of camaraderie and the actual hierarchies that are quickly established amongst the men, but also, and far more explicitly, through their relationship with the other; the women who come to visit them, and Pepino, an Italian migrant. Through the denial of complicity with moral ambiguity, the inscription of the cultural distortions on to the bodies of the other[37] – the projections that multiply the identity of the other, but in turn preclude any engagement with the subjectivity of the other – the local males are presented as attempting to occupy a space in which their identity is seen as the alternate of the other. Their identity is a reaction against the other, remaining distinct from it, and refusing to acknowledge any active dialogue, with the other that may draw them beyond certain limits. In the final scene it is Robin, the youngest character of the novel, who emerges utterly estranged from his countrymen and turns to the Italian migrant in the hope of finding an alternative.

> He wanted to ask him if it was the same in his country. Signor Baldino laughed when he saw the boy looking at him and said in his own language:
>   You must come to Reggio, you must come and see the shop!
>   Robin Garton could only guess at the meaning of what the Italian said. He went on staring at the laughing face and the white bandaged arms, as he had stared at so much, and tears came into his eyes. After a few seconds he knew the tears were there. For the first time in his life he was not ashamed of them.[38]

The Foot of Clive is set entirely in the hospital ward named Clive. The ward is mapped out like a body and the action is located in the foot. There are few specific references to England, but the novel intends to create a microcosm in which the English can be examined. In the Oedipal tale the foot is synecdochically related to the fears of castration, and in this novel Berger explores the Oedipal anxieties of four men.

Apart from generalised descriptions of the city and the sky which anonymously enter and exit like the passing clouds, the only detailed references to the outside world are the descriptions of a patient's wife, mother or daughter. To focus more explicitly on the strictures of the social order, Berger erases any specific reference to place but projects all the consequences of place and culture directly on to the appearances and mannerisms of the women. Like strangers, women are introduced to expose further the flaws in the cultural world which only Englishmen fully inhabit. The identity of women and strangers is not posterior to but concurrent with the multiple projections of fantasies which create a sort of palimpsest, where the original identity has been effaced to make room for subsequent inscriptions, and the repetition of this procedure occasionally brings to light the multiple layers of identity. The posterior identity of a stranger or a woman is thus a fragment of the new composite identity that is instantaneously projected upon them as they enter into discourse.

When considering the contestatory nature of Berger's writing and the crucial position that he constructs for the other, it is not sufficient to question the general positions that are demarcated in this process, but it is also necessary to question the specific engagement with the subjectivity of the other – in short, not only an investigation into where the other is, but also an investigation into whether, or how, the other speaks. Does Berger repeat or challenge modernism's incorporation of the other; situating the ambivalence of the other within an aesthetic that subordinates it to another level of objectification? For instance Andreas Huyssen[39] argues that the male modernists co-opted the 'figure' of woman in order both to re-invent transcendentalism and to reposition the borderline between aesthetics and politics. (A similar argument could also be levelled at the way other cultures were introduced and a new form of primitivism was celebrated within modernism.) While the dilemmas of femininity became the subject of modernist literature these very tensions were negated as they were reified within the pre-given aesthetics of modernism that inevitably returned the subject to the position object.

Whether he is describing their actual visits or a reverie involving a woman, Berger represents the arrival of the woman as the arrival of the repressed. English women are singularly portrayed as the epitome of exaggeration. Unlike the men whose own distortions become apparent through their discourse, the women are seen as disfigured from the outset. Their authenticity is denied by the stultifying burden of obligations and duties which implicitly deny them a sense of freedom and hence meaning to their actions. To the narrator this is apparent even in the way they walk:

> The visitors raced into the ward. Those in the lead looked as though they were winning an egg-and-spoon race. They have only one hour. Many run out of conversation within 20 minutes. But in prospect an hour always seems too short. It is measured against the endless present which existed before the ambulance arrived, or the little suitcase was packed and the man walked out of the house into the hospital. They would like to fly like birds to a sill. Instead they must walk as fast as possible without breaking into a run, along passages, up stairs, down wards – all with floors treacherously slippery. This is why those in the lead give the impression of winning an egg-and-spoon race.[40]

But why does the narrator repeat his first impression, and whom is he trying to justify himself to? Is this repetition a defence against any immanent feminist criticism? Does he already thereby admit the legitimacy of the claim that his observation, which subordinates women as it denigrates English manners, is merely a superficial observation, a paper-thin stereotype, another of the infamous clichés which mask rather than reveal identity. For it is common in misogynist literature to represent women as possessing distorted bodies as a metaphor for man's discontent with the moral order that surrounds him.[41] Does Berger's narrator fit into this recurring scenario where man, feeling unable to cope with the negative characteristics inside him and generally perceiving a profound lack of love, seizes any opportunity to attack and denigrate all other expressions of love? As in the classical exhibition of projective identification, man's primary defensive strategy is to project his own anxieties and fears on to woman. Woman is seen as both the cause and carrier of all the things that repulse man; by identifying her as the problem he also justifies the blame that he pours on to her. The desire to heap blame goes by unquestioned. This negative and spiralling projection is also confirmed by Pepino, to whom English women are not only foreign and ugly, but also unnatural!

They wore shapeless colored clothes and satin blouses. They carried brown paper parcels. They were short with broad but stiff bottoms. Their hair was fizzy and thin. Perhaps women in England went bald. When they reached their men they hardly kissed them. They just touched their foreheads with their lips – as you do when you kiss the cross. And all the time they whispered as if they were in church. He began to become convinced that England was like Russia. Across the seas or plains it lived a life of its own. No foreigner could really understand them. They had their own laws. He could easily imagine that women in England had their babies in secret, going away to a secret little room.[42]

If the narrator and the stranger both fail to show any sensitivity in their perception of the women, then this shortcoming fades into insignificance when compared with the violent and grotesque fantasies of the Englishmen. For these men the entrance and exit of women is always mediated by a destructive fantasy. The private fears of the men are explicitly related to sexual betrayal and the woman's physical presence is never neutral, it is always held somewhere between a domestic fiction and their pornographic imagination.[43] Take for example a scene in which two jokes are told. The first joke is built around a suppositional naivety that is eventually disclosed as a perversion. It involves a married man who lost his testicles in an accident. He goes to a doctor, who says he might be able to help but it was a question of experimenting. He fits him with a dog's pair and asks him to inform him of how he is getting on. The patient returns after a fortnight and laments that while they worked, it was certainly not what it had been once. He is refitted with a ram's pair, and still it didn't seem to do the trick. Eventually the doctor has him fitted with a pair of monkey nuts. The patient did not come back for two months. When he did, the doctor asked him what had happened and why he looks so miserable. The patient explained: 'Why – he'd not been able to find a willing monkey in the whole of . . .'.[44] The narrator claims that this joke succeeded because it played 'with the shapes you may notice or imagine when your eyes get accustomed to the dark of Clive',[45] whereas the second joke offered by an enlightened foreigner, which sarcastically castrates the male fantasies, falls flat: 'Do you know the difference between an abominable snowman and an abominable snowwoman? Two abominable snowballs',[46] The wit of this joke fails as it threatens to illuminate the darkness in which the men prefer to live and dream:

> Into this dark many women enter. The official visiting hours of the afternoon is only a formal confirmation of the endless visiting that continues throughout the night. These women assume such postures, act in so extreme a way, uphold and destroy such fundamental values that by contrast it is the night nurse who appears disembodied.[47]

Doubt and misogyny

While the narrator's and the stranger's conscious perception of women equates them with a perceived moral inversion, the native's unconscious reveals a deeper misogyny which is further related to a repression of complicity with moral ambiguity.[48] The most telling example of misogyny is a character who epitomises the sensibility of normality and fair-play. Harry goes about his day efficiently and as actively as possible, takes pleasure in his neatness and is appropriately described as the 'trade union type'.[49] It is Harry's sense of orderliness which secures his tolerance but also curtails his identification with the other. For example, when looking at Pepino he remembers the plight of the Italians during the war, his perception of Pepino swells with the combined memory of previous injustices, but then as if this feeling is inflating or distorting his judgement, he frames, checks and almost annuls them by qualifying his empathy with the other to a vacuous pity for the 'Latins'. Nothing further is thought, the feelings have been cut off, and the imaginative projection ceases at the very point where a metaphorical connection could have been made. Hence 'Harry won't have to imagine now what it is like to wake up with one hand. The danger point has been passed'.[50]

Harry's schema is organised around an antagonistic opposition between doubt and certitude. These polarities are sexualised in such a way that the masculine occupies the rational, conventional and neutral and the feminine the irrational, exaggerated and ambiguous. It is this symmetry which Berger most deeply wants to rattle. First we note Harry's wife challenging this order: 'It's not tolerance, she says to him, it's just mental laziness'.[51] Then this refusal to acknowledge his own repressiveness is most severely tested by the admission of a captured killer, Jack House, into the ward. Harry is the first to find out the status of the new stranger, and he is also the first to realise the potential threat arising from moral ambiguity. He can see how it is not only upsetting the order (masculine domain), but also introducing chaos (feminine): 'it will all be whispers and gossip. He can see it now. They'll act like a bunch of women. Jaw, jaw, jaw and then up into the air about nothing'.[52]

Harry consistently strikes out at and blames the 'feminine element in his fellow men'[53] and his misogyny is inextricably bound to a profound fear of doubt, ambivalence, darkness and the multiplicity of things. This dread is echoed in a bizarre dream where he is given a mission to construct the original infinity with only nothing as the source: he falls into a vertigo where he experiences a sense of not knowing where to begin because everything leads 'to the next, to the next, to the next, and all were inseparable'.[54] This equation of doubt in origin with the infinity of destiny is redolent of the fear of the uncanny, the *unheimlich* fear of the womb, the original nothing and infinity of origin. When Harry first decided to keep the identity of Jack House a secret it was because 'He visualizes the *open questions as holes* into which he can see patient after patient falling. And he decides it is best to keep quiet'[55] (my emphasis). Harry's silence is the result of the inability to reconcile more than one contradiction. Dilemmas compound as his encounter with the uncanny unfolds his implicit repressiveness and misogyny into the very tissues of his exterior tolerance and rugged reticence.

How can we explain these fantasies and fears? Is woman merely the object that man misrepresents, or is the confrontation with woman also a confrontation with the unknown that can displace the very tenets of certitude? It is clearly inadequate to argue that the imaginary feminine space becomes another arena in which man can exercise his authority over woman, and that this serves no other purpose than to truncate the image of woman in order to bolster the sagging self-identity of man. Ascertaining the misrepresentation of woman is not just an identification of man's transgressions, but must also entail the starting point of an investigation into the 'itinerary of man's desire'.[56] This 'itinerary' demands deeper investigation, for within it we may explore the very imbrication of the self and the other that is constitutive of the process of identity. Analyses which simply halt their inquiry at the point of exposing the negative cultural representations *of* woman do little to explain the contradictions *in* identity, and ultimately are subject to the same criticisms that have been levelled against the assumption that the truth and the real self will be unveiled once the exploitative layer of ideology is exposed. For reciprocity and mutuality – the potency of any form of dialectic between man and woman – is once again precluded and deferred by the masculinist assumption that the true self is always hidden from view.[57]

The uncanny and nostalgia[58]

It often happens that neurotic men declare that they feel there is something uncanny about the female genital organs. This unheimlich place, however, is the entrance to the former Heim (home) of all human beings, to the place where each one of us lived once upon a time and in the beginning. There is a joking saying that 'Love is homesickness'; and whenever a man dreams of a place or a country and says to himself while dreaming: 'this place is familiar to me, I've been here before', we may interpret this place as being his mother's genitals or her body. In this case, then, the unheimlich is what was once heimisch, familiar; the prefix 'un' ('un-') is the token of repression.[59]

But why are the female genitals related to the secret place, why should the archetypal point of origin be a subject of repression and why is this process of investigating the past, consciously or unconsciously, inscribed in sexualized metaphors? For if the male genitals are associated with plenitude and not lack, with surety and knowledge rather than doubt and ambivalence, then this explains why Harry attributes irrationality and ignorance to the 'feminine element', but it does not explain his fear. His fear is explained by his dual alienation; the discovery of his own castration which is coupled with a resentment against the futility of nostalgia for the mother. Since the mother doesn't possess the phallus then the return to the surety of the womb is precluded – projecting the maternal space as the 'ground' of the archetypal homeland to an irretrievable past, separating the subject from the familiar and rendering everything foreign. Hence Harry cannot admit the 'feminine element' without exposing his own fears. He must conceal the absence of the phallus, for, like the uncanny, it is that which 'ought to have remained secret and hidden but has come to light'.[60]

The appearance of the uncanny in Jung's writing is likened to the emergence of a repressed conscience, Jung extended Freud's metaphors as he criss-crossed them over and against sexual identities and surfaced with the image of 'woman in man'. With this ambivalent combination he saw the uncanny as the pendulum which swayed between threat and promise, claiming that 'It is tragic that the demon of the inner voice should spell the greatest danger and indispensable help at the same time'.[61] Between apocalypse and salvation, the uncanny offers to thrust one into the fullness of life, or to be the harbinger of death.

The uncanny comes *between* common sense and the rational process of intellectual inquiry. It emerges from and cleaves apart both the pre-existence of limited certitudes and the explanatory power of open-ended illuminations. It does not belong to an either/or binary opposition, but to the more nebulous yet equally insistent category of the neither/nor. Perhaps the encounter with the uncanny is central to any experience of estrangement and alienation: a taste of the exilic in the heart of the homeland. The uncanny is a dread which jolts perceptions, dislocates names and identities, blurs the boundary between the familiar and the foreign – but where does such a dread come from?

Freud begins his investigation of the uncanny by questioning its conventional definition as simply 'that class of the frightening which leads back to what is known of old and long familiar'.[62] The paradoxical meaning of the uncanny is more explicit in the etymology of the German *unheimlich* than its English equivalent. The conceptual opposition between the familiar and the foreign in *unheimlich* is an oscillation which has the word *heim* (home) at its radix. He qualifies this opposition by acknowledging that it is not a reciprocal relationship: 'We can only say that what is novel can easily become frightening and uncanny; some new things are frightening but not by any means all. Something has to be added to what is novel and unfamiliar in order to make it uncanny'.[63] For Freud this opposition is a paradox because the feeling of uncanniness cannot be simply reduced or solved by rational illumination, hence he disputes that the unsettling residue of the uncanny is the result of intellectual (un)certainty.

To explore this paradox further Freud returns to the definition of the word *heimlich*, whose meaning is compounded with contradictory associations: on the one hand emphasising domesticity and intimacy in human values (when referring to animals and things it mentions those which are tame and companionable or homely and familiar), on the other hand suggesting the act of concealment and withholding, 'kept from sight', a secret often referring to a sexual matter whose appearance must be kept hidden. Freud seizes upon the ambivalence that is contained within this word to explore the borderline between the foreign and the familiar. Putative opposites *heimlich–unheimlich* exhibit shades of meaning which are identical.[64] Freud concludes the first stage of his investigation by emphasising that it is the ambivalence in the one that brings it closer to the other.[65]

Thus we may extrapolate and consider how the ambivalence in the self leads to an attraction with the other but also facilitates the return from the other, and the return is the journey which either affirms or denies the resonance and existence of the other. To scrutinise this borderline Berger arranges his characters like a series of variously attracting and repelling magnets, and it is through the rupture of the uncanny that the symmetry of these dynamics is displaced.

Throughout *The Foot of Clive* there is a constant reference to news. The news is what happens outside, people take a newspaper home and from the inside read about the outside world. The news is ubiquitous, it 'falls everywhere like snow',[66] but home is where the shock of the news is meant to stop: 'The last barrier against consequence is the home'.[67] One of the events singled out by the narrator is the arrest of a murderer. 'His name is Jack House. It is alleged that he shot a policeman when he and his accomplice were trapped during a bank raid in Liverpool'.[68] Jack House was injured in the process of being arrested and consequently brought into the 'foot' of Clive for minor surgery before he goes to his certain hanging.

Jack House's admission into the ward has challenged the conventional borderline between inside and outside. His presence has plunged his neighbours into a story that they cannot narrate. Their proximity to this news-event and the absence of a clear entrance or exit from it has rendered their preconceived judgements impotent.[69] For here the presence of the other is disrupting both their ability to narrate and to act rationally, they do not as yet know how to tell this story, or what to do, they have found themselves *in* another story which seems to be above their control and now they feel helpless.[70]

Jack House never speaks, and apart from a few glimpses to and from the operation room he is never seen. Kept behind screens, under constant police surveillance, he is not exactly in any position to offer a threat to the other patients and yet they are all, in one way or another, terrified of him. He has yet to be tried, yet they are all convinced that his hanging is inevitable. So is he already dead? Symbolically it seems he is. For the others are obsessed with him in the way people are obsessed with a dead person or a lost lover; they are constantly addressing him and implicitly acknowledging their own insecurities in a retrospective voice, simultaneously trying to justify their past and ameliorate their present. Yet if he is not dead then whose ghost is haunting them? Is it Jack House's future ghost that is haunting them in the present?[71] The judged one becomes the silent judge, and the conflict between judgements intensifies as proximity with the uncanny is increased. Dilemmas are sustained because, as Harry foresaw, Jack House symbolises a moral void which is both irresistible and a threat: they feel compelled to fill this void but realise the danger of being lost in it.

Freud's definition of the uncanny ultimately returns to the 'primal' fear of castration, but only after a process of self-scrutiny which has the power of splitting the subject. The repetition of the foreign, its resemblance with the familiar, not only objectifies as it splits the self but also 'renders it possible to invest the old idea of a "double" with a new meaning'.[72]

The presence of Jack House not only ruptures the conscience of his neighbours but also initiates a number of imaginary trials where each actor persecutes himself as he is interrogated by the others, but the self that survives these imaginary trials emerges twofold.[73] The incommensurability of these identities is stated but not developed. Berger shows how the foreign can rupture the familiar old borderlines, but cannot illuminate how the subsequent sutures transform or repeat themselves in the new realities. For in the end he does suggest that the old borderlines are restored, and the deeper effects of estrangement, like the future, are left as hypotheses. Robin's final gesture of mutuality with Pepino epitomises the very barriers between the self and the other. They simply misunderstand each other and are left with the rhetoric of hospitality. But what is the significance of such gestures, are they to be dismissed as empty or naive? At this vital point Berger fails, he reaches the 'limits' of mutuality and the novel ends.

Prawer argues that the uncanny in literature has always been central to the ways in which artists can represent the question of homelessness. He concludes his essay with two examples: for Goethe the artist's function is 'to make us feel at home in a world changing so rapidly that our intellect can scarcely keep pace with it', whereas Kafka offers a complementary lesson, perhaps more pertinent for our modern times, the need to 'focus an awareness of homelessness, articulate a feeling of strangeness and disorientation, keep us alive to the possibility of orders of existence that cannot be assimilated in the categories of our waking consciousness'.[74] Sociology can also be characterised by this dual response to the question of ontological homelessness in modernity.

Origins of sociology and nostalgia

Nostalgia is conventionally understood as a passive or negative emotion, it is thought that because of nostalgia one's presence in the present is hampered, one holds back from an active engagement and prefers to wallow in the infinitely regressing recesses of the past. Nostalgia is something people suffer from, it is not normally seen as a gift, let alone as a whetstone upon which critical insights can be sharpened. The etymology of nostalgia bears out this stigma, as it originates in the Greek where it referred to the 'pains for home'.[75] The pain of nostalgia was recognised as manifesting in three forms: a wish to return to place, a wish to return to time, and a regret for having gone to the wrong place. The first two wishes can be understood as being motivated by drives to return to an earlier state, which was not only more satisfying but also a clearly known state. However the third aspect of nostalgia contains a sense of transgression which is motivated by a desire that *cannot* be defined as belonging to the past. There is the attending paradox, a yearning for something that has never been known. Here the regret of nostalgia arises from an unsatisfied desire. Jane Gallop focuses on this paradoxical desire, which never locates satisfaction, to explain the relationship between Freud's claim in his essay 'The Uncanny', that homesickness is a longing to return to the womb of the mother, with Lacan's claim that the alienation of the subject is in the discovery of the ubiquity of castration. Gallop argues that

> If we understand the nostalgia resulting from the discovery of the mother's castration in this way, then the discovery that the mother does not have the phallus means that the subject can never return to the womb. Somehow the fact that the mother is not phallic means that the mother as mother is lost forever, that the mother as womb, homeland, source, and grounding for the subject is irretrievably past. The subject is hence in a foreign land, alienated.[76]

As modernity is so often seen as a journey away from the pre-modern, nostalgia re-enters as a way of reflecting back, making sense and working out one's bearings while in the midst of journeying. Nostalgia arises from the perceived gap between intentions and consequences, resemblances and identities, appearances and essences. Nostalgia is usually understood as the rebounding away from the threatening aspects of the present and the search for safer grounds in the past, but implicit in this very manoeuvre is an attention to the unnamed aspects of the present. It is this element of nostalgia which can yield critical insight, and paradoxically work towards naming the present.

Stauth and Turner argue that the emergence of sociology, as a discipline, is coeval with a specific sense of alienation in modernity, and that 'One of the most powerful metaphors of sociological analysis is that of nostalgia'.[77] The critical stance which subjects the present to scrutiny is usually driven either by a projection into the past with a sense of plenitude and integrity, or by an imagined sense of unity in the future. The nostalgic paradigm is at the centre of all major sociological critiques of modernity. Stauth and Turner argue that critics who felt this sense of exile from language and social practice have emphasised four specific forms of displacement: (1) the value and continuity of history with a firm sense of location; (2) a wholeness that can embody and exercise moral certainty; (3) an individual autonomy which can sustain genuine social relationships and give strength to the practices of everyday life; and (4) a sense of simplicity and spontaneity which in all its lightness and almost transparency lends the weight and stamp of authenticity to the above expressions.[78] The nostalgic comparisons are motivated by a sense of sedimented moral unity and spiritual integrity which gave social existence a sense of purpose and meaning that modernity lacks, and because of this perceived sense of lack, the melancholic 'sufferer' of nostalgia condemns the world as she or he feels that it is but a shadow of the 'real' reality.

Nostalgia has been so much at the centre of critiques of modernity that Alice Jardine felt compelled to reject nostalgia as a critical tool, for it seemed too deeply grounded in a 'melancholic search for a recognisable solution'.[79] While she cites examples which do tend to blunt the critical edge of nostalgia as they merely recycle the regressive male fantasies,[80] there is however, no need to assume that such uses exhaust the potential of all subsequent appropriations of nostalgia. Following Spivak's example[81] I would argue that nostalgia can be strategically internalised and affirmed in vastly differing ways. For if the 'double displacement' of the other is to be undone, then it is necessary to begin from that position of displacement and to remember that nostalgia is not singularly about loss.

Nostalgia for the future

It is from this position that Stauth and Turner look to Nietzsche for a new direction and for insight into the radical potential of nostalgia. For Nietzsche nostalgia was not a way of measuring the discrepancy in the present, his 'aim was not to look backwards to a moral security but forwards to a revaluation of values' and his 'proclamation about the death of god was not a call to fundamentalism but, on the contrary, a forward-looking utopian gesture'.[82] Nietzsche's nostalgia is beyond the wish to return to an idealised state in the past. Nietzsche's recalling of nostalgia was not the recollection of objects known in the past, the object he is calling for is unknown even to fantasy. It is that 'indefinable something' which Gallop claims is the result of primary repression, both 'primordially and structurally excluded' from consciousness, to which we cannot return, because this nostalgia is married with the object of desire.[83]

To appreciate Nietzche's proclamation we need to radicalise the differentiation between the normative universal from the pathological particular, the elevating from the depressive components not just in nostalgia but in all criticism which is premised on some mythical totality. Both the negative and the positive forms of nostalgia share 'a feeling of being joined to something wonderful and captivating'.[84] The sense of pleasure is achieved through an idealisation of the past, a yearning for a suppositional union within a perfectly enclosed time and space. In the psychoanalytic context this is interpreted in metaphors related to the maternal womb. But nostalgia also entails an ability to reconcile the bittersweet irreversibility of time, to acknowledge that the past is irrevocably over; and rising from this perceived rupture between past and present is the process of naming: identifying, bridging the gap between the tenses and the consciousness of difference.[85]

The key to nostalgia is its spur to identification. Thus the unnamed parts of reality, those which are adjacent to consciousness but often repressed because of their putative foreignness, are introjected and assimilated by the process of naming. Nostalgia thus moves beyond the retreating perspective, towards an assertive vision of the future, beyond a lazy complaint and towards the construction of oppositional systems and possible utopias.

Nostalgia: a little patch of heaven, or the place where everyone dwelt once upon a time and in the beginning

It might seem a paradox to suggest that nostalgia is as much future-oriented as it is concerned with the past, just as it is paradoxical to say that visionaries are melancholics who have invested themselves with the necessity of 'having' to 'speak the truth without having the authority to speak it',[86] and so it could be said that travellers who leave one point are often (and even before departure) actually searching for their place of origin. The quest for belonging is so vigorously sought that it uproots and displaces the very possibility of ever finding the ultimate point of arrival.

The country from which we come is always the one to which we are returning. You are on the return road which passes through the country of children in the maternal body. You have already passed through here: you recognize the landscape. You have always been on the return road. Why is it that the maternal landscape, the heimisch, and the familiar become so disquieting? The answer is less buried than we might suspect. The obliteration of any separation, the realization of the desire which in itself obliterates a limit; all that which in effecting the movement of life in reality, allows us to come closer to a goal, the short cuts, the crossing accomplished especially at the end of our lives; all that which overcomes, shortens, economizes and assures satisfaction appears to affirm the life forces. All of that has another face turned toward death which is the detour of life. The abbreviating effect which affirms life asserts death.[87]

A sense of displacement in the present space and time usually implies a command for a deeper integrity between past and present. And so nostalgia and utopia can be found enmeshed in the one place. The sympathetic and stable space is already lost before it can be found in the imaginary, always set a little beyond reach; inaccessible, secret, private and distant. 'The garden must be deep in a wood, and have walls round it. Paradise, they say, means walled garden in Persian.'[88]

This enclosed garden[89] is the container of both the general and the local, the part and the whole: both nostalgia and utopia are visions which synecdochically play with a sense of omnipotence and the universal – a state of purity and a sense of infinity, both the beginning and end of all dreams. The certitude of home which is the base of these yearnings is the hope of assigning an incontestable identity to the self and its relationship with all others. For if the home is the womb plus the phallus, then it is not just home, it is also utopia. In this home the gap between identity and resemblance will have found closure, a once and for all reconciliation. However, since we are precluded from such a home and there is always a gap between identity and resemblance, then this is also where the uncanny conjunctions of desire and nostalgia begin. The utopian and nostalgic desire, whether it be an advance or a return, is nevertheless a simultaneous call for a mythic unity of given certitudes and stable identity.

For the separation and rupture that nostalgic and utopian thinking confronts is also a search for integration, it seeks a space where the inside and outside dichotomy isn't a means of exclusion but is overcome by a more generalised and totalising schema of inclusion. Exile is both the process and the position that marks the inadequacies of the home and the ardours of the unhomely life. The desire for transgression is also a yearning for another closure. This journey is a search for a centre, which has overcome any contestation with the peripheries, it is an 'ideal' centre which knows of no outside and so can be composed only of an inside which is total and complete in itself. It is by virtue of such a centre/home – both abstract and concrete – that identities can ever be rendered in a static and absolute form, attaining both the originary and the eternal. But it is also by virtue of its abstraction that such a centre/home is never attainable. Both exile which is unliveable and the home which is unattainable are centres which remain uninhabited. The congruence of the nostalgic and the utopian in Berger's narratives is such that they are both articulated in sexual metaphors. Both the nostalgic return to the maternal space and the utopian advance to woman always represent for Berger, as Jardine noted about other theorists of modernity, 'the *space* at the end point of man's symbolization'.[90] For when Berger is evoking the unrepresentable specificity – the 'firstness' of sexuality which renders language foreign to its being and declares that the potency of contingency is such that the only poem that can be written about sex is 'here, here, here, here – now'[91] are we not again inside the womb, under the silken sky, utopia – the place without place, the image beyond images?

From crisis in male identity to the return to woman

Corker's Freedom was Berger's third novel, his second since he decided to live outside England, and, like *The Foot of Clive*, this novel is almost exclusively set in a few small and enclosed spaces. Similarly the events are confined to a very small passage of time.

In one crucial passage the question of naming and its relationship to space is drawn all the way back to the primal conflicts of identity, from the child's ambivalent departure from the protective space of the mother's womb to the confrontation with an open-ended antagonism with identity that is conferred by the name of the father:

> I have kept certain things in these cupboards since I was four, kept them secret and for myself. I cannot know what is in these cupboards for I only recognize by night and then I recognize their familiarity rather than their identity. They are my unidentifiable toys. They are what I saved from that time, now long ago, when I first moved in and had a roof over my head instead of the silken sky. There is also the danger of fire. My house William will be ashes when I die. I shall be myself no more. The house and I must end together. But we did not begin together. I came before the house.... Before I moved into my independent name, everything around me under the silken sky confirmed that I was the centre of the world and mother the space I inhabited... My name wasn't me. It hadn't been given me. I moved into it with all my accessories, but I had not built it... At first it seemed likely that Father had built my house for me... I was frightened because I feared that I was not living in the house which was mine but which was also the house he granted me... it was not until one month ago that I knew for certain that there was no supplier, that there was nobody to whom I could appeal... that the person I had inhabited since the day the silken sky was rent was mine to do what I liked with. Then I knew I was alone... I matter, I matter, but I do not know how to think it.[92]

In this passage Corker's identity is poised between the distinctness offered by the name of the father and the pre-nomial other which is equated with the space of the mother, he says: 'Before I moved into my independent name, everything around me under the silken sky confirmed that I was the centre of the world and Mother the space I inhabited...' Here the locus of the primal idealisation and subsequent alienation is situated in the space the child shared with the mother. Entering the home-name of the father, the child is exiled from the omnipotence of the mother.

The antagonism between the name of the father and the space of the mother is played out against the finite significance of house and the infinite 'silken sky'. Corker wants to reject the fixity of the father, to leave the house in which his name was given a place to live in, but to which he feels he doesn't belong. But where to go, how can he make sense of his mid-life solitude, will the 'silken sky' still be witness to his centrality without the omnipotence of the mother's gaze? And who is the essential 'me' which isn't 'my name', the 'I' which has all the 'accessories' and 'unidentifiable toys' that moved into this prefabricated name? The identification of this prior identity is not as significant as the recognition of the gap between the prior and the given identity. This is what constitutes the void which Corker needs to redress and perhaps it is from this abyssal heterogeneity that Berger's imaginary can also find an uncanny locus of beginning.

The constitution of a void at once marks the points of rupture and the necessity of the journey: the lack, or the loss of the maternal space in the male's identity. The void in the male self is thus figured as woman, and as writing is an attempt to approach this alterior space it must thus be written as the search and the hope of coming into contact, again, with woman.

The will to emancipation, and the recollection of this primal exile are both premised on the murder of the father. But the refusal of the father's name which, in psychoanalytic terms, is linked to castration, also yields a crisis in the order of the symbolic. In the space of the mother, the question of matter didn't matter, the return to this space is an escape from the tyranny of representation. But after having lived in the house of the father, the step out cannot be taken without an experience of dread. In the midst of crisis – between an unnameable exile and the necessity to find the old-new self – Corker finds hope but only 'through' his idealisation of women. The crisis of male identity is displaced as it is renamed in the quest for women.

On the night that he has callously given notice to his sister that he intends to abandon both her and their paternal home, Corker gives a lecture on his travels to Vienna. In other places the timeless and desexed present exists, for as he tells his assistant Alec, when asked what he does in Vienna: 'I live! . . . The Viennese have the secret of how to live. They are the most cultivated people in the world. You don't have to "do" anything'.[93] Spurred on by the presence of a young woman – his flirtatious relationship with her can be described only as platonic lust, whereas for her it was just the means of getting the necessary information so that her boyfriend could rob his office – Corker begins to shift his account of Vienna from its usually precise and meticulous list of dates, architects, rulers and battles to an impassioned reverie on mutuality and an absurd description of the utopias that were moored in the dreamy harbours of his private life. Meanwhile Corker's office, which is not just his place of work (his ego) – in the vacant space above it he intends to establish his new identity (his alter-ego) – is being robbed. Should we ask why Corker allowed himself to be betrayed, or perhaps is the more important question, why did Corker need to base his image of freedom on an idealisation of the trust between man and woman, and to what extent did the necessity of this idealised relationship actually delude him about his possible future selves and the identity of the other?

The ultimate hollowness of Corker's freedom can resound only within the formal problematics of Berger's narrative and (to repeat Spivak's phrase) 'the itinerary of man's desire that creates such a text'.[94] For both are equivocally drawn by the interconnected strategies of figuring the unnameable and the need to know woman. Corker's own paranoia, which is framed between the loss of maternal identity and the discomfort caused by the strictures of the paternal identity, echoes the author's struggle with the boundaries of narrative. Spivak's comment on Hegel and Derrida can again be transposed to Berger's novels: 'the discourse of man is in the metaphor of woman'. Woman stands at each impasse in man's identity, yet the representation of the unnameable which rescues the narrative from the abyss of silence – the 'silken sky' – is also woman. The eternal figure of woman thus not only redefines the boundaries of male identity but extends the limit of the unrepresentable through what Alice Jardine calls the *'banalization* of castration' by the male authors of modernity.

Perhaps this ambivalence in the articulation of identity needs to be explored further. If we recall the dread Harry experienced in the dream I referred to earlier and place it beside Corker's dread, and more generally relate it to Berger's representation of the crisis in identity, we will understand how the depths of aporia are sexualised and how woman defines the limit of language. Jardine argues that in modernity the countenance of the unknown has been continuously represented by the figure of woman:

> First of all, the indistinctness and distortion of the visage, the descent into the uncharted space of night, has everything to do with the infantile exploration of the mother's face – the first point of reference mapped by the infant in search of the breast. But second and most important, it has always been the woman's figure, her lack of visage, of individual traits, of identity and humanity, that has saved the male artist.[95]

Time, exile and woman

Berger consistently argues that the concept of timelessness has been banished by the culture of positivism in modernity;[96] he also claims that the experience of time precedes that of space in human consciousness.[97] Through the act of storytelling, he signals the defiance of both the banishment of timelessness and the separation of the temporal and the spatial. Berger tells stories which illustrate the desire to transcend time without self-deception: they are based on events where endeavour and imagination are merged, where contemplation reveals 'simultaneity instead of sequence, presence instead of cause and effect, ubiquity instead of identity'.[98]

Yet more often than not, the metaphor that traces out the enigma of time, or brings about the union of the temporal and the spatial, is based on the representation of woman. In the novel *A Painter of Our Time*, there is an entry in Janos's diary which discusses the process of memory and idealisation. In this passage Janos decides that there are two ways in which this can operate, and that only the exile, who is haunted by the absent presence of the women in his past and his mother-country, can appreciate the difference. Woman, homeland and time are brought together in this reflection on two representations of women. In Titian:

> there are elisions there, too, but they are a tribute only to the unreasonable adoration one feels in the face of the fact, they are a tribute to the unknown quality that jostles the known facts – not to the kind of memory that does not jostle at all. The Giorgione is a virgin dream, poignant in its ignorance. The Titian is the memory of a woman who was once all that the picture pretends. The point is too fine perhaps for any except an *emigre* who both dreams of and remembers the women of his own country. Katinka. My age.[99]

The memories which stimulate anticipation, which separate the events of the past in order to vitalise their meanings in the present, the idealisation which holds up rather than denies liminality, this is the memory which Janos prefers, but it also coincides with the significance that Berger attributes to storytelling:

What separates the story-teller from his protagonists is not knowledge, either objective or subjective, but *their* experience of time in the story he is telling. (If he is telling his own story the same thing separates him as story-teller from himself as subject.) This separation allows the story-teller to hold the whole together; but it also means that he is obliged to follow his protagonists, follow them, powerlessly, *through* and *across* the time which they are living and he is not. The time, and therefore the story, belongs to them. Its meaning belongs to the story-teller. Yet the only way he can reveal this meaning is by telling the story to others.[100]

In *A Painter of Our Time*, Berger reflects on the relationship between an experience and its representation as art. The example he cites is love-making. What separates the two he concludes 'is not a barrier in space' but a 'barrier in time'.[101] Since art is not for the preservation of experience but for interpretation, then the meaning must lie between the past and the future, not simply in the idea or the intention behind the work, but through the conjunctions of its reception. Then Janos concludes that 'when an artist works, he straddles time'.[102] Love-making is no innocent example, it is also that which straddles time, in Berger's eyes, and the émigré artist is the privileged agent for the redemption of the timeless, by sublimating as he substitutes love for art in the act of making love to time. And again we can ask, where does this position the woman?

To return to the genderisation of visage let us look again at the opening sentences of the long passage previously quoted from *Corker's Freedom*: 'I have kept certain things in these cupboards since I was four, kept them secret and for myself . . .' The enigma of the contents in the cupboard is the mystery of time and sexual difference. The hint to this is found much later in the preamble to the central essay of *G* which is called 'A Situation of Women'. Here Berger begins with the involuntary recollection of a friend. Memory in this instance seems to recreate a moment in the past and also to anticipate an imminent experience. This coincidence of past and future in a single 'prescient' flash is a mystery that defies containment within the arbitrary – it suggests the ambivalence of grasping but not holding, the alluring alteriority of something familiar whose attracting energies are equally matched by a repelling momentum that pulls it away, towards something foreign. Berger compares this feeling to a

never seen object in the dark, we can feel our way over some of its surfaces. But we have not identified it.

The way my imagination forces me to write this story is determined by its intimations about those aspects of time which I have touched but never identified. I am writing this book in the same dark.[103]

It is also not a coincidence that these meditations on the split and enfolding nature of time which serve explicitly as an analogy for the tensions of the author's imaginary, also implicitly structure the dominant characteristic of his abstract portrayal of bourgeois women – their schizophrenic passivity:

> A woman's presence was the result of herself being split into two, and her energy being inturned. A woman was always accompanied – except when quite alone – by her own image of herself. Whilst she was walking across the room she was weeping at the death of her father, she could not avoid envisaging herself walking and weeping. From earliest childhood she has been taught and persuaded to survey herself continually. And so she came to consider the surveyor and the surveyed within her as the two constituent yet always distinct elements of her identity as a woman.[104]

The portrayal of the incommensurability of women's identity neatly reflects the paradox of woman in man's imaginary. On the one hand woman must wait for man to come into being, but on the other hand the split in her identity implies not only that there is a side of woman that man can never realise, but also that this opposition precludes her from ever entering the real. The surveyor and the surveyed within woman are already there to render everything illusory, shuttling her from lack to discontent: 'For a woman the state of being in love was a hallucinatory interregnum between two owners, her bridegroom taking the place of her father, or later, perhaps, a lover taking the place of her husband'.[105]

G is an exploration of three moments in time: childhood, sexuality and revolution, all of which stand either outside or directly opposed to the homogeneous calendar time. The book is not just about the different ways the past can be articulated in the present, but more specifically about how the past relates to the present in the very process of thinking through one's actions while actually performing them. It is about the instantaneous consciousness of similitude and difference of one identity from that of another. As Berger says of the protagonist when describing his consciousness during his first sexual encounter: 'Her difference from him acts like a mirror. Whatever he notices or dwells upon in her, increases his consciousness of himself, without his attention shifting from her'.[106] However, it is not just that the difference between past and present is analogous to the difference between man and woman, but rather, and once again, it is the metaphor of woman which articulates the unknowable for man, and in this case the historical process.

In a passage where Berger attempts to describe the dislocation of time between G's falling off a horse and his apprehension of pain,[107] Berger replays this confrontation with the limits of representation; probing for the unarticulated sediment that skims the surfaces of consciousness. The 'unimaginable' slowness of time during the fall can be evoked only by an excessive attention to physical details and an unarticulated sense that the authority implicit with age had taken different proportions. Berger explains G's courage and control over pain by claiming that in the fall he merged with time, G became ageless. His return to consciousness is the return to his 'normal' age with the sedimentary memory that in the spectre of death action and consequence, image and object appear juxtaposed but also distant and discontinuous with each other. G's return to consciousness empowers the narrator to rebind these relationships – to put a roof over them. Berger notes that it is the presence of home that offers the final protection against the dread of death: 'In the time which his fall and his pain arrested, he found a home'.[108] It is the finding of a home which saved G from his fall and also restored coherence to the narrative. This mythical home is at the centre of G's personal quest and running through this quest is also the narrator's struggle to articulate the enigmas of experience. It is unclear what or where this home is. Berger admits that he cannot describe it in the duration of the fall, but he is able to make an unqualified assertion concerning its presence – perhaps the existence of this home is composed paradoxically by the generalised memories of home that supposedly rush out in the split second of danger, and a retrospective projection based from the actual home in which G awakens.

Berger ends this half-lit passage with a quotation from R. G. Collingwood which explores the paradoxes of historical consciousness:

All history is contemporary history: not in the ordinary sense of the word, where contemporary history means the history of the comparatively recent past, but in the strict sense: the consciousness of one's own activity as one actually performs it. History is thus the self-knowledge of the living mind. For even when the events which the historian studies are events that happened in the distant past, the condition of their being historically known is that they should vibrate in the historian's mind.[109]

Collingwood's philosophy of history stands in contradistinction to Croce's. Croce argued that history must proceed by recreating the needs that brought about the events of the past, whereas Collingwood insisted that history is not a 'scissors-and-paste affair' and knowledge is not gained by rearranging the events of the past.[110] For if the past exists at all, its trace must have survived in the processes of the present. History begins with the discovery of these traces and proceeds with the investigation into the relationship between the processes that link the past and the present. The difference between Collingwood's and Croce's philosophy of history echoes the difference between the normal time and the undefined other moments of time that Berger is attempting to articulate in *G*. Berger is continuously working with this idea of the overlapping moments in time, exploring the compulsion to call forth a moment from the past and seeking its resonance in the specificities of the present, and illustrating both the contiguity and the residue of the past in the present. For Collingwood, historical consciousness admits nostalgia and repetition neither as antiquarian nor passive modes but as the necessary means to the critical act of thinking through the situation and powers of the individual. Interestingly Collingwood's metaphor for relating time is based not on linear succession from the past to the present, but the 'incapsulation' of the past in the present.

It is this idea of incapsulation which is also at the centre of G's sexual desire. In recounting G's first sexual experience Berger describes it as a journey to a mythical place – the womb, the past, perhaps both?

Let us go to that place.
He unhesitatingly put his hand on her hair and opened his fingers to let it spring up between them. What he feels in his hand is inexplicably familiar . . .
Her cunt begins at her toes; her breasts are inside it, and her eyes too; it has enfolded her.
It enfolds him.
The ease.
Previously it was unimaginable, like a birth for that which is born.[111]

In his autobiography Collingwood describes more explicitly the meaning of incapsulation to his theory of history and further relates the persistence of the past to the process of desire.[112] He basically argues that events pass away but that processes are passed on by being incapsulated in the desires of the present: 'In subsequent life the desire is what I call incapsulated'. The relationship between the past and the present is not an open-ended one because the question of the past 'arises' out of the desires of the present. But what is the nature of this desire? Is this quest – which proceeds via an imaginative projection of the self into the space of the other[113] – coterminous with the appropriations of the writing effect that Jardine defined as gynesis? Could it be said that this conception of time is another configuration of the eternal woman – that the incapsulation of the past in the present is analogous to the encapsulation of man in woman? Collingwood's idea of history and Berger's representation of sexuality reveal the uncanny path of nostalgia as male identifications weave themselves inside and outside the metaphor of woman whilst searching for the lost origin: the home for which there is a pain.

This question of woman's identity being inside and outside of man's is inextricably bound up with Berger's image of the idealised other – the intimate and the stranger; the person inside you and the person outside you; your origin and your destiny. When a woman submitted herself to G she did so because she found in him the possibility of realising the very paradox of desire. And it is her desire that Berger supposedly expresses when he draws up this myth from Olympus:

> When Zeus, in order to approach a woman he had fallen in love with, disguised himself as a bull, a satyr, an eagle, a swan, it was not only to gain the advantage of surprise: it was to encounter her (within the terms of those strange myths) as a stranger. The stranger who desires you and convinces you that it is truly you in all your particularity whom he desires, brings a message from all that you might be, to you as you actually are. Impatience to receive that message will be almost as strong as your sense of life itself. The desire to know oneself surpasses curiosity. But he must be a stranger, for the better you, as you actually are, know him, and likewise the better he knows you, the less he can reveal to you of your unknown but possible self. He must be a stranger. But equally he must be mysteriously intimate with you, for otherwise instead of revealing your unknown self, he simply represents all those who are unknowable to you and for whom you are unknowable. The intimate and the stranger. From this contradiction in terms, this dream, is born the great erotic god which every woman in her imagination either feeds or starves to death.[114]

Ultimately the identity of G is a combination of the permanent metic and the identity of desire itself:

> When analysed, sexual desire has components which are violently nostalgic and lead us far back as the experience of birth itself: other components are the result of the ineradicable appetite for the unknown, the furthest away, the ultimate of life – which can finally only be found in its negation – death. At

the moment of orgasm these two points in time, our beginning and our end, may seem to fuse into one. When this happens everything that lies between them, that is to say our whole life, becomes instantaneous. It is thus that I explain the protagonist of my book to myself.'¹⁵

The gap between the exile and the native in *A Painter of Our Time*, like the gap between the stranger and the intimate in *G*, is the fundamental gap of difference between the known and the unknown. With metaphor such opposites can be brought together, and for Berger the very act of writing becomes the metaphor for enfolding differences, and that metaphor is woman. Identity is constituted out of the need to pluck something familiar out of the uncanny darkness of non-identity. The gap within identity is split, the alterior part becomes woman, enabling the male writer to constitute identity at the precise moment in which he is enunciating a crisis. The irrepressible attraction to the other, and the reinscription of the self in the very evocation of the other, has echoes of the critique of the misogyny that underlined the modernist aesthetic. But if we listen again, these echoes also displace the very identity that such an aesthetic tried to ground. The writing self, by acknowledging that it is scarcely to be grasped without the other, reneges its own purity and pluralises the ground of its possible selves. The final question remains, is the recognition of the exile of man another exile for woman — rendering the other to the alterior, a further step into the beyond?

Exile and the intellectual in modernity

Writing about the possibility of critical thought — the intellectual as a dissident — Kristeva observes that the conjunctions of modernity invariably lead to exile. Kristeva claims that the condition of modernity is marked by the subject's exile from the unitary status of the home. This displacement from the site on to which the permanence of identities was previously fastened is also linked to a crisis in the order of the symbolic, or what Kristeva calls 'the death of the name of the father'. If home is the shelter that sustains connections between family, country, language, and religion, then exile, since it is the condition that uproots all these bonds, must be the banishment of the symbolic process that fixes meaning into unitary locus:

The exile cuts all links, including those that bind him to the belief that the thing called life has a Meaning guaranteed by the dead father. For if meaning exists in the state of exile, it nevertheless finds no incarnation, and is ceaselessly produced and destroyed in geographical and discursive transformations. Exile is a way of surviving in the face of the dead father ...'[116]

The exile which Kristeva evokes does not directly approach the condition experienced by a refugee, who is expelled simply because of what he or she is. Kristeva is referring to deracinated intellectuals whose contestation with their given cultural and historical position occurs on qualitatively different terms. By the intellectuals' very relationship to discourse, the patterns of loss and the resources for redemption that they express are different from those of the refugee.[117]

Not all forms of exile are equal. The displacements, for example, that Berger describes in the stories that involve the peasantry cannot be compared with those in his first four novels. There may be similar themes intersecting them, but the difference in their historical and cultural grounding (urban versus rural, modern versus the vestiges of the pre-modern in the periphery of the modern) defines their contrasting construction of hope and redemption.[118]

The novels are premised on the displacement or alienation from the certitudes of identity and the struggle to find a sympathetic space within modernity in which identity can be re-located. Berger's characters are portrayed as either resisting this search or else being frustrated by it. The sympathetic space which they are either denying or pursuing is an unalienated sense of mutuality. The parallels that can be drawn from this search for mutuality, and the journeying from exile to home, lead to the conclusion that the return home, and the arrival into this space of mutuality, are never to be found. While both can be yearned for through an uncanny mixture of nostalgic and utopian desires, their presence is always precluded from modernity.

Does the absence of mutuality in Berger's novels return us to the tragic sense of exile, where hope and identity are simultaneously annihilated? Or are these very yearnings by his characters a lever into a new sense of identity, paradoxically offering a trace of the pre-modern as well as calling for salvation from the beyond? The evocation of these desires returns us to the form of exile that Kristeva identifies as intrinsic to the intellectual of modernity.

Kristeva is no subscriber to the view that exile simply yields irredeemable loss, with identity being either banished to the nebulous infinity or wiped clean out of existence. The condition of exile does present a dual threat to identity, but arising from this confrontation is a third element which turns the two forces of negation into the drive for affirmation. From the loss and refusal of exile, Kristeva finds grounds for new forms of reconciliation. In the attempt to escape the strictures of the past a new identity is formed as it embraces the other. This embrace, however is not a submission to the other, but a marriage of ambivalence. This desire for the other has opened both the path into exile and the possibilities of the reconciliations that release exile from its overwhelming negativity. Kristeva outlines the three stages of exile. Firstly, there is the 'shattering' of the primary narcissism – the departure from the home does entail the loss of certitudes and symbolic protections that entangled identity with truths and beliefs. Secondly, exile is no longer the condemnation to a ritualistic disembowelling or a reactionary petrification in no-man's-land, but rather it marks the possibility of escape from the strictures of 'paternal death' as it inevitably marshals the confrontation with the other. For Kristeva the meaning of exile in modernity is defined by the simultaneous enunciation of the absence of love, with the death of the name of the father, thus converting the primary 'shattering' into a form of liberation. For if there can be 'no release from the grip of paternal death' without exile, then exile is also the springboard into the possibility of love. Kristeva insists that both the privileged place of social transformation and the act of loving are outside the death of the father; the object of love is 'the transposition of love for the other'.[119] Kristeva shifts the focus of exile from a lament over the plenitude in the past and a resentment against the lack in the present to introduce the third element: an affirmative reconciliation with liminality, fragmentation and difference. The ruptures may be premised on the violence and the negation in exile, but exile itself necessitates an ambivalent identification that goes beyond the violence and negation of the 'shattering' of the primary narcissism. Exile is no longer the disavowal of the past but a reinscription of identity, it 'bounces back to me echoes of a territory that I have lost but that I am seeking within the blackness of dreams . . . territory of the mother. If this heterogeneous body, this risky text provide meaning, identity and jouissance, they do so in a completely different way than a "Name-of-the-Father."'[120]

The resilience of identity in exile that Kristeva speaks of must not be confused with the transcendence of self that romantics aspired to in the process of journeying away from home. The scars of the past are not erased but become the very marks of memory, identity is found not in the journeying away, but is coterminous with the search for the 'lost territory' of the mother. Kristeva stresses that the crucial fantasy of the maternal space that is nurtured by the adult is not based on an idealised archaic mother, it is not to the figure of mother, but rather, it is to the shelter of the idealised relationship which binds mother and child, that the adult returns to, as the exilic rush of anguish threatens to collapse identity. It is in that unlocatable yet 'discreet cult of the Mother',[121] that the artist simultaneously demands maternal love to overcome the unthinkable dread of death and claims it as a substitute for the loss of meaning.[122]

In order to critique modernity Kristeva privileges the sensibility of the artist and woman, for she sees their identities as traversed by the contradictions of exile – inevitably split between the unnameable other and the threshold of sociality. Both artist and woman must face the frontiers of representation and return with the 'uncanny' expressions of something personal and asocial. For Kristeva, the hope for social transformation does not arrive in a language of certitudes and purities, but rather it is in that sullied contestation that surfaces between the voices of authority and common sense: 'The language of exile muffles a cry, it doesn't ever shout'.[123]

Kristeva equates the language of dissidence with the exile's experience of the foreignness in language. The oppositional qualities of a dissident must thus be registered primarily in their relationship with language, exile signifies the gap between fluent mother tongue and the translated other tongue, heightening the suspicion against neat correspondences. By being always out of place, the exile must also speak of that which is missing. Inserted into a different flow of time, the exile is conscious that it is language which is also alienated from its objects, that words are not quite the things that they seek to represent, and that language can only achieve its own transparency as long as its users have internalised the laws of difference, repressed the lack in language and forgotten the arbitrariness with which the symbolic order has projected values. The exile who stands at the junctures of alienation with language cannot only thus remind the native of the intrinsic foreignness of all language, but can also feel empowered to challenge the very structures of exchange *in* language. The exile as a dissident primarily speaks of the opaqueness, the absence, or the warp of language. Thus the resonance of the exile's dissidence depends on how deeply and how variously we see the question of identity being related to language.[124] For Kristeva, the question of language is inextricably bound to the representation of territory. The ability to name – to place – is to enter the symbolic.

Laughter is the marker of the present time and place, and entry into language is the first victory over the mother.[125]

The search for the 'lost territory' of the mother by the author is not just an attempt to transgress the limits of representation, but paradoxically, by constituting this 'atopia', there is also an attempt to reconstitute the tremulous site of identity. At the precise moment in which its very grounding is most deeply threatened, identity resurfaces.

Notes

1   J. Mitchell *The Selected Melanie Klein*, Harmondsworth, Penguin, 1986, p. 26.
2   H. K. Bhabha 'Interrogating Identities', *Identity*, London, Institute of Contemporary Arts, Documents, 6.
3   J. Berger *And our Faces* . . ., p. 91.
4   J. Berger *Pig Earth*, p. 6.
5   S. Freud *Collected Works*, XXI, London, Hogarth Press, 1960, pp. 103–4.
6   J. Berger *G*, London, Weidenfeld & Nicolson, 1972.
7   A. C. Jardine *Gynesis, Configurations of Woman and Modernity*, Ithaca, Cornell University Press, 1985: 'Gynesis – the putting into discourse of 'woman' is that *process* diagnosed in France as intrinsic to the condition of modernity; indeed the valorization of the feminine, woman, and her obligatory, that is, historical connotations, as somehow intrinsic to new and necessary modes of thinking, writing, speaking. The object produced by this process is neither a person nor a thing, but a horizon, that toward which the process is tending: a *gynema*' (p. 25).
8   G. C. Spivak 'Displacement and the Discourse of Woman' in M. Krupnick (ed.), Bloomington, Indiana University Press, 1983. However, what must be emphasised, and this is Spivak's lesson from Derrida, is that not all male discourse simply appropriates woman as an instrument of masculinist self-assertion. While we can observe the questioning of some of the binary oppositions which framed misogyny and which privileged the centrality of man, what is also apparent is that even when man declares is own displacement as he ushers woman in as the object he can only 'problematize but not fully disown his status as subject' (p. 173). Yet even in this scheme woman is still defined by the negative of the masculinist binary opposition, she still remains in the generalised terms of 'the faked orgasm and other varieties of denial' (p. 170) and this is the lesson that Spivak returns to Derrida.
9   J. Berger *A Painter of Our Time*, London, Secker & Warburg, 1958.
10   *Ibid*, p. 79.
11   *Ibid*, p. 189.
12   *Ibid*, p. 99.
13   *Ibid*, p. 71.

14 *Ibid*, p. 50–2.
15 S. Stewart, *On Longing: Narratives of the Miniature, the Gigantic, the Souvenir, the Collection*, Baltimore, Johns Hopkins University Press, 1984.
16 *A Painter of Our Time*, pp. 142–5.
17 *Ibid*, p. 119.
18 Susan Stewart also draws a correlation between the form of representation and the relationship to the past: *op. cit*, pp. 66–9.
19 *A Painter of Our Time*, p. 94.
20 For most of his critics these contradictions were seen as evidence of the inauthenticity of Berger's character, arguing that this character emerged more from Berger's politics than from his observations in life. They not only missed Berger's point on the paradoxes of integrating politics and art, but also erased the very question of the incommensurability that lies within the character of an exile. See for exmple, P. Ignotus, *Encounter*, 65, February 1959; S. Spender, *The Observer*, 9 November 1958; and R. Wollheim, *Spectator*, 14 November 1958.
21 *A Painter of Our Time*, p. 127.
22 J. Berger, *The Success and Failure of Picasso*, p. 126–8.
23 *A Painter of Our Time*, p. 17.
24 *Ibid*, p. 14.
25 *Ibid*, pp. 80–1, 91.
26 *Ibid*, p. 165.
27 *Ibid*, p. 17.
28 *Ibid*, pp. 189-90.
29 *Ibid*, pp. 9-10.
30 *Ibid*, p. 24.
31 *Ibid*, pp. 82–4.
32 *Ibid*, p. 25.
33 *Ibid*, p. 189.
34 *Ibid*, p. 190.
35 It is interesting to note that while Berger has been criticised for writing books in which the heroes all seem to share the same qualities and resemble Berger's political aspirations, nobody has noted the fact that is the opposite which may be true, that Berger is writing about the heroes who are precluded from his society, not about the resemblance between himself and his aspirants in a socialist world, but about the difference and distance between what he is and what is his other. Much has been made by Berger's reviewers of his identification with, his desire to merge with, the heroes of his text and many have made the obvious comparison between John the narrator and John Berger the author (see B. Niven, *The Labour Monthly*, September 1961 and J. Newton, *Cambridge Quarterly*, winter 1967). But one biographical detail which does seem illuminating, and remarkably unnoticed by his critics, is that when the author decided to trust more in his imagination, to give up his regular post as art critic for the *New Statesman* and become a freelance essayist and novelist, he did not stay 'home' but rather he left the 'insular island' which he so often identified as a place of fragmentation, a parochial place of decline and decay – a space which can at best be used as men often use women, a launching pad into the other – to write fiction he went abroad, to the continent.

36 'Raising Hell and Telling Stories', John Berger talks to Janine Burke, *Art Monthly*, March 1989, p. 3. This stance of simultaneous love and hate which Berger claims is absent in the English culture is one of the saving graces that Janos acknowledges in Max: 'He has not adopted the English attitude to friendship which precludes love on the one hand and the right to attack fiercely on the other. Friends have a duty to attack – to tear the pretensions off like dressings from a wound that needs the light. The English undestand none of this. If you are friends with a man in England, as we understand the word *friend*, you are considered a homosexual' (*A Painter of Our Time*, p.50).

37 Pepino is an Italian immigrant who is injured in the crash of the aeroplane that brought him to England; his severed hand signifies the loss, the failure of his own journey.

38 J. Berger *The Foot of Clive*, Harmondsworth, Penguin, 1970, pp. 156–7.

39 A. Huyssen, *After the Great Divide*, London, Macmillan, 1988. Huyssen emphasises the political ends but fails to relate them to the literary authority. Perhaps too swiftly, he equates the uses of the authorial 'I' and the elision of the problematics of subjectivity within the literary text as an extension of the imperious and transcendental space of male identity in modernist aesthetics. Following on from Christa Wolf's criticism of this aesthetic's inability to engage with subjectivity and its need to distance itself from reality via a defensive strategy against reality – 'warding it off, of protecting against it' (p. 47) – he rightly observes that the authorial 'I' always remains above the merely personal, and it becomes a convenient means whereby the male author can both insert himself into and also escape from the points of crisis. Thus the arrival of the transcendental is read as both the signal of the threat of the real and the last protective barrier into which the male self is marshalled.

40 *The Foot of Clive*, p. 78.

41 K. M. Rogers *The Troublesome Helpmate: A History of Misogyny in Literature*, Seattle, University of Washington Press, 1966, p. 227.

42 *The Foot of Clive*, p. 79. Needless to say the only woman portrayed in an unequivocably positive light is Pepino's wife; the narrator describes her through a juxtaposition of images which suggest an idealised combination of practicality, fecundity and sensuality (p. 12). Even the Matron, the only woman with unquestioned authority, is tainted with a hint of misogynism: 'she likes the boys best' (p. 89), we are complicitously informed.

43 *Ibid*, p. 86.
44 *Ibid*, pp. 23-25.
45 *Ibid*, p. 25.
46 *Ibid*, p. 25.
47 *Ibid*, p. 25.

48 The obvious scenes which testify to this are Ken's fears of contributory negligence to the death of a motorcyclist, in the accident which hospitalised him, along with the sexual betrayal of his wife; and Cyril's Christian dogmatism which also harbours a secret guilt for having raped his wife and the fantasy of his wife's bestiality.

49 J. Berger, *The Foot of Clive*, p. 13.
50 Ibid, p. 47.
51 Ibid, p. 48.
52 Ibid, p. 51.
53 Ibid, p. 58.
54 Ibid, p. 95.
55 Ibid, p. 49.
56 To use Spivak's phrase.
57 Such are the limitations of Huyssen's polemic against modernism for its incorporation and fetishisation of the feminine space (p. 45).
58 This section takes many of its cues from S. Gunew, 'Home and Away', in P. Foss (ed.), *Island in the Stream*, Leichardt, Pluto Press, 1988. Gunew relates the uncanny to the dislocative enunciation of nostalgia which lies in the twixt of alienation and the recognition of new landscapes in the writings by migrants in Australia.
59 S. Freud 'The Uncanny', *Art and Literature*, Harmondsworth, Penguin, 1985, p. 368.
60 Ibid, p. 345. For an interesting reading of Freud's essay which relates the vision of what is lacking in the mother to the terror of absence and the consequences that this has for the constitution of the engendered subjects, see M. Jacobus *Reading Woman: Essays in Feminist Criticism*, London, Methuen, 1986, p. 258.
61 Quoted in S. S. Prawer *The 'Uncanny' in Literature*, Monograph of the Inaugural Lecture delivered at Westfield College, London, 1965, p. 13.
62 Freud, 'The Uncanny', p. 340.
63 Ibid, p. 341.
64 Ibid, p. 345.
65 Ibid, p. 347.
66 *The Foot of Clive*, p. 17.
67 G, p. 52.
68 *The Foot of Clive*, p. 17.
69 Ibid., p. 62. See also Dai's description of the fox, particularly his analogy with the psyche of the killer, the one who wants to live but is caught on the wrong side of the wire: 'the killers want to live. They dream of settling down. But their earth is in the woods, on the outside of the wire-netting. And so always the wire-netting is between them and what they need to live. The wire-netting runs right through their brains. They are artful. They plan their way in. They try to foresee all the possible contingencies. They have sharp ears and sharp eyes . . . They are on the far side and they find themselves trapped; so they kill. They kill in the hope of escaping, in the hope of getting back to their earth. They kill to live, I tell you, just like foxes!!' (p. 116).
70 Ibid, p. 62.
71 Here it is akin to Novalis' s aphorism: 'Where there are no gods, ghosts hold sway'. Or to put it in Buber's words, who saw the uncanny manifesting itself as a material alienation that filled the void of a spiritual disenchantment, 'The uncanny is something that helps to pierce the protective armour assumed by modern man in his endeavours to shut out the call of the beyond' (both Novalis and Buber are quoted in Prawer, *op. cit*,

p. 16). Why do their fears take the shape of the tame and companionable dogs and their alter ego expressed in the fox? The dogs at first serve as the metaphorical expression of the uncanny, but once the unconscious is unleashed the distinction between the material and the imaginary becomes erased, so the dogs move from being loyal but fickle to the point that their treachery abandons their 'inherited faith in man' (p. 32). Later it is disclosed that 'The dogs, who once only dared to enter dreams, have been emboldened by the last day's events. They can now be heard in the foot of Clive when all are awake. Each man knows a dog is near, and this knowledge transforms his surroundings. The six of them are alone in a place they hate. They are trying to hurry on, to be rid of the dogs, to return to their own comforts' (p. 109).

72   Freud, 'The Uncanny', p. 357.
73   *The Foot of Clive*, pp. 135–46.
74   Prawer, *op. cit.*, p. 25.
75   In the seventeenth century a Swiss physician, Johannes Hoffer, applied the term to Swiss mercenaries whose fighting in distant lands was jeopardised by the recurrence of this feeling of homesickness and whose symptoms included despondency, melancholy, anorexia and suicide attempts. See J. Hoffer (1678), 'Medical Dissertation of Nostalgia', *Bulletin of History of Medicine*, vol. 2, 1934, pp. 376–91.
76   J. Gallop, *Reading Lacan*, Ithaca, Cornell University Press, 1985, p. 148.
77   G. Stauth and B. Turner, *Nietzsche's Dance*, Oxford, Basil Blackwell, 1988, p. 28.
78   *Ibid*, pp. 30–1.
79   A. Jardine, *Gynesis*, p. 68.
80   Jardine cites Lasch's critique of mass culture as a society without a father; Baudrillard's critique of the repressiveness of rationality via a recuperation of the feminine principle of seduction; and Steiner's chastisement of women for their loss of the genius based on the inner speech and intimacy, as examples following the nostalgic paradigm purely in terms of melancholic languor (pp. 67–8).
81   G. C. Spivak, *In Other Worlds*; see in particular section one.
82   Stauth and Turner, pp. 53–4.
83   See Gallop, p. 151.
84   H. Kaplan, 'The Psychopathologies of Nostalgia', *The Psychoanalytic Review*, vol. 74, no. 4, winter 1987, p. 466.
85   See J. Berger, *A Fortunate Man*, p. 119, on anguish and different time-scales.
86   Auden quoted in T. Coherty, *On Modern Authority*, Brighton, The Harvester Press, p. 47. See also chapters 1 and 2 on exile and the home in literature.
87   H. Cixous, 'Fiction and its Phantoms: A Reading of Freud's The "Uncanny"', *New Literary History*, vol. VII, no. 3, spring 1976, p. 544.
88   *The Foot of Clive*, p. 136.
89   Compare with Kristeva's metaphor of the maternal space as 'walled city'.
90   A. Jardine, *Gynesis*, p. 87.

91 *G*, p. 111.
92 J. Berger, *Corker's Freedom*, London, Writers and Readers, 1979, pp. 35–8.
93 *Ibid*, p. 49.
94 Spivak, 'Displacements', p. 191.
95 A. Jardine, *Gynesis*, p. 78.
96 J. Berger, 'Once upon a Time', in C. Rawlence (ed.), *About Time*, London, Jonathan Cape, 1985, p. 15.
97 *Ibid*, p. 25.
98 *Ibid*.
99 *A Painter of Our Time*, p. 66.
100 'Once upon a Time', p. 28.
101 *A Painter of Our Time*, p. 118.
102 *Ibid*, p. 119.
103 *G*, p. 148.
104 *Ibid*, p. 149.
105 *Ibid*, p. 152.
106 *Ibid*, p. 107.
107 *Ibid*, pp. 50–4.
108 *Ibid*, p. 52.
109 *Ibid*, p. 54.
110 R. G. Collingwood, *An Autobiography*, Oxford, Oxford University Press, 1939, p. 141.
111 *G*, p. 109.
112 Collingwood describes incapsulation as 'my name for such facts as this – familiar enough to everybody – that a man who changes his habits, thoughts etc, retains in the second phase some residue of the first', *An Autobiography*, p. 141.
113 'In re-thinking what somebody else thought, he thinks it himself. In knowing that somebody else thought it, he knows that he himself is able to think it. And finding out what he is able to do is finding out what kind of a man he is', *ibid*, pp. 114–5.
114 *G*, p. 133.
115 *Ibid*, p. 142.
116 J. Kristeva, 'A New Type of Intellectual: The Dissident', in T. Moi (ed.), *The Kristeva Reader*, Oxford, Basil Blackwell, 1987, p. 298. However, I am aware of Rosi Braidotti's astute critique of Kristeva in her inspiring book *Patterns of Dissonance*, Cambridge, Polity, 1991, where she argues that Kristeva overgeneralises the intellectual's claim to dissidence as she elides the important questions concerning women's identity formation through the abstraction of the figure of woman that challenges the symbolic order. My interest in Kristeva's writing is focused on the illumination of the experience of exile that results from the insertion of the figuration of woman into the symbolic.
117 G. Bowmann 'Tales of the Lost Land', *New Formations*, no. 5, 1988, pp. 31–52. Bowmann outlines the differences between acounts of Palestinian identity and nationalist consciousness, from the texts of a displaced refugee in Lebanon, a 'bourgeois' Palestinian intellectual in the United States, and a Palestinian lawyer in the West Bank.

118 It is for these reasons that the short stories concerning the peasantry *Pig Earth*, *Once in Europa*, and *Lilac and Flag*, are not incorporated in this analysis. This project marks a separate stage in Berger's thinking and deserves consideration from a different perspective.

119 J. Kristeva, *Desire in Language*, ed. L. S. Roudiez, Oxford, Basil Blackwell, 1987, p. 149.

120 *Ibid*, p. 163.

121 J. Kristeva 'Stabat Mater', *The Kristeva Reader*, p. 177.

122 For example, the numerous references to 'walled gardens' in *G* and similar edenic metaphors which resemble the space of the womb in Berger's other novels are far more expressive of this crisis than the biographical essay on the relationship to his mother: J. Berger, 'Mother', *Keeping a Rendezvous*, New York, Pantheon, 1991, pp. 43–52.

123 J. Kristeva, *The Kristeva Reader*, p. 298.

124 See J. Gallop 'The Mother Tongue', in F. Barker *et al.*, (ed.), *Politics of Theory*, Colchester, University of Essex, 1983, p. 53, in which she argues that while a speaker in a foreign language is in a position to remember the symbolic, a foreign language cannot insure one's dissidence. Gallop then claims that, by privileging the exile vis-à-vis language, Kristeva repeats as she reverses the projection of difference intrinsic to the castration complex, hence empowering the exile over the native. For another account which also sees Kristeva's self-privileging of exile as 'emblematic of the displacement systematically theorized as the work of the heterogeneous semiotic', see M. Atack 'The Other: Feminist', *Paragraph*, vol. 8, Oct. 1986, p. 30.

125 J. Kristeva, *Desire in Language*, p. 289.

Postscript

Faith without certitudes

> The starting point of critical elaboration is the consciousness of what one really is, and is 'knowing thyself' as a product of the historical process to date, which has deposited in you an infinity of traces, without leaving an inventory, therefore it is imperative at the outset to compile such an inventory.
>
> A. Gramsci
>
> What we ought to do is retrace not the biography of a writer but what could be called the writing of his work, a kind of ergography.
>
> R. Barthes
>
> There is never a single approach to something remembered. The remembered is not like a terminus at the end of a line. Numerous approaches or stimuli converge upon it and lead to it. Words, comparisons, signs need to create a context for a printed photograph in a comparable way; that is to say, they must mark and leave open diverse approaches. A radial system has to be constructed around the photograph so that it may be seen in terms which are simultaneously personal, political, economic, dramatic, everyday and historic.
>
> John Berger

This book began as a doctoral dissertation. In the preliminary drafts of this dissertation the assigned role for Berger's texts was secondary. My primary intention was to examine the relationship between the experience of exile and the representation of identity. Berger's texts would enter to probe the boundaries and question the silences within this discourse. The attempts to write such a dissertation were becoming increasingly pedantic and the results were always very unsatisfying. Nevertheless I persisted, as someone does when they are trying to dig themselves out of a hole: up and out seemed to be the only option. Fortunately this trajectory was interrupted by a trip 'home'. On my return to Cambridge, confronted by a rather shapeless dissertation, I commenced the process of 'writing up'. This proved to be more than an exercise in tightening up or restructuring the argument; it was a period in which my whole methodological approach altered. I found myself attempting to construct paths by starting with Berger's texts and assembling an order by intuition rather than the subordination of these texts to pre-existent schemas. The change was, at the time, almost imperceptible – the themes that I was preoccupied with were still the same, the only difference being that the relationship between them had been 'vitalised'. This eventually led me to realise that the various themes that I had identified in Berger's work, and which I wanted to discuss in abstract, were not only deeply embedded in each other but were also the key components to his generalised perspective. The themes were so interconnected that they had become indistinguishable from his method; to separate was to neutralise them because, more than anything else, they were dependent on the force, the tension that was the consequence of their being put together. The irony of my methodological reversal was doubled both by the realisation of the old lesson that all substantive projects are cross-hatched by the processes of intuitive imagination, and the understanding that the twin components in Berger's metaphorical perspective were exile and empathy. The two themes that I was trying to examine in isolation were to make themselves available only as a dual process which would always lead to a third term, which was itself renewed as it replayed the critical path of metaphor. The impact of this lesson was, however, not confined to witnessing the processes of a dialectical imagination.

From the outset I have been convinced that both the experience of emigration and the exilic tension between absence and presence is the continuous subject for Berger. The persistence with which he returns to this subject is not the consequence of an obsession which flattens every other object as it is brought in relation to it, nor is it a fixation that imposes an imperious judgement on all the other subjects that are brought into its domain. Rather it reveals the *pulse* in the bias of his imagination, and reflects the oscillating pattern with which his termperament returns to and departs from an inexhaustible question. The continuities in Berger's diverse writings are thus found in the insistence to confront the tension between the order with which disparate subjects present themselves to him, and the order with which he represents the discontinuous. 'Writing up' is thus not merely the process of making the substance of thought more accessible to the other, but also the consequence of the patterns in self-consciousness.

Something of the other's soul can be glimpsed between the panoply of identities that are staged in the text and the author's signature. The circle of understanding that I am attempting to describe in relation to Berger's texts relies on a degree of parallelism between a personal project and epochal transformations. So how does the intersection of Berger's themes and method offer a perspective on the 'spirit' of modernity? Looking at the texts individually, an immediate answer comes to the fore. By articulating the incommensurable moments in the migrant's entry into the metropolis and the histories that are truncated or silenced for the sake of 'progress' and 'development', Berger identifies the disjunctures of modernity. But when examining the texts cumulatively (and not necessarily in the order in which they were written), and when considering the persistent cross-hatching of theme and method, which like a fingerprint or a scar is reproduced despite the cellular transformation of the body, here we can see an omnidirectional relationship between the destiny of a personal project and a historical phenomenon.

In biographies the link between the personal and the historical has often been made in symbolic terms, whereby correspondences are fixed by equating the part with the whole. This form of linkage presupposes an untenable conflation of the universal with the particular. The connection between author and epoch that I am interested in is far more open-ended; it is an allegorical rather than a symbolic relationship; it is a search for a correlation between trajectories, rather than for the icons which contain the 'sign of the times'.

There are conventional structures for housing an author's work. Either it is related to an established tradition of critical thought or its development is aligned with a social movement. With Berger's texts such a method of encasing would invariably negate the very processes that I am intending to elaborate. The appropriate metaphor that characterises the trajectory of his work is that of the journey. For his writing embodies not just a fascination with migration but also a migrant's perspective. The generative element in Berger's mode of thinking is the *distance* berween names and things, or in his own formulation, 'the gap between the given and the desired'.

The nature of this conflict, between the processes of imaginative experience and the received categories or sentiments from a dominant culture, will not be properly understood if critical discourse reproduces the oppositional structures which sustain the latter at the expense of the former. Both in fiction and in art criticism, Berger has offered numerous portrayals of a hero, and at the centre of each is a representation of a vision whose affirmative example is simultaneously expressed through the heroes' unflinching faith in their own imaginative experiences and a profound scepticism about the society they are situated in. By focusing on the insistence to negotiate the tension between the materiality of the present and the alterity of the future, Berger reveals both the partial overlap in, for instance, the critical longings of Marxism and Romanticism, and the potential space for an alliance with diverse historical figures, all of whom have attempted 'to say that which was never meant to be said'. Berger's journey is therefore not a defence of a critical tradition but an exercising of the critical will.

There is no independent truth upon which all hopes of arrival are staked. Confirmation of Berger's journey is not mapped by fixed co-ordinates. This loose but ongoing trajectory could be read as a benign metaphor for self-understanding in modernity. It is not that his writings offer an apologetic history of the transformations in modernity, but rather that they translate and utilise the vicissitudes of modernity. It is in this way that the truths of an epoch can be read from the irreducible contours of a life's project. His ethics are guided not by *a priori* principles but by the context of dispossession and the resistance to an oppressive silence. The only philosophical principle that Berger has internalised so deeply, that it surfaces as an intuitive belief is that truth is always on the other side of the 'screen' of clichés that constitutes the ideology of the dominant class. This principle which shrewdly examines utopian or totalising claims is also the basis of Berger's commitment to hope, for its capacity to critique the present is not premised on a return to an idealised point in time or space, but on the convertibility of the past and the future in the work of the present.

The journey into metaphysics is always underwritten by the political. While the allegorical relationship between author and epoch can be traced through the repetition of theme and method, what it consistently leads to is an ambiguous discovery: there is the realisation that the path of this journey incessantly re-invents its origin and its destiny by establishing a continuous relationship between the self and the other. Thus the attempt to trace this relationship can only lead back and in upon itself, much like the structure of a helix. This circuitous path between the self and the other is very familiar to all story tellers. Hence the certitudes and the generalisations that are a hallmark of Berger's style are not so much an expression of the desire to pronounce with authority, or to declare the superiority of one logic by inverting another, but rather they reveal how the assemblage of disparates once subjected to the criss-crossing pattern of comparison may yield hints and conclusions that can serve as both questions and solutions.

The metaphor of the journey – which includes the utilisation of the migrational predisposition with a critical perspective on modernity – has implications for the position of the modern intellectual. Having experienced the dismantling of one schema of interpretation, the migrant is always in the position not only to substitute the 'old' for the 'new' but also to consider the relationship, the gap between different schemas, and consequently offer interpretations which are the result of *both* or *neither*. This perspective, as it re-examines the relationship between names and things, admits a view which is unacknowledged by the conventions of critical thinking. For the duality in this mode of thinking does not necessarily demand that one polarity should subordinate the other but beckons a possible third position. Thus the migrant perspective is not only a means to express the repressed but a desire to reach for another space – a potential which results not from the interiority of either polarity but from the hybridity within each duality. In this sense the intellectual's intended audience is the imaginary audience of *différance*. Displaced from the privilege of addressing an exclusive audience, the modern intellectual is also dislodged from the practice of working with a subject that possesses fixed boundaries and a unified theme.

Select Bibliography

WORKS BY JOHN BERGER
BOOKS

A Painter of Our Time, London, Secker & Warburg, 1958.
Permanent Red, London, Methuen, 1960.
The Foot of Clive, London, Methuen, 1962.
Corker's Freedom, London, Methuen, 1964.
The Success and Failure of Picasso, Harmondsworth, Penguin, 1965.
A Fortunate Man: The Story of a Country Doctor (with Jean Mohr), Harmondsworth, Allen Lane, 1967.
The Moment of Cubism and Other Essays, London, Weidenfeld & Nicolson, 1969.
Art and Revolution: Ernst Neizvestny and the role of the Artist in the U.S.S.R., London, Weidenfeld & Nicolson, 1969.
G: A Novel, London, Weidenfeld & Nicolson, 1972.
The Look of Things, edited by N. Stangos, Harmondsworth, Penguin, 1972.
Ways of Seeing (with S. Blomberg, M. Dibb and R. Hollis), based on the BBC Television Series, Harmondsworth, Penguin, 1972.
A Seventh Man (with J. Mohr and S. Blomberg), Harmondsworth, Penguin, 1975.
Pig Earth, London, Writers & Readers, 1979.
About Looking, London, Writers & Readers, 1980.
Another Way of Telling (with Jean Mohr), London, Writers & Readers, 1982.
And our Faces, my Heart, Brief as Photos, London, Writers & Readers, 1984.
The White Bird, edited by L. Spencer, London, Chatto & Windus, 1985.
Once in Europa, New York, Pantheon, 1987.
Goya's Last Portrait (with Nella Bielski), London, Faber & Faber, 1987.
Lilac and Flag, New York, Pantheon, 1990.
Keeping a Rendezvous, New York, Pantheon, 1991.

Bibliography

Essays and reviews from *The New Statesman*: 1951–61

1951
Young Contemporaries at RBA Galleries, 3 Feb.
Edward Wadsworth (1889–1949), 10 Feb.
The London Group, 17 Feb.
Louis Marcoussis, 24 Feb.
Humphrey Jennings (1907–1950), 3 Mar.
Untitled, 17 Mar.
L. S. Lowry, 24 Mar.
William Gear, 14 Apr.
Bernard Buffet / Algernon Newton, 21 Apr.
British Painting, 1925–1950, 5 May.
Splendid Occasions / Masterpieces of Victorian Paintings at the V&A, 19 May.
Abstract Painting, Sculptures and Mobiles, 2 June.
Traditional Art from the Colonies, 9 June.
Two British Painters, 16 June.
Blake's Tempera Paintings, 23 June.
Brobdingnag, 30 June.
British Painting 1925–1950, 7 July.
Graham Sutherland, 21 July.
Sickert, 4 Aug.
British Abstract Painting, 11 Aug.
Lithographs by Toulouse-Lautrec, 18 Aug.
Treasure Trove, 1 Sept.
Ceri Richards, 15 Sept.
Paintings of Jamaica, 22 Sept.
Charles Malfrey, 29 Sept.
Ganymed Reproductions, 13 Oct.
Josef Herman, 20 Oct.
Sven Blomberg, 3 Nov.
Keith Vaughan, 10 Nov.
Present Painting, 17 Nov.
London Group, 24 Nov.
George Mellemish / Lilian Colbourn, 1 Dec.
John Craxton, 8 Dec.
Jankel Adler 1895–1945 & Bernard Meninsky 1891–1950, 15 Dec.
Degas Bronzes, 29 Dec.

1952
Francis Bacon, 5 Jan.
Julian Trevelyan / Lyonel Feininger, 12 Jan.

For the Future, 19 Jan.
William Turnbull / Balthus, 26 Jan.
Graham Sutherland Portrait of Lord Beaverbrook, 2 Feb.
Ruszkowski, 9 Feb.
Viero Da Silva / Barns Graham / Merlyn Evans / J. D. Innes / Affandi / India House Show 16 Feb.
Winifred Nicholson / Cartier Bresson, 23 Feb.
Nicholas de Stael, 1 Mar.
Peter Lanyon, 15 Mar.
Photographs from Life magazine / Carel Weight, 22 Mar.
Direct Communication: Five Young French Realists, 29 Mar.
Geoffrey Clarke / Peter Potworowski / Fifty Years of Dutch Painting, 5 Apr.
Jacques Villon, 12 Apr.
Arts of India and China / Ingredients of Taste, 26 Apr.
Emilio Greco / Guido Pajetta/Studio Group, 3 May.
The Royal Academy, 10 May.
Affandi and Other Indonesian Painters / Victor Pasmore / Lucien Freud, 17 May.
Three Women Painters, 24 May.
Ravenna Mosaics, 31 May.
The Biennale, 5 July.
Recent trends in Realist Painting, Eugène Delacroix, 12 July.
The Art of Gandhara, 19 July.
Master and Decadents, 26 July.
Primitives and Sophistication 9 Aug. Reply, 2 Aug.
AIA Exhibition, 16 Aug.
Contemporary Lithographs, 23 Aug.
Six Young Contemporaries, 6 Sept.
Ben Enmonwu / Kokoschka, 20 Sept.
Jacob Bornfriend, 4 Oct.
Terry Frost, 11 Oct.
Temptations of Talent, 25 Oct.
Elisabeth Frink / John Harvey / Michel Werner. 1 Nov.
John Piper / Elinor Bellingham-Smith. 15 Nov.
Zao Wou-ki. 22 Nov.
Alvaro Guevara (1894–1951), 29 Nov.
Contemporary British Painters, 6 Dec.
Contemporary Ceylonese Paintings, 13 Dec.
Definitions, 20 Dec.
Max Ernst, 27 Dec.

1953
Peter L. Peri / Orpheus and Prometheus, 3 Jan.

Bibliography

Looking Back, 10 Jan.
Drawings and Sculptures by Georg Ehrlich, 17 Jan.
Return to Realism, 15 Mar.
The Unknown Political Soldier, 21 Mar.
Brian Robb, 28 March.
Recent Paintings by Yves Alix / Correspondence, 4 Apr.
Alphonse Quizet, 11 Apr.
Machine-Life Paintings, 18 Apr.
Andre Minaux / Twentieth Century Form, 25 Apr.
Rodin, 2 May.
Le Corbusier / Ceri Richards, 9 May.
Three Sculptors, 23 May.
Courbet's Art and Politics, 30 May.
British Life, 13 June.
Public Sculpture, 4 July.
Rowlandson and Gillray, 11 July.
Mary Cassatt (1845–1927), 18 July.
The Young Generation, 25 July.
Judgement on Paris, / Sculpture by Gordon Herick, 1 Aug.
Twelve Australian Painters, 8 Aug.
Fashionable Blinkers, 15 Aug.
Hazel Turnbull, 22 Aug.
Drawing is Discovering, 29 Aug.
Josef Herman, 3 Oct.
Renoir, 10 Oct.
Four Painters, 17 Oct.
Andrew Forge, 24 Oct.
Taste and Soccer / Jugoslav Medieval Fresco / Painting into Textiles, 31 Oct.
A Set Problem, 7 Nov.
Derrick Greaves, 14 Nov.
A Degas Nude, 28 Nov.
Portrait of the Artist as an Acquisition, 3 Dec.
Jewish and Other Paintings / Profile of Moscow, 12 Dec.
Soviet Values, 26 Dec.

1954

Carnival Painter, 16 Jan.
Art in Ceylon, 23 Jan.
Soviet Aesthetics, 6 Feb.
Charles Ginner, 13 Feb.
Rebeyrolle and Stanley Spencer, 20 Feb.
Piltdown Sculpture, 27 Feb.
Six Young Painters, 6 Mar.

Light and the Party Line, 13 Mar.
Paintings by Stefan Knapp, 20 Mar.
Art is Slow, 27 Mar.
Landscapes as Close-ups, 3 Apr.
Drawings and Watercolours by Hokusai, 10 Apr.
Keith Vaughan / Sculpture Vacuum, 17 Apr.
Victor Pasmore, 24 Apr.
Round the Galleries, 1 May.
Academy Life, 8 May.
Why Picasso?, 15 May.
The Gourmet, the Shepherd, and the Critic, 22 May.
Bonnard and Others, 29 May.
Art and Architecture, 5 June.
Two Masterpieces, 12 June.
Goya, 19 June.
Round the Galleries, 26 June.
The Heroism of Cézanne, 3 July.
Delicacy and Gentility – Giorgio Morandi, 10 July.
A Nude and Reflections, 17 July.
Cameras and Lies, 24 July.
Paintings by Harold Wood / George Catlin, 31 July.
The Glut in Art, 7 Aug.
Patience, 14 Aug.
Isolation and Freedom, 21 Aug.
The Cosmopolitan and the Village Pump, 22 Aug.
The Impossible Student, 11 Sept.
The Innocent and the Guilty, 18 Sept.
John Bratby, 25 Sept.
Ancient and Modern, 30 Oct.
A Dickensian, 6 Nov.
Henri Matisse, 13 Nov.
A Comparison, 20 Nov.
Watteau and Chardin / T.U.C. Sculpture, 4 Dec.
Fernand Léger and the Future, 18 Dec.
Une Saison en Enfer, 25 Dec.

1955
David Jones, 1 Jan.
The Height of Superficiality, 8 Jan.
Aunt or Arbiter, 15 Jan.
Painting and Oil, 22 Jan.
The Reaction of the Young Contemporaries, 29 Jan.
The Missing Example, 5 Feb.

Bibliography

Louis Le Brocquy, 12 Feb.
Two Views / The Siege of the Ivory Tower, 19 Feb.
An Indian Painter, 26 Feb.
Martin Bloch, 5 Mar.
Bernard Buffet, 12 Mar.
Guttoso, 19 Mar.
Round the Exhibitions, 26 Mar.
Round the Galleries, 2 Apr.
Appreciation, 9 Apr.
Mud and Other, 23 Apr.
The Morality of Competition, 30 Apr.
Carl Frederick Hill / The Nylon Academy, 7 May.
That Man Again, 23 June.
Shame and Tenacity, 2 July.
The Limits of Dumbness, 16 July.
Painting as Passion, 23 July.
Social Realism and the Young, 30 July.
The Flesh and its Denial, 13 Aug.
Real Oils, 20 Aug.
L'Envoi for Léger, 27 Aug.
Drawings by Edward Ardizzone, 27 Aug.
A Skin Painter, 10 Sept.
Around and About, 17 Sept.
Critic's Choice, 23 Sept.
Michael Ayrton, 1 Oct.
The Ideal State of Art / The Indian and the Sensitive Man, 8 Oct.
Reproductions and Lithographs, 15 Oct.
Murder, 22 Oct.
Auntie Becomes Sally, 29 Oct.
Julian Trevelyan and Kathleen Allen, 29 Oct.
Abandon Hope, 5 Nov.
St Vincent and Gabriel The Magnifying Glass, 12 Nov.
Paintings by Ginette Rapp, 19 Nov.
Good Painting / Man Within A Frame, 26 Nov.
Round and About, 3 Dec.
Greaves and Hogarth, 10 Dec.
English Taste in the Nineteenth Century, 17 Dec.
Homage to Bernard Berenson, Géricault, 24 Dec.
Style and the Man, 31 Dec.

1956
The Unrecognized, 7 Jan.
Several Exhibitions, 14 Jan.
The Battle 21 Jan.

The Face of Nature, 28 Jan.
Edward Middleditch, 11 Feb.
The Child, The Mystic and The Landlady, 3 Mar.
Time's Winged Chariot, 17 Mar.
De Stael, 24 Mar.
Dusk and Dawn, 31 Mar.
O Flatterer! / Ceri Richards, 14 Apr.
Round the Galleries / Looking Forward, 28 Apr.
Practice and Prestige, 5 May.
Polish, German, Italian, 19 May.
King of Geometry, 2 June.
Through the Gate, 16 June.
Rebeyrolle and Picasso, 30 June.
The Biennale, 4 Aug.
Millet and Morality, 8 Sept.
Tooths and Bones, 22 Sept.
Exit and Credo, 29 Sept.
The World's Yours, 13 Oct.
An Art-Historical Expedition, 15 Dec.

1957
Death of a Hero, 12 Jan.
Vincent Their Vincent, 20 Apr.
Grace and Pedantry, 13 July.
Artists and Schools, 27 July.
The Example of Mireille, 10 Aug.
Days and Nights, 14 Sept.
The Regent's Dumb School, 26 Oct.

1958
Comme Ci Comme Ca, 4 Jan.
Candlepower and Le Roi Soleil, 11 Jan.
The Art of Assassination, 18 Jan.
Roses by Other Names, 25 Jan.
Art Schools and Vital Statistics, 1 Feb.
Rough Justice / Action Painting, 15 Feb.
The Art of Emmer, 22 Feb.
The Star of Cubism, 1 Mar.
An Immortal Progress / The Idealist's Progress, 8 Mar.
Some New Moon, 22 Mar.
Success and Value, 5 Apr.
She Shall be Called Woman, 12 Apr.
Letter, 20 Apr.
Not So Modest, 3 May.

Bibliography

The Art of Unlived Life, 10 May.
Three Landscapes, 17 May.
The Engineer as Prophet, 7 June.
The Difficulty of Being an Artist, 14 June.
Brill and de Francia, 21 June.
Viennese Diary, 28 June.
Round the Galleries, 5 July.
Italian Diary, 2 Aug.
Italians and Modigliani, 9 Aug.
The Banale, 16 Aug.
Major at Wigan, 30 Aug.
George Fullard, 6 Sept.
Frisco Ten Holt, 20 Sept.
The Place of Thy Tent, 4 Oct.
Different Logic, 18 Oct.
The Falsifiers / East German Art, 25 Oct.
Free to Starve / Art Show, 8 Nov.
The White Cell, 22 Nov.
Darkness is Zero, 29 Nov.
Imaginary Illness, 13 Dec.
Controlling the Spin, 27 Dec.

1959
Radio Rescue / Russian Art at the Academy, 3 Jan.
A Belief in Uniform, 17 Jan.
News from the World, 24 Jan.
Reproduction of a dry point etching by Peter Peri, 31 Jan.
Me Too, 7 Feb.
Autographs, 14 Feb.
A Dialectical Masterpiece, 21 Feb.
Robbed, 28 Feb.
Round the Market, 14 Mar.
Bon Courage, 21 Mar.
Poussin at Dulwich, 4 Apr.
Who Are You?, 11 Apr.
For Whom is the East East?, 9 May.
Five Ways of Looking at a Tree, 23 May.
Pre-Naturalism, 30 May.
Gods and Critics, 6 June.
No Still Life, 13 June.
Artists against the Bomb, 20 June.
This Century, 20 June.
George Fullard and Karl Wescke, 18 July.
The Ambush of Reality, 25 July.

Romantic Notebooks I, 1 Aug.
Romantic Notebooks II, 8 Aug.
Through the Bars, 22 Aug.
The Weight, 19 Sept.
Unlikely Virtue, 3 Oct.
From Umbria to the Moon, 10 Oct.
The Hero, 14 Nov.
People in a Final Tree, 21 Nov.
A Stick in the Dark, 28 Nov.
Wasps in the Jam, 19 Dec.

1960
Only Connect I, 20 Feb.
Only Connect II, 27 Feb.
Thicker than Water, 16 Apr.
Dear Sir, 21 May.
Paradise Lost, 13 Aug.
Explanations in Purgatory, 24 Sept.
Museum Mandarins, 15 Oct.
The Barricades of Art, 29 Oct.

1961
Zadkine's Hand, 13 Jan.

Books containing essays by Berger

'Introduction', to E. Duff, *How We Are*, London, Allen Lane, 1971.
'Introduction', to H. F. Daniel, *Enclyclopedia of Themes and Subjects in Painting*, London, Thames and Hudson, 1971.
'A Philosopher and Death', in E. Fischer, *An Opposing Man*, translated by Peter and Betty Ross, London, Allen Lane, 1974.
'Problems of Socialist Art', in L. Baxandall (ed.), *Radical Perspectives in the Arts*, Harmondsworth, Penguin, 1972, pp. 209–23.
'Boris', in B. Buford (ed.), *Granta*, 9, Cambridge, 1983, pp. 23–51.
'Once upon a Time', in C. Rawlence (ed.), *About Time*, London, Cape & Channel 4, 1985, pp. 8–28.
'Question of Geography' (with Nella Bielski), in B. Buford (ed.), *Granta*, 13, Cambridge, 1984, pp. 73–116.
'A Story of Aesop', in B. Buford (ed.), *Granta*, 21 Cambridge, 1987, pp. 11–20.
'Walking Back Home' (with Sylvia Grant), in C. Killip, *In Flagrante*, London, Secker & Warburg, 1988.

Film Scripts

Salamander. (with Alain Tanner)
The Middle of the World. (with Alain Tanner)
Jonah who will be 25 in the year 2000. (with Alain Tanner)
Play Me Something.

Translations

G. Goedhart, *Helene Weigel, Actress*, A Book of Photographs. Text by Bertold Brecht (with Anya Bostock), Leipzig, VEB Editions, 1961.
Bertold Brecht, *Poems on the Theatre* (with Anya Bostock), Middlesex, Scorpion Press, 1961.
Aimé Césaire, *Return to My Native Land* (with Anya Bostock), Harmondsworth, Penguin, 1969.
Nella Bielski, *Oranges for the Son of Alexander Levy* (with Lisa Appignanesi), London, Writers & Readers, 1982.

SECONDARY SOURCE

Adorno, T. W. *Minima Moralia*, translated by E. F. N. Jephcott, London, Verso, 1974.
— *Prisms*, translated by Samuel and Sherry Weber, Cambridge, Mass., The MIT Press, 1981.
Adorno, T. W., W. Benjamin, B. Brecht, E. Bloch and g. Lukács, *Aesthetics and Politics*, London, Verso, 1986.
Anderson, B. *Imagined Communities*, London, Verso, 1983.
Arac, J.'(ed.), *Postmodernism and Politics*, Manchester, Manchester University Press, 1986.
Arato, A. and E. Gebhardt (ed.), *The Essential Frankfurt School Reader*, Oxford, Basil Blackwell, 1978.
Arendt, H. *The Origins of Totalitarianism*, London, Andre Deutsch, 1986.
Bachelard, G. *The Poetics of Space*, translated by M. Jolas, Boston, Beacon, 1969.
— *The Poetics of Reverie*, translated by D. Russell, Boston, Beacon, 1969.
— *The Psychoanalysis of Fire*, London, Quartet, 1987.
Barthes, R. *The Pleasure of the Text*, translated by R. Miller, New York, Hill & Wang, 1975.
— *Image, Music, Text*, translated by S. Heath, London, Flamingo, 1977.
— *The Grain of the Voice*, translated by L. Coverdale, New York, Hill & Wang, 1981.
— *Empire of Signs*, translated by R. Howard, London, Jonathan Cape, 1982.
— *Sade, Fourier, Loyola*, London, translated by R. Howard, London, Jonathan Cape, 1977.

— *Mythologies*, translated by A. Lavers, London, Granada, 1982.
— *Michelet*, translated by R. Howard, Oxford, Basil Blackwell, 1987.
Baudelaire, C. *The Painter of Modern Life and Other Essays*, London, Phaidon, 1969.
Berger, P. L. *The Homeless Mind*, Harmondsworth, Penguin, 1973.
Benjamin, W. *Illuminations*, translated by H. Zohn, London, Fontana, 1982.
— *One Way Street*, translated by E. Jephcott and K. Shorter, London, Verso, 1985.
— *Understanding Brecht*, translated by A. Bostock, London, Verso, 1988.
— *Moscow Diary*, translated by R. Sieburth, Cambridge, Mass., Harvard University Press, 1986.
Berman, M. *All That Is Solid Melts Into Air: The Experience of Modernity*, New York, Simon and Shuster, 1982.
Bhabha, H. K. *Nation and Narration*, London, Routledge, 1990.
Blanchot, M. *The Space of Literature*, translated by A. Smock, Lincoln, University of Nebraska Press, 1982.
Brecht, B. *Poems 1913-1956*, London, Methuen, 1976.
Bourdieu, P. *Outline of a Theory of Practice*, translated by R. Nice, Cambridge, Cambridge University Press, 1987.
Brownlie, I. *Principles of Public International Law*, Oxford, Clarendon, 1979.
Burger, P. *Theory of the Avant Garde*, translated by M. Shaw, Minneapolis, University of Minnesota Press, 1984.
Camus, A. *The Rebel*, Harmondsworth, Penguin, 1982.
— *The Myth of Sisyphus*, London, Penguin, 1988.
Caute, D. *Collisions*, London, Quartet, 1974.
Cavafy, C. P. *Collected Poems*, translated by E. Keeley and P. Sherrard, London, Chatto & Windus, 1978.
Certeau, M. de *Heterologies: Discourse on the Other*, translated by B. Massumi, Manchester, Manchester University Press, 1986.
Clifford, J. and G. E. Marcus, *Writing Culture: The Poetics and Politics of Ethnography*, Berkeley, University of California Press, 1986.
Cohen, N. *The Pursuit of the Millennium*, London, Paladin, 1978.
Collingwood, R. G. *An Autobiography*, Oxford, Oxford University Press, 1939.
Coser, L. A. (ed.), *Georg Simmel*, Englewood Cliffs, Prentice-Hall, 1965.
Davies, A. F. *Essays in Political Sociology*, Melbourne, Cheshire, 1972.
Derrida, J. *The Ear of The Other*, New York, Schoken, 1985.
— *Memoires for Paul de Man*, New York, Columbia University Press, 1986.
Docherty, T. *On Modern Authority*, Brighton, Harvester Press, 1987.
Dyer, G. *Ways of Telling*, London, Pluto, 1986.
Eagleton, T. *Exiles and Emigres*, London, Chatto & Windus, 1970.
Ellman, R. *Oscar Wilde*, London, Hamish Hamilton, 1987.
Fabian, J. *Time and the Other: How Anthropology Makes its Object*, New York, Columbia University Press, 1983.

Featherstone, M. (ed.), *Global Culture*, London, Sage, 1990.
Fernbach, D. *Surveys from Exile*, London, Pelican, 1973.
Fleming, D. and B. Bailey (ed.), *The Intellectual Migration*, Cambridge, Mass., Harvard University Press, 1967.
Foss, P. (ed.), *Island in the Stream: Myths of Place in Australian Culture*, Leichardt, Pluto, 1988.
Foster, H. (ed.), *Postmodern Culture*, London, Pluto, 1985.
Foucault, M. *Language, Counter-Memory, Practice*, Ithaca, Cornell University Press, 1977.
— *Foucault/Blanchot*, New York, Zone, 1987.
— *Death and the Labyrinth: The World of Raymond Roussel*, translated by C. Ruas, London, Athlone Press, 1987.
Freud, S. *On Metapsychology: The Theory of Psychoanalysis*, translated by J. Strachey, Harmondsworth, Penguin, 1984.
— *Art and Literature*, translated by J. Strachey, Harmondsworth, Penguin, 1984.
Frisby, D. *Sociological Impressionism: A Reassessment of Georg Simmel's Social Theory*. London, Heinemann, 1981.
— *Fragments of Modernity*, Cambridge, Polity, 1985.
Fuller, P. *Seeing Berger*, London, Writers & Readers, 1982.
Gallop, J. *Reading Lacan*, Ithaca, Cornell University Press, 1985.
Giddens, A. *The Nation-State and Violence*, Cambridge, Polity, 1985.
Gurr, A. *Writers in Exile, The Identity of Home in Modern Literature*, Brighton, Harvester Press, 1981.
Holst Petersen, K. and A. Rutherford (ed.), *Displaced Persons*, Sydney, Dangaroo Press, 1988.
Huyssen, A. *After The Great Divide*, London, Macmillan, 1988.
Ilie, P. *Literature and Inner Exile*, Baltimore, John Hopkins University Press, 1980.
Jacobus, M. *Reading Woman: Essays in Feminist Criticism*, London, Methuen, 1986.
Jameson, F. *Marxism and Form*, Princeton, Princeton University Press, 1971.
Janik, A. and S. Toulmin, *Wittgenstein's Vienna*, London, Weidenfeld and Nicolson, 1973.
Jardine, A. *Gynesis: Configurations of Woman and Modernity*, Ithaca, Cornell University Press, 1985.
Jay, M. *Adorno*, London, Fontana, 1984.
— *The Dialectical Imagination*, Boston, Little & Brown, 1973.
— *Permanent Exiles: Essays on the Intellectual Migration from Germany to America*, New York, Columbia University Press, 1985.
Kamenka, E. *Nationalism: The Nature and Evolution of an Idea*, London, Edward Arnold, 1976.
Kappeler, S. *The Pornography of Representation*, Cambridge, Polity, 1986.
Kedourie, E. *Nationalism*, London, Hutchinson University Library, 1960.

Kefala, A. *The Alien*, St Lucia, Makar, 1973.
Kracauer, S. *History, The Last Things Before the Last*, Oxford, Oxford University Press, 1969.
Kristeva, J. *Revolution in Poetic Language*, translated by M. Waller, New York, Columbia, 1984.
— *Desire in Language: A Semiotic Approach to Literature and Art*, translated by T. Gora, A. Jardine and L. S. Roudiez, Oxford, Basil Blackwell, 1987.
— *The Kristeva Reader*, ed. T. Moi, Oxford, Basil Blackwell, 1987.
— *Powers of Horror: An Essay in Abjection*, translated by L. S. Roudiez, New York, Columbia University Press, 1982.
Kruger, B. and P. Mariani, *Remaking History*, Seattle, Bay Press, 1989.
Krupnick, M. (ed.), *Displacement, Derrida and After*, Bloomington, Indiana University Press, 1983.
Levin, H. *Refractions*, New York, Oxford University Press, 1966.
Levine, D. N. *Georg Simmel: On Individuality and Social Forms*, Chicago, University of Chicago Press, 1971.
Lyotard, J.-F. *The Postmodern Condition: A Report on Knowledge*, translated by G. Bennington, and B. Massumi, Manchester, Manchester University Press, 1979.
Lyotard, J.-F. and J.-L. Thebaud, *Just Gaming*, translated by W. Godzich, Manchester, Manchester University Press, 1985.
Mackie, F. *The Status of Everyday Life: A Sociological excavation of the prevailing frameworks of perception*, London, Routlege & Kegan Paul, 1985.
Man, P. de *The Resistance to Theory*, Manchester, Manchester University Press, 1986.
Miller, D. F. *The Reason of Metaphor: A Study in Politics*, Delhi, Sage, 1992.
Mitchell, J. *The Selected Melanie Klein*, Harmondsworth, Penguin, 1986.
Nairn, T. *The Break Up of Britain*, London, Verso, 1981.
Nandy, A. *At The Edge of Psychology*, Delhi, Oxford University Press, 1980.
— *The Intimate Enemy*, Delhi, Oxford University Press, 1983.
— *Traditions, Tyranny and Utopia: Essays in the Politics of Awareness*, Delhi, Oxford University Press, 1987.
Nietzsche, F. *Ecce Homo*, translated by R. J. Hollingdale, Harmondsworth, Penguin, 1986.
— *The Gay Science*, translated by W. Kaufmann, New York, Vintage, 1974.
— *Beyond Good and Evil*, translated by W. Kaufmann, New York, Vintage, 1966.
— *The Use and Abuse of History*, translated by A. Collin, Indianapolis, The Library of Liberal Arts, 1965.
Pratt, H. R. *Place and Displacement in Lorca, Cernuda, and Reverdy* (unpublished Ph.D.), University of Cambridge, 1986.
Raphael, M. *Proudhon, Marx, Picasso*, translated by I. Marcuse, London, Lawrence & Wishart, 1980.
Rogers, K. M. *The Troublesome Helpmate: A History of Misogyny in Literature*,

Seattle, University of Washington Press, 1966.
Rose, G. *The Melancholy Science: An Introduction to the thought of Theodor W. Adorno*, London, Macmillan, 1978.
Rundell, J. F. *Origins of Modernity*, Cambridge, Polity, 1987.
Said, E. W. *The Question of Palestine*, London, Routledge & Kegan Paul, 1980.
— *The World, The Text, and The Critic*, Cambridge, Mass., Harvard University Press, 1983.
— *Orientalism*, Harmondsworth, Penguin, 1985.
— *After The Last Sky*, London, Faber & Faber, 1986.
Sartre, J.-P. *What is Literature*, London, Methuen, 1967.
Schutz, A. *Collected Papers, Volume II: Studies in Social Theory*, The Hague, Martinus Nijhoff, 1964.
Seidel, M. *Exile and the Narrative Imagination*, New Haven, Yale University Press, 1986.
Simmel, G. *On Individuality and Social Forms*, Chicago, Chicago University Press, 1971.
Sontag, S. *On Photography*, Harmondsworth, Penguin, 1986.
— *Styles of Radical Will*, New York, Delta, 1981.
Soyinka, W. *Art, Dialogue & Outrage*, Ibadan, New Horn Press, 1988.
Spivak, G. C. *In Other Worlds*, New York, Methuen, 1987.
— *The Post-Colonial Critic*, London, Routledge, 1990.
Steiner, G. *A Reader*, Harmondsworth, Penguin, 1984.
— *Extraterritorial*, London, Faber & Faber, 1972.
Stewart, S. *On Longing: Narratives of the Miniature, the Gigantic, the Souvenir, the Collection*, Baltimore, Johns Hopkins University Press, 1984.
Stauth, G. and B. Turner, *Nietzsche's Dance*, Oxford, Basil Blackwell, 1988.
Szondi, P. *On Textual Understanding and Other Essays*, translated by H. Mendelsohn, Manchester, Manchester University Press, 1986.
Tabori, P. *The Anatomy of Exile*, London, Harrap, 1972.
Torrance, J. *Estrangement, Alienation, and Exploitation*, London, Macmillan, 1977.
Tucker, R. C. *The Marx–Engels Reader*, New York, W. W. Norton, 1978.
White, H. *Tropics of Discourse*, Baltimore, Johns Hopkins University Press, 1986.
Williams, R. *The Politics of Modernism*, London, Verso, 1989.
Wolff, K. H. (ed.), *The Sociology of Georg Simmel*, New York, Free Press, 1950.
— *Essays on Sociology, Philosophy and Aesthetics: Georg Simmel*, New York, Free Press, 1965.

Index

absence, 24, 96, 126–7, 192
abstraction, 42, 44, 97
Adorno, T. W., 42, 57, 82, 83
Affandi, 63
affirmation, 98, 99–100, 148, 181
agency, 5, 12, 80
agonism, 40–1
Ahmad, Aijaz, 88
Ahmet, Seker, 23–4
alienation, 11, 93
altruism, 107, 117
ambivalence, 39–40, 44, 72, 78
  of stranger, 92, 126, 127
anonymity, 122, 135, 136
Antal, Frederick, 37, 83
anticipation, 120, 174, 175
appropriation, 5, 69
Arendt, Hannah, 27
Aristotle, 3, 76
arrival, 96, 112, 113, 114, 115
art, 3, 19–24, 44, 45–55, 149–50
  distance, 73, 74
  individualist, 77
  non-metropolitan, 61, 62, 63
  and politics, 41–5, 59, 64, 67, 136, 147, 158
  and rebellion, 38, 55–6, 78
  social role, 37, 46, 47, 53, 54, 55, 57, 65, 67
  tradition, 78
  see also artists
artists
  exiled, 62, 63, 102

  heroic, 129, 132–3
  liminality, 55, 136
  as prophets, 55, 60, 73
  and public, 43, 46, 47
  social position, 41, 47, 55, 102, 136, 146
  vision, 78, 183
  working methods, 19–24
  see also individual artists
attachment, 3, 6, 8, 14, 52, 55
  to other, 108, 109
Australian painters, 63
authenticity, 11, 38, 167
author, 3, 4–5, 20, 32–3, 69, 128
avant-garde, 41–5, 68

Bachelard, Gaston, 11
Bacon, Francis, 61
Bakhtin, Mikhail, 102
Barthes, Roland, 21, 31–2, 40, 191
Baudelaire, Charles, 136
Bauman, Zygmunt, 42, 94, 95–6
beginnings, new, 148, 149
belief, shattering of, 43
belonging, 90–6, 169
Benjamin, Walter, 14, 48–9, 83, 90, 91, 136, 137
bereavement, 131–2
Berger, John, 2-3
  WORKS: *About Looking*, 14–15; *And our Faces, my Heart, Brief as Photos*, 10–11, 110; art criticism, 3, 19–24, 45–55; *Art and*

Index

Revolution, 53–5, 57, 59; *Corker's Freedom*, 171–4, 175; film scripts, 17; *The Foot of Clive*, 156–66, 173; *A Fortunate Man*, 90–2, 104–5, 105–10, 111–14; *G*, 16–17, 145, 175–80; *Goya's Last Portrait*, 33; *A Painter of Our Time*, 61, 63, 65, 146–56, 174–5, 180; *Permanent Red*, 61–2; *Pig Earth*, 17; *A Seventh Man*, 90, 104, 105, 110–18, 122, 129–30, 135–6; *The Success and Failure of Picasso*, 47–53, 57; *Ways of Seeing*, 36–7
Berman, Marshall, 29
Bhabha, Homi K., 92, 103–4, 143
biography, 191, 193
Blake, William, 77
blame, 145, 159
Blanchot, M., 59–60
Blunt, Anthony, 77
borders and boundaries, 9, 115–16
  of home, 143–6, 164
  transgression, 3, 14, 15–16, 27, 96, 100, 101, 164
Bowmann, G., 189
Brancusi, Constantine, 152
Braque, Georges, 51, 58
Brecht, Bertold, 17, 83, 90, 91
Britain, 46, 62, 66–7, 102, 107, 146–7, 156
Brodsky, Joseph, 97–8
Buffet, Bernard, 77
Burger, P., 41, 42, 43–5

Camus, Albert, 55, 66
capitalism, 36, 65
Carter, Paul, 3
castration, 143, 147, 162, 165, 167, 172, 173
Caute, David, 80
Cavafy, Constantine P., 90
centre, 68, 71, 136, 170
Certeau, M. de, 76
certitude, 65, 95–6, 100, 120, 161, 170, 182
Césaire, Aimé, 84
Cézanne, Paul, 21, 84

change, social, 1, 12, 16, 41, 76
chauvinism, cultural, 134
city *see* metropolis
Collingwood, R. G., 177–8, 178–9
colonialism, 3, 62, 64, 72–4, 92
commitment, 6, 69, 95
  dual, 36, 37–8, 39, 126
common sense, 105–6, 108, 124, 163
Conrad, Joseph, 71, 108
contradictions 6, 17–18, 21, 35, 37–8, 41, 52, 64, 68, 77
  see also commitment (dual); opposition
Coser, Lewis A., 142
Craig, R., 80
creativity, 15–16, 101, 129, 132
criticism, 39–40, 57–62, 65, 66–7
  Berger on art, 3, 19–24, 45–55
  distance, 5, 68
  metaphors for, 8, 13–27
  non-metropolitan, 73, 102–4
  representation, 1, 48–9, 68–79
Croce, Benedetto, 178
cubism, 25, 47, 51, 56–7, 58, 77
culture, 3, 5, 9
  global, 48, 68, 81
  links across, 3, 16, 100

death, 177, 182, 183
de-centring, 3, 75, 100–1
Degas, Edgar, 77
departure, 6, 107–8, 112, 113
Derrida, Jacques, 134, 135, 173
desire, 17, 21, 193, 166, 170, 178–80
detachment, 3, 14, 22, 44, 52, 74
  and attachment, 8, 52, 55
  Berger's, 67
  and exemption, 152
  romantic, 14, 38, 43, 44, 48, 98–9
  see also estrangement
dialogue, 4–5, 46–7, 64
différance, 195
diminution by exile, 9, 10
discourse, 32–3, 76
disembowelment, 9, 10, 182
disintegration, 46, 53–4, 132
dislocation/displacement, 4, 11–12, 67–9, 72, 105, 133

multiple levels, 1, 11–12, 13, 14
  see also under language; women
dissidence, 9, 54, 183
distance
  in art, 73, 74
  author/subject, 69, 128
  critical, 5, 68
  and foreignness, 6, 9, 13
  given/desired, 21
  historian's, 128
  imaginative, 109
  in metropolis, 70, 116
  names/things, 121, 193
  native/exile, 155–6
  and objectivity, 22, 128
  physical and psychical, 95
  romantic, 48
  self/other, 144
  see also near and far
domination, 6, 193, 194
doubt, 65, 160–2
dualisms, 68, 136–7
  see also contradictions

Eagleton, Terry, 69, 71–2
Eisenstein, Sergi M., 17
Eliade, Mircea, 11
empathy, 4, 14, 15–26, 128, 192
engagement, 19, 40, 41–5, 52
Enlightenment, 41
Erikson, Erik Homburger, 130
establishment, cultural, 61, 62, 137, 193, 194
estrangement/alienation, 11
  absence of dialogue and, 64
  Brecht on, 17
  and critical consciousness, 135
  of exceptional painter, 78
  and fixed image, 124
  and freedom, 13, 37, 128
  in identity, 143
  internal, 93
  language and, 32, 183
  Marxist and romantic, 38
  in metropolis, 70
  and objectivity, 125
  pervasive, 146–7
  preceding departure, 13
  in representation, 149
  beyond solidarity, 133
  and transcendence, 68
  and vision, 14, 126, 147
  see also detachment
ethnocentricism, 61, 62
etymologies, 2, 18, 164, 166
'exile', 8–9
exclusion, 6, 18
exemption, 152
exile
  in modernity, 1, 2, 8–13
  primal, 93
  see also individual aspects
expatriates, 69, 73–4
experience, 14–15, 19, 20–1, 121
exploitation, 135
expressionism, abstract, 63

Fanon, Frantz, 103
fantasies, sexual, 145, 157, 159–60, 168, 161–3
Fasanella, Ralph, 22–3
father, 145, 171–2, 173, 180, 182
fear, 9, 161–3, 177, 183
fetish, 103
Fischer, Michael, 101–2
flâneur, 136, 138
Flaubert, Gustave, 98
form, 20, 42, 46, 71
Foucault, M., 31, 32, 56
fragmentation, 9, 10, 182
France, 5, 50, 51, 54, 62, 66
freedom, 20, 38, 43, 51, 73, 173
  and estrangement, 13, 37, 128
  of exile, 74, 97, 133, 182
Freud, Sigmund, 24, 132, 143, 145, 147, 163–4, 165, 166
Fuller, Peter, 33, 37, 79
future, 149–51, 167, 168–9, 175–6, 194

Gallop, Jane, 166–7, 168
garden, enclosed, 170, 190
Gehlen, Arnold, 13, 29
gender, 80, 173–4, 175–6
generalisations, 76–7
genius, 77

Index

Giddens, A., 5, 9
Gilroy, Paul, 102
Giorgione, 174
given and desired, 21, 193
globalism, 48, 68, 81
God, 12
Goethe, Johann Wolfgang von, 166
Gramsci, A., 67, 191
Gris, Juan, 84
group, *see under* stranger
Gurr, Andrew, 73–4
gynesis, 145, 179

Hall, Stuart, 5
Harris, Wilson, 30–1
Hegel, G. W. F., 75, 173
Heidegger, Martin, 24
hell, 52
hero, 21
   artist as, 129, 132–3
   migrant as, 113, 114, 115
hinge metaphor, 47, 64
history 3–4, 13, 31–2, 37, 62, 66
   Collingwood on, 177–8, 178–9
   critical/sentimental, 48–9
   distance, 128
   and identity, 143
   Kracauer on, 127–8
   Nietzsche's wanderer and, 134
   stranger and, 120, 123–4
   truncated or silenced, 20, 193
Hodgkins, Frances, 86
Hoffer, Johannes, 188
home, 11, 12–13, 41, 45–7, 51–2, 93
   borders of, 143–6, 164–5
   certitude, 170, 177
   and engagement, 52
   expatriates and, 73
   and identity, 127, 143, 153, 170, 180
   lack of, 48, 123
   language as, 18–19
   return to, 144, 181
   in romanticism, 143
   the uncanny and, 166
   as utopia, 170
hope, 54, 65, 129, 151, 153, 194
   loss of, 181

pre-migratory, 114–18
house as metaphor, 11
humanism, 37
Husserl, E. G. A., 3
Huyssen, Andreas, 158

idealisation, 107, 108, 129–30, 146
   by memory, 123–4, 174–5
   of other, 179
identification, 10, 20, 25, 26, 46
   and nostalgia, 110, 169
   by opposition, 2, 18, 68, 111
   with the other, 46–7, 50, 62–7, 111, 144–5
   psychoanalytic, 100, 103
identity, 3, 143, 147
   certitudes, 100, 181
   home and, 127, 143, 153, 170, 180
   loss, 74, 97, 146, 171–4, 181
   migrant's, 116, 122, 129, 130
   Nietzsche and, 134–5
   and nostalgia, 74, 146, 170–1
   parents and, 171–2, 173
   representation, 26
   /resemblance gap, 104, 143–4, 167, 170
   resilience, 180–2
   self-, 146
   sexual, 3, 146, 171–4, 178–9
   split, 176
   stability, 130
   of stranger, 2, 92–6
   stranger defines native's, 2, 109–10, 112
Ignotus, Paul, 79
imagination, 102, 109, 114–18, 160–1, 192, 193–4
imprisonment, 131
individualism, 13, 63–4, 65, 77
innocence, 51, 77
integration, 46, 51–2, 75–6, 147, 167
intellectual, modern, 180–4, 195
intention, 39–40, 167
interjacency, 10, 25
intimacy, 22, 121, 164, 179
   critical, 5, 67–79
isolation, 44, 48, 51, 97

James, Henry, 73
Jameson, Fredric, 28, 74–5, 82
Jardine, Alice, 145, 168, 170, 173–4, 179
Jay, Martin, 140–1
John, Gwen, 86
journalism, 16, 57, 60–1
journeys, 1, 96, 107, 112, 182
　distance, 6, 13
　love-making as, 178–9
　as metaphor, 193, 195
　pre-migratory imagining, 114–18
　quest for belonging, 169, 170
Joyce, James, 73, 98, 117
Jung, Karl Gustav, 163

Kafka, Franz, 166
Kedourie, E., 27–8
Kefala, Antigone, 114
Keohane, N.O., 84
knowledge, 15, 33, 107
　group, 119, 120
　self-, 191
　see also unknowable
Kracauer, Siegfried, 123–4, 127–8, 136
Krauss, Rosalind, 33–4
Kristeva, J., 180–4

Lacan, Jacques, 100, 143, 166–7
lack, 98, 119–21, 126–7, 154, 162–3
language
　and alienation, 32, 183
　decentring of self, 100–1
　dislocation, 70, 72, 99, 113–14, 117, 118, 122
　entry into, 143, 184
　as human home, 18–19
　and objectification, 25
　for the other, 27, 119–28
　redemptive, 99, 100
　sacred, 42
　woman and limits, 173
　word/thing gap, 27, 100, 121, 183, 193
　see also etymologies; metaphor; representation; synonyms
Lasch, Christopher, 188

La Tour, Georges de, 22
laughter, 184
law, international, 9
Levin, Harry, 98, 99
liminality, 55, 124, 125–6
　value, 112, 127, 128, 136, 182
Lorca, Federico García, 53
loss, 129, 131–2, 148
　of certitudes, 95–6, 182
　see also under hope; identity; migrant workers; place
Lukács, Georg, 42, 82, 83, 123
Lyotard, J.-F., 26, 41, 42–3, 45, 78, 87

McCarthy, Mary, 54, 73
MacIntyre, Alisdair, 39
mannerism, 19, 71
Marxism, 25, 35–89, 106, 135, 194
master/servant, 25–6, 75, 98, 102
Mazurek, R. A., 80–1
melancholia, 132, 168
memory, 62, 123–4, 130, 174–5, 191
Mercer, Kobena, 102
Merleau-Ponty, Maurice, 66
metaphor, 1, 4, 8–34, 64, 76–7
　links contraries, 17–18, 52, 64
　and critical representation, 8, 40, 60, 69
　exile and empathy, 14, 15–26, 192
　of hinge, 47, 64
　of house, 11
　of journey, 193, 195
　meaning, origin and process, 17–18
　as method, 13–27
　Picasso and, 53
　sexual, 144, 170–1
　of shuttle, 41
　Simmel's use, 107
　time and space united by, 174
　for transience, 96
　woman as, 144, 173, 177, 180
methodology, 13–27, 68, 124–6, 192
metropolis, 67, 70, 110, 116–18
　culture, 70, 74–5, 146, 147, 193–4;
　　Picasso and, 47, 48, 54
Michelet, Jules, 21, 31–2
migrant workers
　hopes, 114–18

Index

identity, 116, 122, 129, 130
  loss: of language, 113–14, 117, 118,
    122, 129; of place, 118
  perception of metropolis, 116–18,
    193
  return home, 113, 114, 115, 118
  time perception, 130–2
  tragedy, 23, 105, 113, 128–35, 181
  and 'welcome stranger', 111–14
Millet, Jean François, 32
mimicry, 103
minorities, rights of, 9
misogyny, 123, 145, 146, 156, 158,
  159, 180
  and doubt, 160–2
Mitchell, Juliet, 143
mobility, 13, 135
modernism, 37, 42, 99–100, 102
modernity, 1, 2, 8–13, 26, 41
  see also individual aspects
Mohr, Jean, 90, 115
Montaigne, Michel Eyquem de, 77
Moore, Henry, 61
mosaic, 77
mother, 143, 145, 162–3, 167
  and identity, 147, 171–2, 173, 174,
    182–3, 184
  mutuality, 144, 156, 173, 181
myths, 93, 179

names and naming, 2
  anonymity, 122, 135, 136
  by differentiation, 2, 18, 68, 111
  of father, 171, 172, 180, 182
  inadequacy, 27, 100, 121, 183, 193
  and space, 171–2, 183–4
  and time, 167, 169
  of unnamed, 106, 109–10, 112, 118
Nandy, Ashis, 16, 25, 98
narcissism, 54, 73, 74, 182
nationalism, 10, 134, 147
nationality, 9–10, 147
native
  distance from exile, 155–6
  and welcome stranger, 2, 105–7,
    109–10, 112, 113
nature, pre-exilic, 143
near and far, 3, 14, 46–7, 68, 93, 95,

112, 127, 136
Neumann, Franz, 9
New Statesman, The, 60–1, 62, 66
Nietzsche, F. W., 49, 133–5, 136, 168
Niezvestny, Ernst, 46, 53–5
nostalgia, 49, 131, 151–2, 166–8
  and desire, 166, 170
  for future, 167, 168–9, 169–70, 181
  and historian, 178
  and identification, 110, 169
  and identity, 74, 146, 170–1
  for integrity of past, 147, 167
  Jewish, 62
  permanent refugee's, 148
  romantic, 15, 38
  and sociology, 166–8
  and utopia, 149–51, 167, 169–70,
    181
  and woman, 179

objectification, 22, 25
objectivity, 16, 72, 77, 125
  and distance, 22, 93, 128
  stranger's, 93, 107, 126
Oedipal wishes, 143, 157
opposition, 35, 38–9, 69
  definition by, 2, 18, 68, 111
  see also contradictions
order and chaos, 26, 161
Ortega y Gasset, José, 52
oscillation, 90
other, the, 97, 146, 154, 158
  abstract attachment, 108, 109
  idealised, 179
  identification with, 46–7, 50, 62–7,
    111, 144–5
  language for, 27, 119–28
  pre-nomial, 171
  and self, 3, 19, 21, 50, 144–5, 164,
    194
particular, the, 71, 72, 77, 193
past
  beginning of conscious, 143–4
  and future, 149–51, 175–6
  integrated, 147, 167
  obsession with, 148, 149
  and present, 178–9, 194

representation, 48–9
peasantry, 17, 35, 105, 181
    see also migrant workers
periphery, 68, 71, 96, 136
perspective, 14, 23, 69, 136–7
phallus, 162–3, 167, 170
photography, 14, 17, 29, 90
Picasso, Pablo, 47–53, 54, 56–7, 58, 61, 152
Pick, Zuzana M., 100–1
place, 18, 67, 69, 107
    loss of, 6, 9, 118, 167
    see also home; space
plenitude, *see* lack
poetry, 3–4, 18
politics, 9, 35, 37–8, 70, 194
    and aesthetics, 41–5, 59, 64, 67, 136, 147, 158
portraiture, 29–30
positivism, 174
post-colonial culture, 61, 62, 69, 98, 102–4
postmodernity, 26, 99–100, 100–1
Poussin, Nicolas, 77
power, 33, 116
Prawer, S. S., 166
pre-modernity, 13, 52, 54, 167
prescience, 175–6
presence, 24; *see also* absence
present, 150, 151, 167, 178–9, 194
primitivism, 49–50, 158
projection, 15, 21–2
propaganda, 59, 61
property, 36
prophecy, 55, 56, 60, 67–79
Proust, Marcel, 123–4
psychoanalysis, 100, 103, 110
purgatory, 54
Pushkin, Alexander S., 55

racism, 102
Raphael, Max, 29, 83
rationality, 41, 72, 77
realism, 17, 37, 42, 69, 70, 73
rebellion, 106–7, 129, 134, 155
    and art, 38, 55–6, 78
    Marxist, 38, 46
recipes, social, 119–20, 126

redemption, 107, 109–10
regression, 166
reification, 123
relational thinking, 77
Rembrandt, 78
representation, 5, 14, 19, 27, 149–51, 183
    critical, 1, 48–9, 68–79
    identification in, 20, 26
    mode and content, 25, 102
resemblance, 104, 143–4, 167, 170
responsibility, 6, 57
return
    home, 113, 114, 115, 118, 144, 181
    to womb, 162–3, 166–7
Robbins, Bruce, 81
romanticism, 26, 44, 47–57, 80
    detachment, 14, 38, 43, 44, 48, 57, 98–9
    on exile, 8, 9, 14, 43
    and Marxism, 35–89, 194
    Nietzsche on, 133
    nostalgia, 15, 38
    transcendence, 182
rootedness, 1, 6, 24, 36, 70
Rousseau, Jean Jacques, 50–1
rupture, 9, 14, 78, 144, 182
Russia, 39, 46, 54, 60, 61

sacred, the, 42
sacrifice, time of, 131
Said, E. W., 4, 9, 16, 22, 27, 92
Sander, August, 14
Sappho, 90
Sartre, Jean-Paul, 52, 66, 80
savage, noble, 50–1
schizophrenia, 176
Schutz, A., 119–22, 124–8
seeing, 22
self
    contestation against, 62–7, 134
    -definition, 67, 68
    disintegration, 132
    extension, 21, 47
    -knowledge, 191
    -observation, 176
    -projection, 50
    -realisation in sex, 108

Index

romantic transcendence, 182
severance from essence, 129
splitting of, 103, 165, 176
see also under other
sentimentalism, 8, 44, 48–9, 54, 68–9, 145
Serge, Victor, 20
service, 65–6, 107, 108
sexuality 143–90
  lack and plenitude, 162–3
  metaphor, 156, 170–1
  and self-realisation, 108
  and time, 174–80
  see also women
shamans, 108, 112
shuttle, 14, 17, 41, 49, 144
signs, 3, 68, 103
silence, 97, 98, 122, 129
Simmel, Georg, 93–4, 95, 125
  near and far, 3, 93, 127, 136
  on stranger, 92, 93–4, 105, 106, 135–7, 138
'sky, silken', 171, 172, 173
social realism, 61, 63
society, 13, 26, 66–7, 120
  see also change *and under* art; artists; stranger
sociology, 5, 26, 124–6, 127, 166–8
solidarity, 125, 126, 133
Sontag, Susan, 98
Soyinka, Wole, 92, 129, 129, 132–3
space, 2, 171–2, 174, 182–3, 184
Spender, Stephen, 79
Spivak, Gayatri C., 5, 30, 74, 75, 92, 98, 102, 104, 137, 145, 168, 173
Stammelman, R., 34
statehood, 9–10
Stauth, G., 167, 168
Steiner, George, 99, 100, 188
stereotypes, 103, 120–1, 122, 146
Stewart, Susan, 185
storytelling, 110, 174, 175, 194
stranger, 90–142
  ambivalence, 92, 126, 127
  as detective, 123
  enlightenment, 104–5, 112, 127, 128
  and group, 41, 94–5, 119–22, 126–7, 133

  as historian, 123–4
  identity, 2, 92–6
  intimate, 179
  liminality, 112, 127, 128, 136
  objectivity, 126
  Simmel on, 92, 93–4, 105, 106, 135–7, 138
  social position, 2, 41, 92–104, 109–10, 119–22, 126–7, 133, 135
  as sociologist, 124–6, 127
  translation, 121–2
  'welcome', 2, 90–2, 105–10, 111–14
  see also migrant workers
subjectivity, 15, 16, 22, 25, 54, 77
  of other, 111, 158
suicide, 91–2, 110
surrealism, 47
synonyms, 2, 8
Szanto, G., 80–1

Tabori, P., 27
Tanner, Alain, 17
time, 23, 129–30, 149, 174–80
  dislocation, 130–2, 152, 153, 177, 179–80, 194
  see also future; past; present
Titian, 174
Torrance, John, 7, 93
tradition, 46, 78, 93, 133, 134
tragedy, 23, 105, 113, 128–35, 181
transcendence, 44, 55, 99
  and estrangement, 68, 74
  of exile, 71–2, 123
  of time, 174
  romantic, 182
  unity, 100
  and woman, 158
transformation, 1, 21, 55, 100, 111
transition, 26, 115, 129–30, 144
translation, 108, 121–2
truth, 20–1, 65, 69, 76, 182
Turner, B., 167, 168
Tyler, Stephen, 82

uncanny, the, 6, 146, 161, 162–6, 170
unheimlich, 161, 162, 163–4
United Nations, 9
universal, the, 71, 72, 77, 101, 193

unknowable/unknown, woman as, 145, 172, 173–4, 177, 179–80
utopia, 52, 149–51, 169–70, 173, 181

value, determination of, 45, 65
values, social, 1, 13
visibility, 21
vision, 14, 22, 23, 24, 78, 126, 147
void, 161, 165, 172

Walker, Ethel, 86
wanderer, Nietzsche's, 133–5
Watteau, (Jean) Antoine, 57
Williams, Raymond, 28–9, 69–71
Wolff, Janet, 138
women, 158-9, 174–80
    blaming of, 145, 159
    in city, 116
    displacement, 86, 145
    and inversion, 159–60
    and male identity, 144–5, 171–4, 178–9
    other as feminine, 154
    patriarchal representation, 36
    self-surveying, 176
    sensibility, 183
    stereotypes, 146
    subordination, 158–9
    and transcendence, 158
    see also fantasies; mother; unknowable
womb, 162–3, 166–7, 168, 170, 171
writing, 3, 17, 20–1